Contents

EVIDENCE VERSUS POLITICS

Exploiting research in UK drug policy making?

Mark Monaghan

This edition published in Great Britain in 2011 by

The Policy Press
University of Bristol
Fourth Floor
Beacon House
Queen's Road
Bristol BS8 1QU
UK

Tel +44 (0)117 331 4054
Fax +44 (0)117 331 4093
e-mail tpp-info@bristol.ac.uk
www.policypress.co.uk

North American office:
The Policy Press
c/o International Specialized Books Services (ISBS)
920 NE 58th Avenue, Suite 300
Portland, OR 97213-3786, USA
Tel +1 503 287 3093
Fax +1 503 280 8832
e-mail info@isbs.com

British Library Cataloguing in Publication Data
A catalogue record for this book is available from the British Library.

Library of Congress Cataloging-in-Publication Data
A catalog record for this book has been requested.

ISBN 978 1 84742 697 0 hardcover

Cover design by The Policy Press
Front cover: image kindly supplied by www.sxc.hu/photo/1240771
Printed and bound in Great Britain by TJ International, Padstow
The Policy Press uses environmentally responsible print partners.

FSC
www.fsc.org
MIX
Paper from
responsible sources
FSC® C013056

To Sonia

List of tables and figures

Acknowledgements

First things first, I would like to thank Ray Pawson, Simon Prideaux and Teela Sanders for their critical comments on various aspects of this work and for their ongoing support. Their opinions and analysis have been invaluable. In particular, Ray Pawson's cajoling, goading and endless advice has made the final product stronger. I would also like to express thanks to Sandra Nutley for her comments on an earlier iteration of the typescript. Appreciation is also expressed to my colleagues in the School of Sociology and Social Policy at the University of Leeds and to Les King for his assistance. Much gratitude is expressed to Laura Hemingway, Ana Manzano Santaella and Elizabeth Monaghan, who proofread various sections and suggested many points for clarification. I hope I will be able to return the favour one day. Any omissions and errors are down to me.

Due recognition is given to the Economic and Social Research Council (ESRC). The research budget that accompanied the stipend awarded to me as a postgraduate helped to cover costs on the various research trips taken around the UK, the data from which feature heavily throughout. I am indebted to various friends in various locations throughout the country and thank them kindly for their hospitality and generosity while I was completing the research for this work and after. A big, arguably the biggest, thank you is also given to the many respondents who gave their time, shared their knowledge, listened more patiently than I deserved and, in many cases, welcomed a stranger into their homes to discuss the finer points of evidence-based drug policy making. Without them the book could not have been completed. Thanks are also due to all at The Policy Press, especially Karen, for her initial support for the book, and Emily and Leila for their patience as I continually struggled with deadlines. On the domestic front, eternal gratitude and love is expressed to my family, in particular, my parents Bernard and Jane, to my siblings and, finally, to Sonia without whom this would not have been possible.

List of abbreviations and key terms

ACF	Advocacy Coalition Framework
ACMD	Advisory Council on the Misuse of Drugs
BSE	Bovine Spongiform Encephalopathy
BZP	Benzylpiperazine
CSR	Comprehensive Spending Review
EMCDDA	European Monitoring Centre for Drugs and Drug Addiction
ESRC	Economic and Social Research Council
EU	European Union
GBL	Gamma–Butyrolactone
IMF	International Monetary Fund
KPI	key performance indicators
MDA	Misuse of Drugs Act (1971)
MDMA	Methylenedioxymethamphetamine ('ecstasy')
MP	Member of Parliament
NGO	non-government organisation
NOMS	National Offender Management Service
NPM	New Public Management
OECD	Organisation for Economic Co-operation and Development
PSA	Public Service Agreement
quango	quasi–autonomous non–government organisation
RBI	Reducing Burglary Initiative
RCT	randomised controlled trial
SSRC	Social Science Research Council
THC	Tetrahydrocannabinol (the main psychoactive ingredient found in cannabis)
UN	United Nations
zero–sum	reducing the role of evidence to a dichotomy of present (evidence-based) or absent (evidence-free) depending on one's view of the policy in question

You say 'evidence'.

Well, there may be evidence.

But evidence, you know,
can generally be taken two ways.

(Dostoevsky, 1866 [2000])

ONE

Introduction

> Science can, indeed, I would argue must, be the prime mediator of policy if we are to minimize the harms of drugs, both medical and social, but science cannot deliver policy because that is the realm of politics. (Nutt, 2010, p 1154)

Towards the end of 2009 a significant schism occurred between the New Labour government and the chair of the Advisory Council on the Misuse of Drugs (ACMD), Professor David Nutt. The origins of this can be traced back to May 2008 when, against the prevailing advice from the ACMD (ACMD, 2008), the government signalled its intention to reclassify cannabis back to a class B drug under the Misuse of Drugs Act (MDA) 1971. Drug classification is a thorny issue. It returned to the media headlines in March 2009 as the Advisory Council considered the legal status of ecstasy. Their report followed shortly after (ACMD, 2009). Among its many recommendations was the call to reclassify ecstasy as a class B substance, a call promptly sidestepped by the government. The government's decision to seemingly ignore outright this advice led to a row – played out in the media – between Professor Nutt and the then Home Secretary, Jacqui Smith. This had been simmering for some time. In an article published in the *Journal of Psychopharmacology*, Nutt had previously suggested that ecstasy was no more dangerous than horse riding (Nutt, 2009). In response, Smith retorted that this was 'trivialising' the dangers of the drug (BBC, 2009).

The episode was a rare public disagreement between the government and the ACMD, who generally share a similar philosophy on the nature of drug classification policy. Broadly, this philosophy states that the classification system should regulate drugs by placing them into a hierarchy based on their perceived harms and dangers. Criminal penalties relating to drug offences should then be relative to the perceived harm of the substance. This is, indeed, the premise of the current tri-partite classification system of the MDA 1971, where controlled drugs are assigned to class A, B or C depending on their perceived harms. The main point of contention here related to the location of certain drugs within this framework and what should be done about it.

Later in 2009, relations between members of the ACMD and the government further deteriorated, culminating with the removal of Professor Nutt by Alan Johnson, Jacqui Smith's replacement as Home Secretary. Johnson accused Nutt of overstepping his remit and of campaigning against government policy. In response to his sacking, Professor Nutt pointed out how the government had 'devalued' the science in their decision-making processes. In a lecture delivered in July 2009 to the Centre of Criminal Justice Studies at King's College London, Professor Nutt made his now familiar claim that based on the existing science both cannabis and ecstasy are less harmful than legal drugs such as alcohol and should, therefore, be downgraded.

Part of the evidence base cited for this claim was research co-authored by Professor Nutt (Nutt et al, 2007) (hereafter referred to as the 'Nutt et al matrix'). Here, the most widely used illegal drugs, along with tobacco and alcohol, were placed in a scale according to the harm they cause drug users with the substances decoupled from the associated penalties. The authors identified three main categories of harm:

- *Physical*, which is an assessment of the propensity of the drug to cause physical harm, for example, damage to organs and systems. There are three separate aspects to this: acute physical harm – the immediate effects linked to the notion of overdose; chronic physical harm – the health consequences of repeated use, such as the link between cannabis and psychosis; and specific problems associated with intravenous drug use.
- *Dependence*, which entails the relationship between the pleasurable effects of the drug and its propensity to induce dependent behaviour both psychologically and physically.
- *Social harms*, which occur in various ways, for example, with intoxication impacting on family, community and social life through costs to systems of health, social care and the police (Nutt et al, 2007).

Of the 20 substances listed in the matrix, ecstasy was ranked 18th in terms of harm, with cannabis 11th and alcohol 5th.

Discussions concerning the evidence base for the UK drug classification system have been prominent in media debates throughout the last decade. Towards the end of the 20th and into the 21st century, there was a tacit realisation that with new knowledge of drugs emerging, the current classification system – laid out in the MDA 1971 – may not be fit for purpose. It was this realisation that, in part, brought about the initial reclassification of cannabis in 2004 from class B to class C. The 2004 cannabis reclassification was a subtle but nonetheless significant change to UK drug policy and acted as a trigger for ongoing debate over the evidence base for the tri-partite structure of the MDA and whether this is the most effective means to regulate drug use.

Although this is the case, it is acknowledged that the practice of enforcing the MDA 1971 increasingly differs from its theory. In reality, little distinction is made in enforcement and punishment terms between class B and class C substances. The boundary between class B and class C became blurry in the aftermath of the 2004 cannabis reclassification, a product of changes made to adjacent legislation. The Police and Criminal Evidence Act 1984 was also altered so that cannabis assumed a unique status as a class C drug as the police maintained the power of arrest for those caught in possession of the drug (Warburton et al, 2005, p 116). Additionally, the Criminal Justice Act 2003 introduced more draconian punishments for supply of class C substances from five years to fourteen years, on a par with those of class B. Increasingly, the three-tier system actually operates as a two-tier system – class A, and everything else. In this light, arguments about whether cannabis, for example, should be class B or class C are in practice debates over minor tweaks in policy that are of dubious relevance in terms of the control of drugs. This does not alter the fact, however, that such debates are highly sensitive and symbolic.

The significance of the removal of David Nutt from his post as the chief government adviser on drugs episode was that it pushed the relationship between the government and its scientific advisers to the top of the news headlines, creating a simultaneous stir in the blogosphere. The 'Nuttsack' affair, as the satirists colloquially (and sarcastically) labelled it, opened up the government to accusations that when it was not entirely prudent, it was not fully committed to keeping one of its earlier and widely acknowledged promises of developing policies with recourse to a robust evidence base, expressed most (in)famously by the then Secretary of State for Education David Blunkett's assertion that:

> Government policy ought to be informed by sound evidence. Social science research ought to be contributing a major part of that evidence base. It should be playing a key role in helping us to decide our overall strategies. (Blunkett, 2000)

As indicated, the events described above illustrate how the connection between knowledge or research production and policy formulation is tumultuous. In recent years, expectations for the conflux of research production for policy formulation have been consolidated under the banner of 'evidence-based policy and practice'. But this term is elusive – there is little agreement on its nature and its purpose. There is a long-standing and embedded tradition of research-led policy formulation in the UK and elsewhere, although there have been various boom and bust cycles in the fortunes of the sciences, in particular, the social sciences and their links to policy. A microcosm of the fluctuating nature of this relationship can be seen over the past 30 years. The 1980s, or 'Thatcher era', was archetypal of a trough. This era of 'conviction politics' witnessed (under the watchful eye of Sir Keith Joseph) the 'near-demise' of the UK Social Science Research Council (SSRC), subsequently renamed the Economic and Social Research Council (ESRC). The loss of the 'imprimatur of science' was significant, as Nutley et al (2007, p 10) identify. For detractors, this was undoubtedly ideologically and politically driven. Callinicos (1999, p 1) points out how the social sciences were on the retreat from the New Right regimes ascendant in Western liberal democracies at the time, with sociology, in particular, seen as a 'stalking horse for socialism'.

If the 1980s were turbulent, as the 1990s progressed an era of renewed optimism emerged as the 'hand of friendship' was extended between the New Labour government and the social science community (Page, 2010, p 335). On assuming power in 1997 the New Labour government promised more accountability in the policy-making arena as part of the 'modernising agenda' (Cabinet Office, 1999a, 1999b; Bullock et al, 2001). For Solesbury (2001, p 6), the modernising agenda was part of a process of the 'opening up' of government. Evidence-based policy making – the development of policies devoid of dogma – was to be one of the various vessels by which this could be realised. Other aspects of this included joined-up, forward, outward, innovative and inclusive policy making (Bochel and Duncan, 2007). Researchers, analysts, policy makers and other interested parties were charged with the task of finding out 'what works' in specific policy domains. This called into question Keynes' well-cited lament, that 'there is nothing the government hates more than to be well-informed; for it makes the process of arriving at decisions much more complicated and difficult' (cited in Mulgan, 2005, p 216).

'What works' became the leitmotif of evidence-based policy and practice. A leading publication in the field (Davies et al, 2000a) illustrated how providing an answer to this most pressing of questions was preoccupying policy makers and researchers in areas as diverse as healthcare, education, criminal justice (particularly in the reduction of crime), social care, welfare policy, housing, transport and urban policy. 'What works' has been described as a 'pragmatic approach' to policy making, being output-driven as opposed to dogmatic. It was also central to New Labour's 'Third Way' philosophy (Hudson and Lowe, 2004, p 223). With this in mind, various nouns have been employed to describe the onset of evidence-based policy making. These include the 'evidence-based agenda', 'endeavour', 'ethos', 'movement' or 'turn' (many of which, incidentally, are employed in this book).

The evidence-based policy-making agenda was also enmeshed with ensuring government policies provided value for money, for example, through evaluation. In this sense, government departments are continuously required to:

> ... review policies ... to determine when the time is right to modify a policy in response to changing circumstances so that it remains relevant and cost-effective; and departments may need to terminate policies if they are no longer cost effective or they are not delivering the policy outcomes intended. (NAO, 2001, p 12)

Central to this process are Comprehensive Spending Reviews (CSRs). These allocate resources for public services to ensure the most efficient way of service delivery. The 1998 Review was, at the time, the largest scale review undertaken in the UK. It introduced Public Service Agreements (PSAs) intended to 'galvanise public service delivery' and to drive 'major improvements in outcomes' (HM Treasury, no date). Hope (2004, p 292) explains how the 1998 CSR was tied into the modernising agenda and was part of the evidence-based policy ethos. It was, he suggests, 'designed to replace the short horizon, partial, political horse-trading among cabinet ministers that had hitherto marred the budgetary process'. Hope continues that all spending departments had to support their claims for funds with evidence of their cost-effectiveness, 'using rigorously analysed evidence, assembled according to its own guidelines'. This was, in turn, part of a drive towards more efficient public service delivery under the guise of New Public Management (NPM).

The NPM project was a continuation by New Labour of the previous Conservative government's stance of governing at 'arm's-length'. The creation of new agencies and executives to detach the running of services from civil service central control was commonplace. Nowhere was this more apparent than in the approach to crime management and criminal justice administration (McLaughlin et al, 2001). The establishment of the National Offender Management Service (NOMS), which subsumed the National Probation Service and the Prison Service, was indicative of this. The arm's-length agencies were responsible for steering public policy through audit and performance appraisal precisely in a bid to make public services efficient and cost-effective (Hope, 2004). This commitment to more efficient public management and other changes in the business of government were representative of new modes of governing coming into fruition at this time, widely described as new forms of 'governance'.

Although intrinsically linked to the New Labour project, the evidence-based policy agenda appears to be shared across the political spectrum in the UK. In 2008, the Conservative Party announced its intention to send all its Members of Parliament (MPs) on compulsory lessons in scientific literacy 'under a plan to strengthen evidence-based policy making' (Henderson, 2008). The Liberal Democrats, meanwhile, have been at the forefront of raising evidence-based policy issues in Parliament under the aegis of the House of Commons Science and Technology Select Committee, chaired for many years by their MP, Phil Willis.[1] In 2006, this Committee instigated a new research agenda where the emphasis was placed not just on how policy is made, but specifically on how evidence is used (or not) in policy formulation (Science and Technology Select Committee, 2006a). It remains to be seen if or how this will continue.

The commitment to evidence-based policy making was initially well received by the research and policy communities alike, but at almost the same time, this enthusiasm has been met with increasing scepticism, based around a number of unresolved issues (documented further in Chapter Three). For the purposes of brevity, they can be summarised in terms of a problematic relationship between the research and policy communities (Caplan, 1979). The emphasis in this book, unless otherwise stated, is on the relationship between the social science community and the political/policy-making establishment. A key issue relates to the impact that politics in the broadest sense, or political expediency more specifically, has on the policy-making process. Political expediency is captured effectively by Pitts' (2000, p 10) and Melrose's (2006, p 31) intuitive assertion that often policy development is contingent on the 'politics of electoral anxiety'. If evidence or research is pointing in the direction of potentially controversial or even unpopular policies then it is likely to be trumped by the occupational conventions of politicians. In most cases, a politician's ultimate goal is re-election in the long term and favourable press in the short term.

It is with this in mind that consummate sound bites, such as 'policy-based evidence', have been coined (see, for example, Marmot, 2004). Here, policy formulation precedes the search for evidence that is then carefully selected to support the initial stance. These accusations of 'cherry-picking', coupled with the blurring of boundaries between the scientific community and policy-making fraternity (Hope, 2004), has led to the frequent conclusion that much public policy is 'un-evidenced' or evidence-free. This pessimistic view of the evidence and policy relationship also has a long history (Finch, 1986; Heinemann et al, 1990; Weiss, 1998). It is suggested here that these issues are particularly acute in heavily politicised policy areas.

Although on some level all policies are politicised, for the sake of this discussion the term refers to those issues when the political stakes are high and when there are 'powerful constituencies' to face down (Tonry, 2004, p 23). They mainly concern issues that often lie at the intersection of autonomous disciplinary boundaries. In addition, heavily politicised areas are those where there is intense media scrutiny of policy, a lack of consensus on its direction, prolonged conflict between competing interest groups and a permeating sense of crisis. This makes politicised areas inherently unstable and unpredictable (Monaghan, 2010). Under the conditions of heavy politicisation, the direction of policy can alter as public and political opinion changes. This process can be very quick or it can be slow, but these policies do not stand still.

The origins of how illicit drug issues became a political concern are closely tied to the politicisation of crime and punishment in the 1980s. It was around this time that various social problems previously regarded as being peripheral to social cohesion came to the fore and were perceived to be in need of 'tougher' sanctions (Rodger, 2008, p 6). For Garland (2001), crime became constructed in this way due to the gradual erosion of professional middle-class support for social and penal welfare responses and an increasingly insatiable appetite for a return to 'justice' approach to punishment. New Right governments in both the UK and the US were alive to these developments and sought to get 'tough on crime'. This rhetoric has set the political agenda in crime control ever since.

This has a significant bearing on the (lack of) impact evidence is perceived to have. Garland (2001, p 132) has pointed out that 'disregarding evidence that crime does not readily respond to severe sentences, or new police power, or a greater use of imprisonment, legislatures have repeatedly adopted a punitive law and order stance'. Perhaps the most obvious example and, indeed, one of the most widely referenced was the pronouncement in 1993 by the former Conservative Home Secretary Michael Howard that 'prison works' as a way of controlling crime. Pawson and Tilley (1997, pp 3-4) pick up the story, suggesting that Howard's instincts 'did not rely on the bedrock of empirical evidence produced by the ranks of criminologists, penologists and evaluators at his disposal. Instead, he figured that armed robbers, muggers and rapists, and so on, safely locked away cannot be at liberty to pursue their deeds'. The telling point here is that the empirical evidence is conspicuous by its absence; indeed, the 'prison works' rhetoric neatly circumvents many years' worth of data concerning recidivism and reconviction rates. As a result of such issues, in his study of English crime control and punishment policy, Tonry (2004, p 146) suggests that when the subject under investigation involves a 'big issue' – by which he means one that is politicised – politics and not evidence 'is the order of the day'.

The idea is that in highly politicised policy areas policies are made with recourse to ideological standpoints and consequently cannot be 'evidence-based'. In essence, evidence is juxtaposed to politics as the driver of policy making. Returning to the example that will be followed throughout this book, with the benefit of hindsight, it is clear that the cannabis reclassification set in motion a train of events which placed the evidence base for the current UK drug classification system firmly on the political and media agenda. The publication of the House of Commons Science and Technology Select Committee report (2006b) was another pivotal moment. MacDonald and Das (2006) claimed that in the light of the Science and Technology Select Committee's findings, the UK drug classification system was actually an 'un-evidence-based mess', a standpoint typical of heavy politicisation. At the same time, however, independent research commissioned for the inquiry suggested that 'recent evidence is feeding into new policy' (Levitt et al, 2006, p xvi).

This book seeks to move beyond such conclusions on the grounds that the relationship between evidence and policy defies such neat categorisation. To all intents and purposes, the established criticisms of the evidence-based policy movement focus on the impact that politics has on the policy process. Drawing on comments made by a renowned social scientist Michael Rutter, Goldstein (2008, p 393) effectively illustrates this in relation to the use of evidence in UK education policy. He claims that a 'somewhat critical, even cynical, attitude towards government use of evidence' has recently emerged. For Rutter, 'the Government definitely does not want evidence, although their rhetoric is entirely different.... They just care about it if it fits their plans' (cited in Shepherd, 2006). Goldstein (2008, p 393) goes on to show how despite making noises to the contrary about how they welcomed research, members of the initial New Labour government actually systematically discredited certain, unwelcome, findings. The case of Peter Tymms and his research on homework is referenced here: Tymms demonstrated that 11-year-olds who do the most homework often perform less well in national tests. This research prompted ridicule from David Blunkett, who stated that nobody with 'the slightest commonsense' could take these suggestions seriously (cited in Nutley and Webb, 2000, p 23).

The current concern is, then, on the interplay between politics and evidence. In politicised policy areas understandings of evidence are clouded by the fact that it is difficult to locate, or can appear spurious, and is often conflated with absence. Although doubt is cast on the claim that 'evidence' will be discarded in policy areas that are highly politicised, it suggests claims that policies that engage with evidence on any level are 'evidence-based' are also logically problematic. It argues that neither standpoint accurately depicts the relationship between evidence and policy making in this scenario. An alternative path is pursued here, which suggests that much can be gained from considering not only what the connection is between evidence and policy, but also by focusing on what constitutes evidence itself and looking at possible manifestations of the connection. Although the 'evidence', in this case as in others, refers to that produced by 'research' (and these terms are used interchangeably, along with 'knowledge' and 'expertise'), there are still discrepancies in the way that these terms are understood. The subtitle to this book refers to the exploitation of research in policy making. Exploitation has more than one meaning, alluding to the way that research is used and misused or ignored in the formulation of policy. As a consequence, this book seeks to provide an analysis of evidence-based policy making that transcends debates about political expediency being the final nail in the coffin for evidence utilisation. Instead, it argues that political expediency provides the context in which evidence utilisation should be explained. This is because we live in an 'evidence age'. As we shall see, information agencies and providers of expertise are deeply embedded in the policy apparatus of various countries, and evidence from research struggles for impact alongside other phenomena such as politics, journalism, think-tanks, special advisers and so on. In what follows, the issue of UK drug classification – a politicised area par excellence as we have witnessed – is used to illustrate the subtleties of evidence use in this context. With this in mind the book is organised in the following way.

Chapter Two provides the background into the nature of evidence-based policy making, locating it in a particularly 'Western' democratic tradition of policy formulation. In essence, it is argued that the research/policy nexus is grounded in a history of Western state (and super-state) formation and tends to be applied in these contexts. The origins and nature of the research and policy relationship in various jurisdictions are documented. In the UK, the origins of this are charted in the work of various 19th-century philanthropists up to its present-day incarnation as evidence-based policy making under the conditions of New Labour's 'modernising agenda'.

Using Chapter Two as a springboard, Chapter Three details some established criticisms of the evidence-based policy-making agenda. Drawing on the work of Weiss et al (2008), these revolve around three main areas: the inadequacies of research and researchers; inadequacies in the context, beliefs and actions of policy makers; and inadequacies in the link between the two groups. A critical appraisal of these critiques is then provided. Discussion then turns to attempts that have been made to transcend this divide. This makes particular reference to the burgeoning literature surrounding knowledge brokering and transfer. It is claimed, however, that any attempts to bridge the divide are beset with difficulties because the connection is not easy to predict. These issues are magnified in heavily politicised policy areas. As this is the case, further consideration is given to the impact that political expediency has on the decision-making process. In particular, the impact of politics and the media on policy issues and the knock-on effect this has for data production in these policy domains is discussed.

Chapter Four provides background information to the case study through which the complex nature of evidence utilisation is explored. It charts the origins and the impact of the implementation of the MDA 1971 and points out how the passing of the MDA 1971 created the first UK government drugs advisory board in the shape of the ACMD. It goes on to explain how until recently the Act has remained relatively stable despite significant perturbations in the UK drug scene from the 1980s onwards. Following on from this, developments in UK drug policy in light of the election of the New Labour government in 1997 are covered. The centrality of drug classification issues in contemporary drug debates is documented and how this links to the evidence-based policy movement. In effect, the 2004 cannabis reclassification, it is argued, witnessed a collision between UK drugs policy and the evidence-based endeavour.

In Chapter Five attention turns to how the evidence and policy relationship in politicised areas can be explored and explained. It considers some theoretical and methodological tools that can be used to explore the nature of evidence use in politicised policy areas. A central premise of the evidence-based movement is that it is consistent with pluralist models of the policy process (Nutley et al, 2007) and many of these have been, or can be, employed in drugs research (Ritter and Bammer, 2010). The first part of the chapter therefore offers an overview of some of the main pluralist accounts of the policy process. Of all the available theories and methods, a modified version of the Advocacy Coalition Framework (ACF) (Sabatier and Jenkins-Smith, 1993b, 1999) provides the most potential for exploring and explaining the evidence and policy connection in heavily politicised areas because of its focus on conflict in the policy arena, conflict being a defining feature of politicised policies. The ACF is not without its faults and some of its key criticisms are introduced, followed by an account of how it can be made applicable in the current inquiry. Moving on, the next part of the chapter connects the history of UK drug policy with the modified version of the ACF. Drawing on the author's own research it introduces the interested coalitions or 'perspectives' engaged in UK drug classification debates.

In Chapter Six, an ACF-inspired analysis of the way that evidence was understood by key players in the policy process in relation to the 2004 cannabis policy change is undertaken. This also draws on subsequent events relating to broader interest in the UK drug classification system. This is done on the premise that to understand the complexities of evidence utilisation it is necessary to unpack appreciations of 'evidence' itself. The chapter takes the following format. The opening discussion focuses on the appreciations of evidence from the various perspectives identified in the previous chapter in relation to the initial reclassification of cannabis. This is followed by a summary of evidence utilisation in this particular subsystem. It is suggested that a plurality of different accounts of evidence can be ascertained. This is interesting in light of the conclusions that are drawn by the various groups documenting whether or not the decision to reclassify cannabis was evidence-based, which, incidentally, mirror those mentioned by MacDonald and Das, and Levitt and colleagues highlighted previously. The chapter then looks at how to explain the various accounts of evidence. The existence of a hierarchy of evidence is put forward here as a possible explanation, but ultimately ruled out on the grounds that appreciations of differing evidence are ideological as opposed to being primarily methodological.

Chapter Seven continues to closely analyse the label of evidence. In doing so, it embarks with a discussion of the wider drug classification system and the nature of drug harm therein. Once more, drawing on the author's own research with key stakeholders in debates over UK drug classification policy, detailed consideration of various appreciations of the role of evidence in the policy process is highlighted. By looking at appreciations of the role of evidence, different interpretations of the role or the position of evidence in policy making are revealed. This is then elaborated on, as something of a paradox is exposed. Although evidence is generally confused and contested, there is a simultaneous correlation among rival groups in the way that its use is understood. Finally, some extended summarising remarks are documented that suggest that to fully comprehend the nature of evidence utilisation in heavily politicised areas, it is necessary to view evidence both as contested, but with elements of certitude.

Based on the findings of previous chapters, Chapter Eight undertakes the task of explaining – via a model of evidence-based policy making – evidence utilisation in a politicised area. It starts with the premise that a key tenet of the politicisation is that policies are always in a constant state of flux as new data and personnel assume key positions in the decision-making process. This impacts on evidence production in the area, which is likewise dynamic. Using the notion of conceptual flux as a starting point, the debate then turns to how this can be modelled. This entails a brief survey of existing models of research utilisation (see also Weiss, 1986; Bryant, 1995). It is suggested that for various reasons these are not suitable for ascertaining the minutiae of the evidence and policy connection in a heavily politicised context. As this is the case, some newer additions to the literature are considered. Of these a newer processual model (Monaghan, 2010) is tentatively introduced as the most suitable means for understanding the complex relationship between evidence and policy formulation.

The book comes to a close with a discussion of what debates relating to evidence-based policy can tell drug policy makers and likewise what lessons from drug policy making can be learned by those advocating that all policies should be made with recourse to a robust evidence base. In doing so, it speculates on what the future may be for evidence-based policy. Even though the road ahead will continue to be perilous, the message is ultimately one of cautious optimism for the evidence movement.

Note

[1] From November 2007 the existing Science and Technology Select Committee became the Innovation, Universities, Science and Skills Select Committee under the same chair. As of October 2009, it reverted back to the Science and Technology Select Committee. Phil Willis did not stand for re-election in 2010.

TWO

The origins and reach of the evidence movement

There are few walks of modern life, both in the West and in other advanced industrialized societies, in which research is not a more or less explicit requirement of plausible public policy or credible argumentation, whether the matter is child abuse or global warming, punctuated equilibrium or consumer debt, lung cancer or affirmative action. Research-produced knowledge is everywhere, doing battle with other kinds of knowledge (produced by personal testimony, opinion, revelation or rumor) and with other pieces of research-produced knowledge. (Apparduri, 1997, p 58)

To fully comprehend the subtleties of evidence-based policy making it is necessary, in the words of Solesbury (2001), to understand from whence it came. It is also important to consider its constituent parts. Later chapters will deal with the concept of 'policy' and how this is to be conceptualised in the context of evidence-based policy making. This chapter, however, focuses on the 'evidence' aspect. We live in an evidence age. Something of a consensus across various disciplines particularly in the social sciences has arisen over the need to engage with the public or to be more 'outward facing'. Murji (2010, p 344) gives a useful overview of this, suggesting that in recent years we have witnessed a call for public sociology (Burawoy, 2005) and criminologies (Chancer and McLaughlin, 2007), engaged anthropology (Erikksen, 2006), alongside more general claims for making theory apply to practice (Smith, 2007). Mulgan (2005, p 216) suggests that the 'Western' world is currently in an era where the demand for knowledge is paramount and where today's citizens are 'far more educated, knowledgeable and confident than their predecessors'. This manifests itself in the fact that they use scientific knowledge to inform a range of choices, for example, from business decisions to dietary preferences. This scientific knowledge is tied in with the notion of 'best practice' that has become paramount in various policy spheres. For Mulgan (2005, p 216), governments are often cajoled into searching for this by the increasing influence of various transnational bodies such as the United Nations (UN), World Bank, International Monetary Fund (IMF), Organisation for Economic Co-operation and Development (OECD) and the European Union (EU). This search for best practice and spirit of coordination is leading to the creation of an evidence-based policy infrastructure across these domains.

Most European and other 'Western Hemisphere' governments have, therefore, committed themselves to a programme of evidence-based policy under the aegis of knowledge-based societies. Here, the development of public policy increasingly calls on independent, expert inquiry. This chapter is concerned with the genesis of this movement. Although an entire book could be filled and would be required to document the history of the research and policy relationship across the globe, the overview presented here focuses on recent developments in this domain drawing on relevant historical debates for context when required. In the first section attention turns more specifically to the research and policy connection. It shows how this nexus is grounded in a history of Western state formation and tends to be applied in these contexts. The origins of the research and policy relationship in various jurisdictions, including the US, the EU and the UK, are documented to indicate this. In the UK the origins of the work of various 19th-century philanthropists are charted up to the present-day incarnation as evidence-based policy making, stemming from New Labour's modernising agenda. In the second section, an overview of the changeable nature of the research and policy connection is discussed in the lead up to New Labour's modernising agenda and the realisation of evidence-based policy. Finally some summarising remarks are given.

Primacy of the research and policy connection in the 'Western Hemisphere'

The onset of evidence-based policy making was initially an Anglo-Saxon development (Solesbury, 2001; Boaz et al, 2008). For Solesbury (2001, p 6), it was characterised, first and foremost, by a 'utilitarian turn' in research, whereby researchers were required to produce work that was not only 'useful' but 'useable'. In other words, this is research that helps 'not just to understand society but offers some guidance on how to make it better'. It can be claimed, however, that it has actually been a 'Western' preoccupation. In the West there has been an intimate, if often at times, fractious, relationship between the policy-making and research communities (Anderson, 2003). Drawing on the work of Jann (1991), Anderson (2003, p 82) points out how in Europe, the empirical research tradition has been intrinsically linked to data collected by authorities or the state. Durkheim's (1952) *Suicide* is a classic example. The emerging US tradition of conducting field research and data collection, exhibited in the early studies of the Chicago School, reached European shores sometime later. As a consequence, compared to European standards, US public policy research training exhibited 'a preference for data rather than theoretical understanding' (Anderson, 2003, p 82). Both arenas shared the will to develop policy in relation to data. Indeed, that policy should be based on some kind of evidence, research or expertise has for a long time been seen to be common sense in most parts of the Western Hemisphere.

Despite disparities between them, the US, continental Europe and the UK also enjoy or endure a much different relationship between social science and policy making than in areas where the state was, and continues to be, relatively weak. Referring to an 'information society', Miller (1995, p 167) demonstrates why this is not being ushered in universally, suggesting that there is a distinct difference between nations that are 'information-rich' (advanced Western capitalist states) and those that have 'no access to advanced data and technology resources'. For Miller, the key issue here is that those who can enjoy the spoils of an advanced technological infrastructure are able to reap the benefits that this privileged position enables. Those countries with access to limited resources are 'forced to make international policy decisions on the basis of inadequate or incomplete information' (Miller, 1995, p 167). It must be stressed that even though a country may be information-rich, access to this information remains unequal and even those in privileged positions may still be reluctant to engage in this form of decision making. Yet it is the opportunity afforded to do so that is the present concern.

Various social processes impact on a country's capacity to create a knowledge production infrastructure. For Anderson (2003, p 83), the shrinking of the welfare state in the US and many Western European states, combined with the decline and subsequent collapse of Communism in Eastern Europe, resulted in a situation where state funding for higher education and scientific research in the public sector was both less benevolent and less secure. The developed nations of Western Europe, North America and other similar systems were able to absorb this through their established university network, so that the research and policy connection could be maintained. Similarly, in these countries a private sector research industry is now firmly embedded in the scientific community. In other locations this was not the case and not always the intention.

Anderson (2003, pp 82-3) points to various examples where producing scientific findings or providing an infrastructure of data collection devices through which to formulate national policies is not the primary concern. Such governments eschew the use of scientific research in policy formulation, privileging instead the guidance provided from religion, personal intuition or household networks (Anderson, 2003, p 83). For Anderson, the social sciences in particular are dispensed with and have virtually no role in the creation or assessment of public policy in this context. She states that this goes a long way to explain why, for example, in 1998, when asked what Libya's inflation rate was, 'neither the Governor of the Central Bank of Libya nor his director of research knew the answer' (Anderson, 2003, p 89). In other cases, outright hostility towards science seemed to be clearly an expression of government policy. Thus at the turn of the millennium, the official population figure for the entire Kingdom of Saudi Arabia was a state secret and half the volume of economic transactions of Egypt went unrecorded (Anderson, 2003, p 89).

Outside Africa and the Middle East, Anderson points out how the social sciences and their role in policy formulation have fluctuated. These fluctuations stemmed not so much from hostility as from the capacity of the state to subsidise social research and its associated infrastructure. For instance, the fiscal crises of the state in the 1980s in Latin America 'undermined previously generous state funding for higher education' (Anderson, 2003, p 84). Meanwhile, in India there was a reduction in expenditure on social science research, although the government attempted to compensate for this via tax breaks for private supporters and sponsors of social research. It is not the intention to suggest that policy development outside the West is somehow irrational or to make a normative assertion that it is less effective; the point is that an enduring, if not un–turbulent relationship between evidence production and policy making, is predominantly a 'Western' phenomenon. This relates to the culture of scientific endeavour that has developed in these areas and how this is closely tied to state and even 'super-state' formation, in the case of the EU.

History of the research and policy connection in Europe

The connection between evidence and policy in the EU (and its member and associated states) is longstanding, although evidence-based policy per se is not the currency. Instead, the literature focuses on knowledge utilisation and the role of expertise in policy making. It is acknowledged here that there are also significant differences within unitary member states as regards evidence-based policy making. For a discussion of some of these readers should consult Nutley et al (2010).[1]

Specific features of the EU's bureaucracy have also been identified which make it suited to a 'knowledge-based' approach to public policy making. For instance, it has been argued that the EU is primarily a regulatory (as opposed to redistributive) 'state' (Majone, 1996) and, as such, knowledge rather than money is the key resource in policy making (Radaelli, 1999, p 759). The nature of policy making in the EU means that the European Commission, as the institution dominating the initiation and implementation stages of policy, has been the focus of attention. The Commission, as a bureaucratic actor – although one with relatively limited in-house expertise across the EU's policy sectors (Cini, 1996) – has always relied on outside sources for the detailed knowledge necessary in the drafting of effective policy proposals (Peters, 1994). As such, it has actively sought outside expertise. In other words, precisely due to its relatively small workforce, the European Commission is dependent on external actors for informational resources necessary to the development of its policies. The Commission official staring at a blank piece of paper has been receptive to those actors in possession of informational resources with a desire to influence the policy agenda (Mazey and Richardson, 1999).

In short, traditionally the knowledge–policy nexus has been framed largely in terms of the need to make effective policy. The focus here is, then, on the generation of effective policy proposals, and mirrors the Commission's own argument that expertise is necessary for 'better policies'. Statements made by the European Commission provide an insight into its views on the necessity and existence of an evidence base for EU politics. They also indicate a commitment to developing public policy around expert knowledge. The governance White Paper of 2001 (European Commission, 2001), which sought to make changes to the way the EU used the powers given by its citizens, identified the need for 'better policies, regulation and delivery' as one of four broad 'proposals for change'. It acknowledged the role played by experts in preparing and monitoring decisions. It further approved the reliance of the Commission on specialist expertise in order to anticipate and identify problems requiring common European action, and furthermore, in explaining the logic of this necessity clearly and simply to the public.

A relatively new development in the discussion was the way in which the Commission accepted that the use of expertise – as with so many other aspects of its activities – had fallen foul of public confidence and that changes were needed in order restore this:

> It is often unclear who is actually deciding – experts or those with political authority ... a better informed public increasingly questions the content and independence of the expert advice that is given ... expertise is usually organised at the national level. It is essential that resources be put together and work better in the common interest of EU citizens. (European Commission, 2001, p 19)

To this end, the White Paper called for guidelines on the collection and use of expert advice in the Commission to provide for the accountability, plurality and integrity of the expertise used. This resulted in the 2002 Communication *Improving the knowledge base for better policies* (European Commission, 2002), which outlined some principles and guidelines on the collection and use of expertise by the Commission. In this, the Commission reiterated its insistence that expertise plays a key role in a dynamic knowledge-based society, outlining the twin objectives of establishing a sound knowledge base for policy and ensuring that this process was credible.

The first of these aims is consistent with the claim that expertise is a component of 'better policies' and, as such, can be seen to contribute to the output-oriented legitimacy (Scharpf, 1999). But the second aim appears to be about addressing 'input-oriented legitimacy'; 'no matter what seems to be the "right" decision for those involved in the advisory process, it is essential that interested parties and the public at large are themselves convinced that decisions are sound' (European Commission, 2002, p 3). The Commission, it seems, was acting in response to the suspicion that the public had viewed the use of expertise as pernicious and overly technocratic. More recently, the Commission's Transparency Initiative has also addressed the need for openness at this preliminary stage of the policy-making process (Cini, 2008).

The activities of the Commission have been the focus of empirical research, but discussions about the role of knowledge in EU policy, as suggested, have not specifically drawn on the evidence-based policy literature. As Radaelli (1999) notes, they have found expression along several other dimensions. These include studies of professionalism and technocracy in bureaucratic behaviour and network governance, in particular, through advocacy coalitions (Sabatier and Jenkins-Smith,

1993b, 1999) and epistemic communities. The latter have been particularly prominent (Verdun, 1999; see also Richardson, 1996a; Zito, 2001; Dunlop, 2007). According to Haas (1992, p 3), an epistemic community is 'a network of professionals with recognised expertise and competence in a particular domain and an authoritative claim to policy relevant knowledge within that domain or issue area'. Richardson (1996b) argues that 'the politics of expertise' as practised by epistemic communities 'has become especially important in situations of loose networks and a high level of uncertainty' (p 48). Alongside these descriptive accounts of the knowledge–policy nexus, however, there has emerged a critical dimension, arguably a response in part to the Commission's linking of expertise to 'good governance'. Concern is expressed in some studies of the tyranny technocracy (Albaek, 1995; Parsons, 2002) and the 'dark side' of expertise (Fischer, 1990). The picture of a technocratic EU is one where expertise is the sole basis of authority and power, as opposed to democracy based on legitimate consensus, free elections and participation (Radaelli, 1999, p 758).

The legitimacy dimension of the knowledge–policy nexus is addressed further by Boswell (2008), who argues that knowledge and expertise actually performs a crucial function for the Commission in helping it to substantiate and legitimate its policy proposals. Boswell identifies a series of characteristics of the Commission that make it amenable to using expertise as a legitimating or substantiating factor. Among these are the fact that its role and competence are continually questioned (especially the work of certain directorate-generals) and that it is a technocratic actor whose actions are based on rationalistic decision making. Broader policy communities, for example, asylum and immigration, also use and value expertise as these are contested policy areas. Although the use of knowledge and expertise is important in these respects, it is also crucial for the Commission to 'signal' that it is using knowledge in the development of its proposals. In essence, the use of expertise within the EU has taken a reflexive turn.

Yet despite the emergence of a literature on the descriptive and normative dimensions of expert knowledge in EU policy, there is much that is not known about what expertise is. Neither is it clear when, how, where and by whom it is or should be incorporated into the EU policy-making process and with what consequences for effective and democratic governance. Such issues, it is argued in this book, also plague evidence utilisation in politicised areas. This is interesting as the discussion of expert knowledge in EU policy making has taken place alongside but has rarely interacted with the evidence-based policy paradigm that has dominated similar discussions in one of its member states (the UK), and is increasingly becoming prominent in allied territories (North America). Indeed, closer examination of the evidence-based policy paradigm in the US and the UK reveals significant overlap with the knowledge–policy nexus in the EU. Consequently, many of the problems identified with evidence-based policy making (and proposed solutions) may resonate in other similar jurisdictions.

History of the research and policy connection in the US

It is acknowledged that the US is not representative of all of North America, but for current purposes discussion is restricted to this domain. The relationship between the social sciences and policy formulation in the US can be described as 'intense', stemming from long intertwined histories. Regarding the origins of the social sciences in the US, Anderson (2003, p 3) states that they were 'born as the handmaidens of democracy and industrial capitalism in the formation of the American state'. In effect, the social sciences are closely tied in with the project of American liberalism. The history of the relationship between the social sciences and federal government policy making in the US has been widely documented (Lynd, 1940; Lyons, 1969; Caplan, 1977; Lindblom and Cohen, 1979; Scott and Shore, 1979; Weiss, 1995; Anderson, 2003). One common thread running through these accounts is the sense of strain between the two protagonists. Lyons (1969) referred to the connection as an 'uneasy partnership'; Weiss (1995) refers to it as 'haphazard'; whereas Anderson (2003) points out the 'vexatious' character of the bond.

This is all a far cry from the vision outlined by one of the earliest aficionados of research-based policy in the US, Donald Campbell, in his 'experimental society':

> The United States and other modern nations should be ready for an experimental approach to social reform, an approach in which we try out new programs designed to cure specific problems, in which we learn whether or not these programs are effective, and in which we retain, imitate, modify or discard them on the basis of their apparent effectiveness on the multiple imperfect criteria available. Our readiness for this stage is indicated by the inclusion of specific provisions for program evaluation in the first wave of the "Great Society" legislation and by the current congressional proposals for establishing "social indicators" and data banks. (Campbell, 1969, p 409, cited in Pawson, 2006a, p 2)

It is questionable whether Campbell's vision of the experimental society ever was, or could be, realised. Indeed, the strain and turmoil in the relationship between the science and policy communities stems from growing reservations over the ability of the social sciences to provide the answers to social problems. This is documented in further detail in the following chapter. For now, the origins of the vexatious connection are outlined. Weiss and colleagues (2008, p 31) have charted the research and policy connection in the US, pointing out how 'social science organisations repeatedly called on the federal government to make increased use of the knowledge that the social sciences have to offer'. This gathered apace in the 1960s as the National Academy of Sciences (1968) and the National Science Foundation (1968) produced reports to that effect. This was bolstered by the war on poverty, a key driver in promoting the utility of research and evaluation to policy, and it is in this context, incidentally, that Campbell's pronouncements were made.

In the US, the 1960s was, then, an era of unprecedented opportunities for the social sciences. John F. Kennedy recruited many high-powered social scientists into his policy community and Lyndon B. Johnson's embrace of 'the interventionist state' under the aegis of the Great Society made all seem well (Anderson, 2003, p 30). The enthusiasm was to be short-lived, however. This related, in part, to the sheer intricacies of policy challenges that proved to be much less predictable than first thought. The impact was far reaching. Not only was there tangible dismay on behalf of the scientific community at the limitations of their authority, but the then existing cosy marriage of social science with policy formulation resulted in a backlash from the general public due to the failure of government policies over Vietnam and poverty. Social scientists were seen as being complicit in their development and therefore came to be seen as morally bankrupt.

In effect, dubious foreign policies in South East Asia along with other unpopular domestic policies such as educational segregation meant that social scientists were seen as an extension of government instead of a critical friend whose task was to 'speak truth to power' (Anderson, 2003). The outcome of this was significant unrest on and off campuses in the US. This coincided with a strengthening of the Civil Rights movement, which gained increasing notoriety with support from a sizeable student lobby railing against their 'establishment' professors. The academics retreated to their universities and shied away from political involvement to concentrate on the advancement of the discipline of social science itself. It is this quandary that best sums up the vexatious relationship between social research and policy formulation in the US. While the social sciences have been intrinsically linked to the formation of the US state and the advancement of American liberalism, social sciences also have a duty of care to ensure their own longevity. Episodes such as those of the 1960s neatly illustrate this and this has left a lasting legacy in the US (Wilensky, 1997).

Despite these upheavals, some semblance of a relationship between the research and policy communities in the US remains. For instance, both worlds interact in the area of evaluation research, of which the US has a well-developed infrastructure (for example, see Alkin, 2004). Commentators suggest, however, that this does not necessarily translate into a cosy relationship with the political process. For Nutley and Webb (2000, pp 31-2), this is partly down to the 'fragmented and decentralised political economy' of the US. They contrast this with the more '"corporatist" European systems (such as those found in Sweden, Norway and Austria)' that 'foster dialogue between researchers, bureaucrats and politicians'. Although the evaluation and policy analysis industries are 'less well developed' in these states, there is a clear sense that research findings find their way into policy analysis more routinely than in the US, where 'often single issue research, focusing on short-run effects' is frequently used for political ammunition rather than holistic policy planning.

Although this is the case, evidence is proving a resilient player and remains firmly part of the political lexicon. In an address to the National Academy of Sciences, Barack Obama determinedly emphasised the centrality of science to decision making, concluding that 'we need to engage the scientific community directly in the work of public policy' (Obama, 2009, cited in Clear, 2010, p 2). Similarly, in a recent debate on healthcare reform in the US, President Obama echoed many sentiments uttered by Tony Blair and the New Labour cabal almost a decade earlier:

> Part of what we want to do is to make sure that those decisions are being made by doctors and medical experts based on evidence, based on what works. (*Newsweek*, 2009)

History of the research and policy connection in the UK

We have already seen how the development of the evidence-based policy paradigm, in these terms, was initially a British phenomenon (Boaz et al, 2008). Here, the relationship between applied social research and policy making has a long history. Indeed, Parsons (1995) suggests that it is as old as the state itself. It has also been well documented that one of the first works of what is now referred to as 'political science' – Thomas Hobbes' *Leviathan* – was intended as a guide for those in the English Parliament who were questioning the sovereignty and wisdom of King Charles I (Stokes, 2007). It was, thus, an exercise in the encouragement of policy learning. In 1651 Hobbes stated:

> I recover some hope that one time or other this writing of mine may fall into the hands of a sovereign who will consider it himself (for it is short, and I think clear) without the help of any interested or envious interpreter; and by the exercise of entire sovereignty, in protecting the public teaching of it, convert this truth of speculation into the utility of practice. (Hobbes, 1651/2004, p 155)

Hobbes recognised that some relationship between scholarly practice and policy formulation was a desirable enterprise. In a remarkable example of prescience, he also noticed that it would be necessary for research to be 'short' and 'clear' for this relationship to bear fruit. One is reminded here of Weiss's (1993) finding that research for policy has to be succinct because politicians spend such little time in their day actually reading and therefore require information that can be easily digested in bite-size chunks.

Hobbes was not the only figure from the history of philosophy and related disciplines to express desire for his work to influence policy. Weiss et al (2008, p 31) point out how this was a goal for Thomas Malthus, Karl Marx and Herbert Spencer. It was not until the 19th century, however, that the relationship between research and policy became consolidated. Early examples of this include the work of the Royal Commission on the Poor Law 1832–34, through to that of philanthropists such as Charles Booth and Seebohm Rowntree, whose pioneering studies of London and York, respectively, saw the development of the social survey method and an attempt to 'scientifically' measure the nature and extent of poverty in Victorian society (Bulmer, 1982).

Continuing into the 20th century, studies by Sydney and Beatrice Webb along with the influence of A.L. Bowley gradually saw the institutionalisation of social research and social science in academia and within government (Bulmer, 1982), a tradition continued by Richard Titmuss (Mann, 2009). Government recognition of the significance of social research as a key tool in policy development gained increasing momentum with the publication of several key reports. According to Nutley and Webb (2000, p 17):

> The Haldane Report in 1917 reviewed the government's provision for research and argued that it should be substantially expanded. One of the principles expounded in this Report related to the need for a separate government research department (rather than research units within each government department) to ensure that research is given its own voice and that results are not subordinated to administrative interests. Subsequent government reports – Clapham Report (HMSO, 1946), Heyworth Report (HMSO, 1965) and two reports by Lord Rothschild (Rothschild, 1971; HMSO, 1982) – revisited such issues.

The 1982 Rothschild report is of particular significance. It advocated that government departments should seek to strike a balance in their commissioning of work so that research was not directly critical of policy, but also made a concerted attempt to challenge the scientific and policy status quo.

Running alongside increased governmental capacity in the production of research for policy was the expansion of academic institutions and infrastructure directly for this purpose (Parsons, 1995). Nutley and Webb (2000, p 17) explain that the relationship between the research and policy communities up to the 1960s was premised on a model of social engineering, whereby research 'could and should be of direct use to government in determining and achieving its social policy objectives'. Clear parallels can therefore be drawn between the US and the UK at this time regarding what the perceived ideal relationship between the social science community and the political establishment should be. If the 1960s represented the high point for social engineering, then the 1970s and 1980s witnessed a move towards its nadir. Booth (1988, p 224) picks up the story:

> In both the UK and the USA at roughly the same time, and prompted by roughly the same motives, there occurred a quickening of official interest in the use of social science for policy making. Government funds were channelled into the expansion of the social sciences; there was a rapid increase in expenditure on social research; and social

scientists were drawn into government. For a while optimism ran high that a new partnership was in the making. Before long, however, strains began to show as the overblown expectations of each side were dashed. Social scientists complained that nobody listened to them and their work was ignored. Policy-makers chuntered about the irrelevance of the research they commissioned. Both retreated into their bunkers.

The bunkers, 'chunterings' and strains highlighted here are in fact nothing new. In the US, as we have seen, this was a product of political tensions relating to the ongoing Vietnam War and the Civil Rights movement. In the UK, this was attributed to the decline of the post-war consensus, stemming from a realisation from the political left that 'previous attempts at social engineering through education (and elsewhere) had largely been ineffective' (Finch, 1986, p 35).

One outcome of the demise of the post-war consensus and the failure of social engineering was, from the 1970s onwards, the rise in the 'number, type and variety of think-tanks' (Nutley and Webb, 2000, p 18). These have contributed to an increasing pluralism in the community of evidence production and the wider policy process. They have also contributed to the partisanship noticeable in many areas of policy, particularly those that fall under the banner of heavy politicisation. Around this time changes in the allocation of government funding for research can also be identified as the research council network became consolidated. Through research councils, the government has managed to keep the independent research infrastructure at arm's-length from the decision-making process (Nutley and Webb, 2000, p 19). For the social sciences, this has been particularly problematic. It is germane to remind ourselves at this stage that the social sciences were routinely dismissed by the Thatcher government in the era of conviction politics underpinned by a New Right ideology and that the SSRC ceased to exist in that form as questions were raised about its 'scientific' credentials. In effect, in the 1980s in both the US and the UK a culture of mistrust emerged between government and the social science establishment. New Labour's commitment to evidence-based policy making can be seen as a signal that it intended to reverse some of the later trends. Central to this was the attempt to heal wounds under the conditions of the 'modernising agenda'.

Fluctuating research and policy connection: policy modernisation and the evidential 'turn'

It is clear that the trajectory by which various jurisdictions have reached the commitment towards evidence-based policy making is different. That said, in all areas evidence is now embedded in the decision-making apparatus. Despite this, it has also been illustrated how the relationship between research and policy making has been complex and fluctuating. This can also be seen in the changing conceptualisation of the way the link between the two phenomena has been conceived. In the 1960s it was claimed that social experiments could shed light on and inform programmes of social reform (Campbell, 1969). Throughout the 1970s and 1980s, the relationship was contextualised in terms of models of 'research utilisation' (Bulmer et al, 1986; Weiss, 1977, 1986; Weiss and Bucuvalas, 1980) and evaluation research (Rossi and Freeman, 1985; Guba and Lincoln, 1989). Into the early 1990s, policy-oriented learning – a close relation of evaluation research – was *en vogue* (Sabatier and Jenkins-Smith, 1993b). And from the 1990s onwards, starting in the UK, 'evidence-based policy' has become the accepted label (Cabinet Office, 1999b).

In effect, on assuming power New Labour promised more accountability in the policy-making arena, as part of the 'modernising agenda' and in the quest to discover 'what works' in public service delivery. The goal was to shake up the nature of policy making, making sure that policies were 'strategic, outcome focused, joined-up (if necessary), inclusive, flexible, innovative and robust' (Nutley and Webb, 2000, p 20). Allied to this was the commitment to ensuring policies were 'evidence-based'. A fundamental change in the culture of policy formulation was required, it was thought, to make this come into fruition. This change entailed placing research and analysis at the centre of decision making.

With the benefit of hindsight, Taylor (2005, p 601) speaks of an 'evidential turn' in the language of public policy that accompanied the election of the New Labour administration. He draws on debates occurring in the evaluation literature to illustrate some key points about the political and policy conditions that brought around this state of affairs. Citing the work of various thinkers (for example, Clarke et al, 2000; Glendinning et al, 2002; Newman, 2002; Daly, 2003; Clarke, 2004), he links this to the 'rise of neo-liberalism, public choice theory and new managerialism over the last two decades of the twentieth century'. Through exercising control at a distance corporate models have been employed, as economic efficiency (making policies provide value for money) is crucial for effective governance (Hood, 1995; Stoker, 1998). Linked to these developments, as Taylor subsequently points out, was a move to strip political values out of policy making and replace them with '"objective scientific" evidence of "what really works"'. Along with audit and performance management, evaluation has become a key entry into the lexicon of NPM and the pursuit of what politicians increasingly frame as 'value-free policy' (Taylor, 2005, p 602). In effect, it has become a way of legitimating policy choices.

We have already witnessed how in the EU the use of the best available expertise is being encouraged by the European Commission as a way of legitimising its activities. In the UK, a similar process has occurred although the legitimacy of the policy-making apparatus does not receive the same level of scrutiny. It is widely accepted that some evidence should be underpinning policy formulation and this is broadly considered to be a sensible development. This does not mean that the endeavour has been straightforward; nor does it mean that issues of legitimacy are banished from the agenda completely. It is worth bearing in mind that the evidence turn was part and parcel of wider policy developments occurring towards the end of the 20th century, broadly referred to as changes in governance.

Stoker (1998) has identified how governance is an inherently slippery term, with numerous possible meanings and applications. Broadly speaking, it can be said to refer to changes in the activity and composition of the government; in other words, governance 'refers to a set of institutions and actors that are drawn from but also beyond government' (Stoker, 1998, p 18). In this sense, as has been stressed, it is consistent with the evidence turn in that the latter, for Solesbury (2001), sought the 'opening up' of government. Although this is generally seen to be desirable, it does also raise an issue of legitimacy. This is because the mode of governing assumed by the opening up of governance is contrary to the 'typical' British system of governing typified by the 'Westminster' model. This issue will be discussed further in Chapter Five, but for now it is apposite to say that the Westminster model is characterised by a solitary centre of power. This is power in terms of ownership of the means of legitimate violence and coercion. Further aspects of the Westminster model are 'parliamentary sovereignty, strong cabinet government and accountability through elections' (Stoker, 1998, p 19). These things are, however, undermined by governance and, by association, the commitment to evidence-based policy making. Indeed, it was such issues that resulted in an aversion to technocracy (Clarence, 2002).

Despite the fact that the Westminster model has been widely discredited in that the government has always been a multifarious system with many loci of power and 'diverse links between many agencies of government at local, regional national and supranational levels' (Clarence, 2002), the model still retains some currency. This is because, in the words of Sabatier and Jenkins-Smith (1993a, p 2), it provides a 'commonsense understanding' of the decision-making process and consequently, garners support from the general public. In essence, for many, the ideal type of the Westminster model is favoured. Stoker suggests that empirical work conducted by Miller and Dickson (1996) reveals similar findings relating to the structures of local government that the public tend to favour 'top-down' models of decision making. This represents something of a paradox in that although the evidence movement seems to enjoy widespread appeal, it presents a challenge to popular (if problematic) notions of 'good' governing.

It has already been pointed out that the move towards developing evidence-based policy and practice was characterised by a 'utilitarian turn' in research. This process was driven largely by the funders of social science, who stressed the benefits of cumulating knowledge in the research enterprise. This model was also typical of the medical research process under the aegis of evidence-based medicine. It is, therefore, no coincidence that as evidence-based policy became the currency of policy making, this brought to the fore the systematic review; this is the strategy of synthesising bygone and hopefully good quality evidence in any given field (Hammersley, 2001; Oakley, 2003; Harden et al, 2004; Pawson, 2006a; Petticrew and Roberts, 2006). Organisations such as the Campbell Collaboration have developed with this in mind. Emphasis from systematic reviews has replaced evaluation research as the strategy of choice for policy makers in justifying their decisions. This is, in part, because systematic reviews or meta-analysis provide an overview of families of programmes or interventions across disciplines, and are therefore seen to be of greater validity than an evaluation of a single intervention or programme.

This is not to say that evaluation research has become entirely moribund. Pawson (2006a, p 8) points to another reason why the evidential centre of gravity has shifted. He suggests that this development relates to the 'stunningly obvious point about the timing of research *vis-à-vis* policy – namely that in order to inform policy, the research must come before the policy'. Systematic reviews are, therefore, promoted as being temporally favourable for policy makers to utilise. Much argument over the methodology of the systematic review has also been a noticeable feature of the evidence movement. These debates are reminiscent and in some ways an extension of the 'paradigm wars' that were prevalent in the evaluation literature in the 1980s and 1990s. They can be characterised for the sake of convenience as a debate between social constructionism (Lincoln and Guba, 1985) and realism (Pawson and Tilley, 1997). Thus a certain degree of methodological jousting as to the most efficacious means to undertake systematic reviews has accompanied the rise of evidence-based policy (see Oakley, 2005; Pawson, 2006a; Petticrew and Roberts, 2006). This can be encapsulated as a debate between the established paradigm of meta-analysis (those preoccupied with maximising external validity and guided by the principles of quasi-experimental research designs; see, for example, the work of the Campbell Collaboration) and alternatives such as realist synthesis.[2]

A further factor often overlooked concerns the issue of where research can or should play a role in policy decision making and what kind of research can be used. This will be returned to in later chapters (particularly Chapter Seven). Palpably, not all social issues lend themselves to systematic review or meta-analysis as the evidence base is not so developed. This is quite different, however, from claiming that evidence is non-existent. As the evidential turn has progressed, it has become quite clear that the label can apply to policy formulation where evidence of some kind has been drawn on in the process of decision making. Indeed, it is not uncommon for policy makers or practitioners to scratch around for 'nuggets' of evidence in this manner and these cannot be ignored (Brocklehurst and Liabo, 2004; Pawson, 2006b). These may be the findings of small *n* qualitative projects or the insights from professional or public opinion among other things. In this way, evidence-based policy making is best thought of as an amalgamation of what Gordon et al (1993, p 5) term 'analysis of policy' and 'analysis for policy', with a broad understanding of what can count as evidence. The implications of what counts as evidence will also be considered in later chapters.

The methodological jousting that has accompanied the evidence movement is closely associated to the various criticisms of the phenomenon that have emerged. Indeed, at almost the same time that evidence gained currency in policy making, significant criticisms of the movement have become widespread. These are documented in the following chapter. In response to these, there has been a toning down of the initial enthusiasm that greeted the evidential turn. This is in part because of the recognition that research evidence is only one player in the decision-making process (Weiss, 1986), sitting alongside other things such as 'polling', where a politician canvasses opinion from constituents, and 'punditry', where special advisers, policy analysts or think-tanks carefully select helpful bits of information on which to justify a pre-existing policy (Pawson, 2006a, pp 5-6). The key point is that evidence is not the only player in the decision-making process, but it is a player nonetheless, and a realistic account of its nature and role needs to be factored in to any explanation of how policies are made. It is to this task that the following chapters are applied.

Summary

This chapter has explained the origins of the research presence in policy development, suggesting that the research–policy nexus as a strategy of policy making is grounded in a history of Western state and super-state formation. This is not to suggest that elsewhere, where this relationship is not so consolidated, policy formulation is somehow irrational or inferior. The origins of the research and policy relationship in various jurisdictions including the US, the EU and the UK have been documented. The idea is that evidence in some form has been embedded in the policy decision-making process in these areas even though its fortunes wax and wane. In the UK, New Labour's modernising agenda for policy making breathed new life into the research communities and has reinvigorated the relationship between social science and government that had deteriorated in the 1980s.

From these discussions, it is clear that evidence-based policy (or the politics of expertise in the EU) is central to contemporary policy agendas. Although this is the case, the relationship between the research and policy communities has been consistently tumultuous, to the point that almost simultaneously the existing enthusiasm surrounding the evidential turn has been somewhat muted. The following chapter takes this as a starting point and considers some of the barriers towards evidence-based decision making as well as potential solutions to how these can be overcome and the implications of these for politicised policy areas.

Notes

[1] A special edition of the journal *Evidence & Policy* vol 6, no 2, published in 2010, offers a useful overview of evidence-based policy making in various countries in Europe.

[2] For a detailed discussion of meta-analysis and an alternative picture of realist synthesis, see Pawson (2006a).

THREE

The two communities of evidence and policy, the challenge of politics and the impact of the media

> The honeymoon of intellectuals and policy-makers is often nasty, brutish and short. (Merton, 1957, p 222)

Chapter Two located the origins of evidence-based policy making in a 'Western' democratic tradition of policy development. It stressed that the relationship between the two protagonists of the tale (researchers and policy makers) has never been straightforward and is blighted by mutual suspicion. Continuing this story, this chapter initially focuses on some established criticisms of the evidence-based policy-making agenda. The policy process has broadened under the conditions of governance. Leaving aside for the moment the way this happens and the equity of it, decision making under the conditions of evidence-based policy making has become diffuse as evidence is canvassed from the social science community to buttress policy formulation. In short, any notions that decision making follows a 'Westminster' model have been further undermined by the evidence turn. It was stressed in Chapter Two, however, that this raised something of a paradox as although evidence-based policy making is widely supported, it also raises an issue of the legitimacy of any administration in that the public are familiar with the Westminster style of decision making (Stoker, 1998).

Along with this paradox some irony underpins the onset of evidence-based policy making. A defining aspect of the movement towards evidence-based policy making was, for Solesbury (2001, p 6), witnessed with the propensity of practitioners and policy makers seeking evidence from research knowledge in a bid to recover some of the loss of public confidence in their activities. The irony here stems from the way that the social sciences, and, indeed, sciences in general, came to prominence as a driver or influence on policy at roughly the same time that public confidence in their activities began to erode. Young et al (2002) illustrate this with reference to the increasing 'uncertainty' of scientific evidence arising from ecological issues such as the emergence of Bovine Spongiform Encephalopathy (BSE). In a similar vein, social theorists such as Beck (1992) suggest that under the conditions of what he terms the 'risk society', scientific evidence is increasingly employed to correct the effects of previous scientific endeavours and innovations. Traditionally, professionals operated like a 'priesthood', reliant on the unquestioning faith of their followers. Increasingly, however, patients, parents, students, clients and customers of all kinds are less and less inclined to take professional views on trust.

The 'informed consent' of the public is needed with the implementation of any intervention, which means that professionals must be ready to explain not just what they advise and why it is appropriate, but also what they know of its likely efficacy (Solesbury, 2001, p 6). This development underpinned the commitment to finding out 'what works' in various policy arenas, even though the professional view may not be seen as the most efficacious option. Boaz et al (2008, p 234) observe of these developments how they have created numerous opportunities as 'budgets for analytical work in government departments and agencies have expanded'. The not-for-profit or third sector has also been involved. Charities such as Barnardo's have demonstrated a commitment to thinking in terms of the evidence base behind their decisions and their advocacy.[1]

There are, however, a further number of recognised and unresolved questions or issues concerning the knowledge–policy nexus and in its guise as evidence-based policy making. These can be translated as criticisms of the applicability of research-driven or research-informed policy formulation, and generally revolve around misunderstandings of the functions of each group by the other. These have become widely documented in the literature. It is fair to suggest that such criticisms, in turn, have not been accepted uncritically. As this is so, this chapter moves on to develop a critical appraisal of the criticisms. Following on from this, the discussion moves on to highlight attempts made to transcend this divide. This makes particular reference to the burgeoning literature surrounding knowledge brokering and transfer.

A central premise of knowledge brokering is that highly skilled actors familiar with the research process and adept at decision making can smooth the transition from evidence production to policy formulation, primarily, but not solely, via open and prolonged dialogue. The following section discusses the potential for this to occur when policy areas are heavily politicised. These are often highly contentious debates, consisting of various actors with differing normative appreciations over the nature and direction of policy. As such, it will be difficult for dialogue to have any meaningful impact on beliefs or action (Sabatier and Jenkins-Smith, 1993a). As this is the case, further consideration is given to the impact that political expediency has on the decision-making process, with a discussion of the impact of politics and the media on policy issues and the knock-on effect this has for data production in these policy domains. The chapter concludes with a summary.

Established criticisms of the evidence-based policy movement

There has been longstanding recognition in the policy analysis literature of the tumultuous relationship between what Caplan (1979) describes as the 'two communities' of research producers and policy makers. This has underpinned many criticisms of evidence-based policy. Taking a lead from Weiss et al (2008),

---

three main concerns can be identified. These correspond to: inadequacies in researchers and research (and their/its utility for policy); inadequacy in the context, beliefs and actions of policy makers and their views of research; and inadequacy in the links between researchers, policy makers and practitioners. These are now discussed in turn.

Inadequacies of research producers and the research produced

It has long been recognised that, particularly in the social sciences, inconsistent and often contradictory findings are commonplace. Mulgan (2005) comments that because all social scientific knowledge is historically contingent and reflexive, it is not always conducive to producing definitive solutions to specific policy problems. For certain thinkers, this critique of the nature of science has gone unnoticed by the government in their quest for finding out 'what works'. Campbell (2002, p 89) suggests that evidence-based policy making has, in fact, been used by the government as a way of neglecting the scepticism that exists within the public towards the scientific community. Clarence (2002, p 4), drawing on the work of Rüdig (1993, pp 18-19), also suggests that through the 'what works' mantra, the government has ignored decades of theory emerging from the sociology of science, highlighting the existence of scientific controversy, that is, the fallibility of scientific evidence and how this is actually an 'intrinsic element of the scientific process' (Rüdig, 1993, p 19). Rosenthal and DiMatteo (2001, p 60) summarise this situation, commenting that in the early part of the 21st century there has been an almost explosive growth of scientific research in nearly every area. In these circumstances 'new findings daily "overthrow" old ones'. Also, some studies 'show effects in one direction and some in the opposite, and some show effects that are close to zero' (Rosenthal and DiMatteo, 2001, p 60). In effect, instead of giving clarification, research findings often mystify central issues in both theory and practice.

A further key criticism of the evidence movement has been the claim that poor scholarship has resulted from the system in which evaluators or evidence suppliers are working. Here phrases like 'quick and dirty' reviews become derogatory titles for work often commissioned by government departments or agencies that rely on speedy access to information. As Weiss et al (2008, pp 31-2) illustrate, 'evaluators often work under limited time constraints with insufficient funds for good comparative design and longitudinal follow up'. To lay these charges solely at the door of 'government' and the demands they place on the research community is somewhat misleading, however. It downplays the fact that most government departments, particularly in the UK (including the devolved administrations), now have or have recently had a bespoke research section, staffed by individuals and teams with significant experience in designing, conducting, analysing and disseminating social research. The fact remains, however, that quite often the social sciences do not have the answers to what policy makers identify as pressing problems. It was this realisation that led Scott and Shore (1979) to their bleak conclusion about the application of sociology for policy.

Inadequacies in policy formulators and their understandings of research

Although in-house research units are commonplace, there are still episodes when significant schisms between the policy-making and research communities have come to light. In his speech given to the ESRC concerning the use of social research by government, former Secretary of State for Education, David Blunkett (2000), stated that he 'felt frustrated' by the tendency for research:

> ... when it does try to be directly relevant to the main policy and political debates, to be seemingly perverse, driven by ideology paraded as intellectual inquiry or critique, setting out with the sole aim of collecting evidence that will prove a policy wrong rather than genuinely seeking to evaluate or interpret impact. A number of studies have tried to claim evidence of poor outcomes when policies have barely been implemented ... we need to be able to rely on social science and social scientists to tell us what works and why and what types of policy initiatives are likely to be most effective. And we need better ways of ensuring that those who want this information can get it easily and quickly. (Blunkett, 2000, para 7)

Blunkett further stated that this is to be achieved by research that paints a coherent picture of how society works, and not by 'worthless correlations based on small samples from which it is impossible to draw generalisable conclusions' (Blunkett, 2000, para 7). He goes on to suggest that studies which combine 'large scale, quantitative information on effect sizes, which allow us to generalise, with in-depth case studies which provide insights into how processes work', are welcome. In response to this, Hodgkinson (2000) pointed out that Blunkett's understanding of social research is inherently positivist. It furthermore neglects the fact that the research design should probably be a product of the research issue under consideration, not a driving force of this (Blaikie, 2000).

In addition to these issues, many researchers and evaluators comment on demoralising research environments, the result of commissioners giving with one hand and taking with the other. Pawson (2006a, p 10) offers the vignette of a situation in which the evaluation of a government initiativecommissioned by one arm of government was under way, before being declared unsuccessful by another, prior to the findings of the evaluation entering the public domain. In a similar vein, Weiss and colleagues (2008, p 33) cite the example of a report from the then Scottish Executive's Social Research and Knowledge Transfer Office (Clark and Kelly, 2005, p 20). This documents how policy makers:

> ... worked to unrealistic, short-term timescales; frequently asked academics to "dumb down" their research findings; sometimes "moved the goal posts" half way through a research project; apparently ignored some research outcomes from projects; did not always take the time to read and analyze full academic outputs; sometimes lost interest in projects or events when policy priorities changed.

Another recent example from the UK illustrates how academics can feel manipulated by policy makers when their research is ripped out of context and misrepresented. Referring to the political risks inherent in scientific knowledge about policies, Hope (2004, p 290) points out that politicians 'may be unable to resist the temptation to use political authority to manipulate the evidence they present in public to produce a more tolerable valuation of their policy', thereby ill-serving the genuine public interest and, ultimately, 'democratic trust in government'. Hope is speaking from experience here as he goes on to document how an evaluation undertaken by a research consortium with which he was involved found less varying rates of success over New Labour's flagship Reducing Burglary Initiative (RBI) policies – part of the Crime Reduction Programme – than did the Home Office's own evaluators.

Hope (2004) suggests that such instances can occur when there is a blurring of the boundaries between research and policy communities and a redrawing of the boundaries between science and politics under the conditions of the risk society. He cites the work of Donald Campbell to illustrate the inherent danger of intertwining the scientific and political communities:

> ... it is one of the characteristics of the present situation that *specific reforms are advocated as though they were certain to be successful*. For this reason, knowing outcomes has immediate political implications ... if the political and administrative system has committed itself in advance to the correctness and efficiency of its reforms; it cannot tolerate learning of failure. (Campbell, 1978, p 80; emphasis in original)

Inadequacies in the connections between researchers, policy makers and practitioners

[handwritten margin note: disstressing]

[handwritten margin note: walk the talk]

For Mulgan (2005), 'democracy' is the reason why there is often a vexatious relationship between policy makers and the research community. Ultimately, politicians have every right to ignore evidence and to follow their instinct. To illustrate this, he cites the example of the paucity of evidence for increasing police numbers 'on the beat' in reducing the amount of crime in any given area. He suggests that politicians frequently ignore this as it is the public's perception that this is the ideal way to solve the problem. Political concerns are thus seen to prevail over the evidence base. Seemingly, there is also a frequent mismatch between the production and consumption of information. Quite often a product of disciplinary conventions of the social sciences, there are frequently large gaps in the knowledge base, precisely in areas of interest to policy makers. It is fair to comment, however, that the natural and physical sciences are also not exempt from this charge.

A further reason for animosity between research and policy communities and one that has already been touched on relates to the respective time frames in which the protagonists work and the language that they use. This is a discrepancy between the compatibility of evidence production (in-depth, detailed and time-consuming analyses of problems) – part of what Pels (2003) refers to as the 'unhastening of science' – and those of policy making (quick-fix solutions to problems). Social research, in most cases, is arduous and is often typified by lengthy, verbose reports, which are frequently of little use for policy makers who require clarity and concision with the key recommendations clearly obtainable. In effect, they require easily digested messages as this is the standard of what is 'useable'.

As was alluded to by Hobbes and touched on in Chapter Two, for research to impact on policy it needs to be presented in a useable format for policy makers. Weiss (1986, p 34), furthermore, suggests that history shows that for a study to have a direct bearing on policy, it takes an 'extraordinary concatenation of circumstances'. Consequently, a great deal 'depends on the efficiency of the communications links', from the research community (often via policy makers' staff) to policy makers. There have been attempts to foster closer relationships between the research and policy community and these are considered shortly. Prior to this it is worth pausing to consider whether the differences between the 'ivory tower' and 'corridors of power' are as stark as the criticisms above imply.

A critical appraisal of the criticisms of evidence-based policy making

The main criticisms of evidence-based policy revolve around the assumption that the differences between the two communities are explicit. This is not accepted universally. Ginsburg and Gorostiaga (2001, p 179), for instance, point out that it does not readily stand up to scrutiny. They suggest three areas in which the 'thesis is built on stereotypical or dominant portrayals of the two cultures'. These are: (a) it presents only one dominant portrayal of each culture; (b) it ignores the heterogeneity of membership in each cultural group; and (c) it overstates the extent to which individuals are members of only one of the two groups. For Ginsburg and Gorostiaga, an alternative portrayal of each culture can be identified which corresponds to the dominant portrayal of the other. In other words, the alternative portrayal of the research community is consistent with the dominant portrayal of the policy/practitioner community and vice versa.

The dominant view of the research culture is that of a firmament committed to the production of 'objective' knowledge that readily lends itself to policy problems. The alternative view is that in actual fact there is little consistency in the research community over the principles of research design. Quoting Pan (1990, p 12), Ginsburg and Gorostiaga (2001, pp 179-80) point out that 'the directions and topics, the research design and methods and the interpretation of the results of research' are all political decisions, stemming from 'deeply held ideological and value differences among scholars'. In this alternative appreciation, attention also turns towards actors who may or may not 'provide the needed or desired resources for scholarly activity'. These groups include the sponsors of research, be they local or national governments, non-governmental organisations (NGOs) or philanthropic organisations. These powerful sponsors can have the power to direct the nature and outcomes of the research towards a specific end and can also decide how far and in what way the research findings are disseminated. Researchers with government contracts will be familiar with the process of research embargoing that often takes place.

A dominant view of the policy or practitioner cultures suggests that they tend to be instrumental in their understanding and use of research, which consists of clear, fixed and internally consistent data for pre-given ends. This contrasts with the alternative view that suggests that practitioners and policy makers engage in a rational and technical decision-making process, whereby the doyens of the policy/practitioner community size up the best course for action among a range of possible scenarios. These alternative perspectives are buttressed by the second aspect of the critique that outlines the heterogeneous nature of both communities.

For Ginsburg and Gorostiaga (2001, p 181), there is a clear division of labour within the research community, between the 'thinkers' (theorists) and the 'doers' (researchers). There are, however, other more pertinent grounds on which to illustrate the differences that exist here. In terms of theorists, there are those who favour 'grand' theoretical explanation and others who stand on the shoulders of Merton (1957), by employing and pursuing 'middle-range' theoretical explanations of phenomena. Drawing on the work of Kuhn (1970), Ginsburg and Gorostiaga suggest that a distinction can also be made between researchers working within the boundaries of 'normal science' and those who are paradigm creators bringing forth a 'scientific revolution'. Beliefs and values also represent an area of schism within the research community. For instance, in the social sciences, different traditions and subcultures (for example, functionalists, conflict theorists and interpretivists) can be witnessed. These have different epistemological standpoints (positivism, interpretivism and critical science) that can lead to different modes of data gathering and collection (experiments and quantitative survey research, participant observation and ethnographic interviewing) (Ginsburg and Gorostiaga, 2001, p 182).

Drawing on a 'world system' approach, they also recognise that there are 'differences in the beliefs and values between groups in centre locations and those on the periphery'. Ginsburg and Gorostiaga (2001, pp 181-2) illustrate how 'through their gatekeeper roles', for example, as editors and conference organisers, some 'theorists and researchers clearly exercise more power than others in shaping the knowledge and ways of knowing in a given field' at a particular moment. In effect, power differentials within universities, faculties and departments can also have a bearing on the nature of knowledge, with the outcome that the research community cannot be seen as a black box. The policy maker/practitioner community is likewise characterised by significant heterogeneity. There is also a specialised division of labour in this sector, with policy makers formulating plans and practitioners turning them into a reality. Furthermore, there are clear differences between the various policy portfolios, for instance, health, education, transport, criminal justice and so on. Even within the same specialist areas, there exists more focused expertise. Thus in education (Ginsburg and Gorostiaga's particular area of proficiency) there are various subsectors such as primary, secondary, further and higher education There are also hierarchies in status and power that characterise the policy maker/practitioner sector. For instance, there are:

> ... potential differences in the power of policy-makers operating at the institutional, local, provincial, national and international levels and to hierarchies among educational practitioners employed at all of these levels (eg director vs deputy director, administrator vs teacher) ... as well as to differences existing between the power and resources of national-level policy-makers in large and small states and between more and less privileged/powerful countries. (Ginsburg and Gorostiaga, 2001, p 184)

Treating the policy sector and research community as a coherent entity is misleading, but it is the separation of the two communities that presents the biggest issue for Ginsburg and Gorostiaga. They claim that this is something of an ideal-type as it does not allow for 'overlapping' or simultaneous membership of both groups (Dobson, 2009; Stevens, 2010: forthcoming). It is not uncommon for researchers and academics to take a secondment into a government department. We have also witnessed previously how government departments are increasingly developing their own infrastructure casting doubt on the mutually exclusive nature of the two communities.

One conclusion that can be drawn from this is that the separation of the two communities is not as pronounced as the critics of evidence-based policy making maintain. Despite this, there are still significant obstacles in the research to policy journey, and Ginsburg and Gorostiaga (2001, pp 186–91) identify six approaches that can be developed to increase 'communication and dialogue' between the two groups. To paraphrase, these include:

- translation/mediation of the data produced and data required by each;
- education to improve the communication between the sectors;
- role expansion which advocates a continuing erosion of the boundaries between the practices of the differing groups;
- decision-oriented research, which is a collective term for various activities that again challenge the general division of labour between the two groups. This involves among other things more 'clinical partnerships', evaluation

research and policy relevant research. The overall aim is to try and understand the information requirements of the client and to meet these. The process is referred to as 'client orientation';
* collaborative action research which again tries to blur the boundaries between the two groups. This follows on from decision-oriented research by advocating mutual reflection and action in relation to research by 'researchers' and also by practitioners;
* collective research and praxis which promotes an expansion of the traditional roles and provides the potential for the most extensive form of dialogue, that focused on the activities of constructing theory and research as well as policy and practice.

There is something of a contradiction here in that the solutions that Ginsburg and Gorostiaga promote are premised on a clear distinction between the two communities. This is a distinction they have previously called into question. Most of their proposed solutions involve opening up channels of communication between the constituencies. In this way, Ginsburg and Gorostiaga must accept the thesis that there are clear differences between them. In recent years there has been a resurgence of interest in how the 'perilous road' from evidence to policy can be circumnavigated (Boaz and Pawson, 2005). Lomas (2000) has suggested that involving decision makers in the research process is likely to yield more evidence-informed policies, and other thinkers have highlighted how one way of increasing the potential for evidence to impact on policy is to employ intermediaries to carry out this function (Sin, 2008). Many labels have been coined to describe this, including 'knowledge transfer' and 'knowledge exchange'. These activities are undertaken by a knowledge broker, intermediary, boundary spanner or research translator (Ward et al, 2009, p 268), and are worthy of further elaboration.

Knowledge brokering and translation: bridging the divide?

Knowledge brokering theory takes as its starting point the view that there is a missing connection in the research/evidence to policy/practice/action chain. A commitment to some kind of 'action research', where policy makers, but more often practitioners, are involved with researchers in the design, application, analysis and dissemination of research, has been seen as one way of meshing the two constituencies together. Knowledge brokering offers another alternative. It advocates the use of key actors 'positioned at the interface between the worlds of researchers and decision makers' (Ward et al, 2009, p 267), who can act as envoys between the two constituencies. These may be individuals, but can also be collectives. In this sense, it accepts that there is some validity to the 'two communities' thesis.

The emphasis on brokering is significant as it serves to create an equal balance of power between the two groups. The broker is supposed to favour neither and to represent the interests of both. In this way, it differs from consultancy as there is doubt about a consultant's capacity for impartiality due to their occupational function in the context of a customer–client relationship (Ward et al, 2009, p 268). Although there is more than one way to achieve knowledge brokering (Oldham and McLean, 1997; Ward et al, 2009), the activity is still beset by problems. Ward et al (2009, pp 273-4) highlight the key drawbacks. Many of these mirror the stumbling blocks of evidence-based policy making. In the first instance, knowledge brokering is time-consuming and labour intensive. This is because in many policy areas the 'evidence base' is often unwieldy and disparate. Consolidating this into a useful package for decision making is bound to be a laborious process, yet decision makers, as we have seen, require knowledge immediately (hence the emergence of the rapid evidence review as a new methodology in recent years).

A further challenge comes from the fact that there is little clarity in the various roles a knowledge broker can occupy. For instance, certain knowledge brokers are required to serve as 'knowledge managers' whose primary task is to share and disseminate knowledge. Others focus on 'linkage and exchange'. Here it is the task of the broker to develop and maintain effective relationships between various stakeholders in the decision-making process. Another distinct role for the knowledge broker is to act as a 'capacity builder or developer'. Here the goal is to foster 'self-reliance in both the researcher and the decision maker' (Ward et al, 2009, p 272). This requires the broker to develop the communication skills of the former and the analytical and interpretive skills of the latter. This snapshot shows the various *modus operandi* of the knowledge broker and how the task can be fuzzy, especially when more than one role is required simultaneously.

In short, the knowledge broker requires an advanced skill set. Ward and colleagues, in their review of this part of the literature, suggest that 'good interpersonal skills and personal attributes such as flexibility, curiosity, and self-confidence' are the generic skills needed. In addition, more specific skills are desirable depending on the brokerage being undertaken. Thus 'the ability to gather, critically appraise, synthesise and tailor research and other evidence' are the key skills of the knowledge or information manager. The 'ability to hear, understand and structure decision-making issues' are further pre-requisites. Meanwhile, if the broker is undertaking a linkage and exchange role, 'communication skills, mediation skills, networking skills and the ability to establish credibility' (Ward et al, 2009, p 273) are the order of the day. A capacity developer, meanwhile, also requires unique attributes. Alongside communication skills, these involve 'teaching' and 'mentoring' skills.

Where one is to find such an accomplished actor is left undetermined, but perhaps the most significant drawback of knowledge brokering, as Ward and colleagues identify, is the lack of evidence about its efficacy. This is particularly problematic when it is remembered that the activity requires significant expenditure in terms of time and resources. This lack of evidence, however, could be an artefact of limitations in research designs of evaluations that have attempted to measure the impact of brokering. As it stands, attempts are being made to come up with some generally agreed principles on which to carry out this task and to evaluate the efficacy of knowledge transfer projects in general (Ward et al, 2009, p 274). It is documented that realist evaluation (Pawson and Tilley, 1997) will be of particular utility here due to the complexity of the interventions under scrutiny, but that (inevitably) more research is needed.

Although Ginsburg and Gorostiaga (2001) and the various advocates of knowledge brokering have prescribed a number of means to improve communication and dialogue between the two communities, it is claimed here (and demonstrated in later chapters) that there is still little guarantee that these will translate into evidence-based policy making. This is especially the case in heavily politicised areas. Here, the evidence to action barriers are magnified and amplified due to entrenched normative beliefs about the way that policy is or should be made. It is very difficult for policy actors to change the beliefs and actors of other policy actors via the use of rationally produced evidence or otherwise (Sabatier and Jenkins-Smith, 1993b). As will also be demonstrated in later chapters, even if evidence does find a powerful sponsor in the decision-making process, this is still no guarantee that it will impact on decision making. This issue is returned to in Chapter Eight when various models of research utilisation are discussed. But this is to jump the gun. For now the precise impact of politics on policy and evidence is worth clarifying. The purpose of this is twofold: first, to illustrate further the difficulties of brokerage in politicised areas and, second, to introduce the difficulties in actually producing evidence for policy under these conditions.

Politicised policies: the impact of politics, the media and public opinion

To all intents and purposes, the established criticisms of the evidence-based policy movement focus on the impact that politics has on the policy process. The political process requires information in haste that the research community struggles to deliver in an acceptable format. In heavily politicised policy areas, this process is further complicated in light of the difficulties in producing or obtaining evidence in the first instance. Before going on to explain this, it is worth reiterating what constitutes heavy politicisation. To recap, there are numerous facets to this. First, the term refers to those issues when the political stakes are high and when there are 'powerful constituencies' to face down (Tonry, 2004, p 23). In this sense, these are sensitive policy areas and evidence often has to jostle for position with what is politically expedient. Second, they are policy areas where there is intense media scrutiny of policy; again this raises an issue for evidence utilisation and production, as we shall see. Third, they are policy areas that often lie at the intersection of autonomous disciplinary boundaries. This means that there can be differing bodies of evidence from differing disciplines drawn on to support or critique the same policy. Fourth, there is a lack of consensus on the nature and direction of policy that again impacts on the understandings of evidence used in decision making. Fifth, there is prolonged conflict between competing interest groups and a permeating sense of crisis. This makes politicised areas inherently unstable and unpredictable (Monaghan, 2010). The direction of policy can alter as public and political opinion changes. This process can be very quick or it can be slow, but policies do not stand still.

In effect, then, heavily politicised areas can be summed up as being characterised by the three Cs of competition, conflict and controversy. In this sense, the notion of competition draws on Mannheim's sociology of knowledge. For Mannheim, competition is one of the principle ways in which the 'social' is structured as 'different interpretations of the world for the most part correspond to particular functions that various groups occupy in their struggle for power' (Mannheim, 1952, p 198). Following logically from the notion of competition is that of conflict. This refers to policies based on competing worldviews or perspectives. These are often simultaneously controversial and are the subject of sensationalist reporting in the media. The media is therefore central to the process of politicisation, and its contribution can be explained by drawing on Chibnall's (2004) analysis of journalism.

In the same way that it is now established criminological wisdom that it is possible for the police to enforce some laws some of the time, it is likewise only possible for the media to report some events some of the time. These events become 'the news'. Choices have to be made about what is covered and how. These are choices about what is 'newsworthy' and this is usually down to the discretion of a newspaper editor or section editor. According to Chibnall (2004), this choice is frequently governed by the need to search for sensational, unusual or dramatic occurrences precisely because this leads to more sales copy. To illustrate how this works in practice, Chibnall suggests that there are certain 'professional imperatives' that informally govern much journalistic practice (see Table 3.1). These generally refer to the reporting of some forms of violence but can be applied generally to anything relating to deviance. These imperatives are accompanied by a process of information selection, which entails careful decision making on the accompanying data to include and what to omit. These professional imperatives governing journalism create a scenario where only certain acts and actors are considered newsworthy – there is thus a restricted media discourse in the reporting of crime, deviance and indeed other sensitive topics.

It has been stated that the reporting of illicit drugs issues has been frequently sensationalised and 'twisted' (Coomber et al, 2000). The way in which the media can distort information relating to sensitive topics was expertly illustrated by Forsyth's (2001) analysis of the reporting of ecstasy-related deaths in Scotland in the 1990s. Forsyth demonstrated how every single ecstasy-related death was reported in the press throughout the decade, by comparing toxicological information relating to drug-related deaths with reportage in Scotland's most popular newspapers at the time. For ecstasy there was a 1:1 ratio between the toxicological information and newspaper reporting. The ratio for amphetamines was 3:1 (for every three amphetamine-related deaths, one was reported in the press). For heroin the figure was 5:1. The point here is that this was related and contributed to a moral panic surrounding ecstasy at the time. One consequence

Table 3.1: Chibnall's professional imperatives of journalism

Imperative	Description
Immediacy	Relates to present events; less concerned with back stories and processes
Dramatisation	Must be dramatic and involve significant degrees of action
Personalisation	Stories often relate to high-profile figures or the 'cult of celebrity'
Simplification	Elimination of any potential shades of grey
Titillation	Reveals the hidden; voyeurism
Conventionalism	Only reports a narrow spectrum of 'conventional' viewpoints
Structured access	Reserves space for the views of experts or authority figures
Novelty	Looks for new angles, speculation and potential twists in a storyline

Source: Adapted from Chibnall (2004)

of this was that rational debate over the dangers of the drug was stifled, creating the illusion that ecstasy represented a greater social ill than was actually the case and distorting the risks associated with other substances responsible for greater numbers of drug-related deaths.

A similar theme can be witnessed in the media furore surrounding changes and debates in UK drug policy over the past few years. These can be characterised using examples from the above list in Table 3.1, in particular immediacy and simplification. Changing the classification of substances is a complex legal process. In recent years the ACMD has advocated various policy changes including the downgrading of cannabis and ecstasy within the MDA 1971. The reporting of these debates in the press has tended not to focus on the complex scientific deliberation and evidence base underpinning these proposals; instead the issue has boiled down to one of politicians being 'hard' or 'soft' on drugs. One outcome of the sensationalist reporting and politicisation of policy are zero-sum views of the evidence and policy connection where evidence is seen to be either present (evidence-based) or absent (evidence-free) (Monaghan, 2010). These criticisms, in turn, have not been accepted uncritically.

It is noted that there are variations in the way that different branches of the media report certain issues. Even within one subsection, such as print journalism, there are clear differences between the broadsheet and tabloid press. One pertinent issue that remains, however, concerns the power the media has to undermine key agencies of the state, or indeed, other actors by directing 'flak' (Herman and Chomsky, 1988) or ridiculing their stances on particular issues (Reiner, 2007). This is particularly true when perceived lenient sentences are handed out to the perpetrators of serious crimes or, for instance, when advocates of drug legalisation or prostitution decriminalisation are dismissed as 'woolly liberals' or 'dangerous radicals'. Media power can therefore influence the policy process via impacting on public opinion and further entrenching the deeply held beliefs of policy actors. Such conditions make politicised policy areas inherently unstable or dynamic. They are, in essence, in a constant state of flux. In such an environment it is extremely difficult to have reasoned debate and, in turn, this has a knock-on effect for the kinds of evidence that can potentially be used in policy formulation. In light of this, Sutton and Maynard (1993, pp 455-6) previously lamented that in the illicit drug field, policy design and execution is 'conducted in an almost data free environment where, because of ignorance, it is impossible to set sensible policy targets, let alone measure the success of spending hundreds of millions of pounds across the Whitehall Departments'. In essence, the arena in which the drug debate takes place can lead to significant problems with the quality of data gathering. For example, data relating to the actual effects of certain drugs are often stifled for ethical reasons (Adler, 1995). The following extract from the oral evidence sessions of the Science and Technology Select Committee (2006b) between the chair, Phil Willis MP, and the then chair of the ACMD, Sir Michael Rawlins, neatly summarises this issue:

> **Q242 Chairman:** Our frustration … is that time and time again you seem to have responded to Members of the Committee that there is a lack of evidence or you have agreed that there is a lack of evidence to make certain decisions. We want to know why the ACMD has not done more to promote research in those areas where there is a lack of evidence. Do you think it is your job to do it or have we misjudged what the purpose of the Committee is?

> **Professor Sir Michael Rawlins:** It is arguable whether it is our job. This is an area in which it is extraordinarily difficult to do research, not just for legal reasons but for real reasons. Would I, for example, be prepared to do volunteer studies with Ecstasy? Would I be prepared to give volunteers Ecstasy? I could probably get the Home Secretary's approval … it is possible. I am not sure I would. I do not know what an ethics committee would think about it, but how would I think about it? We start getting into very real problems of doing research in this area. It is all very well people saying, "You should promote research" but you have to promote research that can be done, not research that we would just like to see. (Science and Technology Select Committee, 2006b, Evidence 15)

A further pressing concern relates to measurement issues surrounding data in politicised areas and the impact this has on evidence use. Again, to develop the example of drugs, the fact that drug use is primarily a hidden activity poses significant problems, particularly when it comes to gauging the scale of the problem. In terms of general prevalence figures, although more recently technologies for undertaking such a task have greatly improved (Stimson et al, 1997; Frischer et al, 2001), they are still beset with difficulties. For example, they are too narrow in their focus and require – but are yet to have agreed on – 'standardised definitions and conceptual frameworks' (Newcombe, 2007, p 33). Consistent with the phenomenological critique of measurement in social research

(Blumer, 1956; Cicourel, 1964), Newcombe (2007, p 33) continues that there is a problem with the use of 'commonsense notions and everyday terms as theoretical concepts and research variables'. Thus:

> Although this is common practice, ordinary language terms are typically laden with value judgements and subjective connotations, and so adopting them for scientific usage requires that they be given standardised operational definition, ideally within a broader conceptual framework. For instance, in the early days of drug prevalence research, it was common for surveys to produce estimates/rates of "recent" or "current" drug users, without any clear definitions of these terms. (Newcombe, 2007, p 33)

This issue is particularly important in the context of drug classification. A key driver of deciphering the evidence base for classification decisions relates to their prevalence. It is important to stress, as Newcombe subsequently does, that recently such terms have been replaced with clearer definitions including lifetime, past month and past year measurements. The juxtaposition of ambiguous measurements alongside more precise ones has meant that estimating long-term trends in the nature of drug prevalence is, inherently, an inexact science as there is clear disparity over what constitutes a 'regular' drug user. Indeed, regular users have been variously defined in surveys as any cases who use between at least three times per year, at least once a week or at least once a month (Newcombe, 2007, p 34). This journey into the problematic nature of research production links us back to the established criticisms of evidence-based policy discussed at the outset of the chapter, in particular, the long-standing and thorny issue of the inadequacy of research and researchers in producing evidence for policy.

Summary

Continuing the background discussion of the origins and fortunes of evidence-based policy making, this chapter has illustrated how recognisable criticisms of the initiative have become commonplace. These generally revolve around suspicion that exists between evidence providers and evidence consumers. Attempts to broker arrangements between the two communities exist, but these are also beset with problems, premised as they are on encouraging dialogue between groups with very different occupational functions. These issues are magnified in heavily politicised areas, primarily a result of the problems in generating evidence in such domains.

This further undermines one of the central premises of knowledge brokering in that in politicised areas it is often difficult to actually obtain the knowledge to broker let alone communicate it to a potentially unreceptive audience.

In effect, problems associated with gathering data in politicised areas obviously have a knock-on effect for the development of evidence-based policies and their analysis. This goes some way to explaining the prevalent viewpoint that UK drug policy and indeed other politicised policies are made in a 'data-free' environment (Sutton and Maynard, 1993). A central argument of this book and one that is backed up by Sutton and Maynard's assertion is that one outcome of the politicisation of policy is that evidence is frequently conceived in what are referred to as zero-sum terms where evidence is either evidence-based or evidence-free.

Such conceptualisations are understandable, but inaccurate. They are understandable because often views of evidence are determined by views of policy. As a result, if a person is critical of any given policy in the first place then they are also likely to be critical of the policy's evidence credentials thus viewing them as un-evidenced. This takes the concept of evidence at face value, but as we have witnessed, there are numerous possible manifestations of what evidence is or could be. Additionally, zero-sum accounts are inaccurate because viewing policy as un-evidenced is misleading and over-simplifies what the connection is between evidence and policy. In other words, political expediency is often seen as a barrier towards the implementation of evidence-based policy, but this ignores the history of the research and policy connection documented in Chapter Two, which has shown that there is a long, if turbulent, connection between evidence and policy in Western societies. In the following chapters a case is put forward that evidence is embedded in the decision-making process and can play a role even in the decision-making process in these contexts. The following chapters illustrate this via the case study of recent debates in UK drug classification policy, a politicised policy area par excellence.

Note

[1] Barnardo's even developed an educational modular resource for practitioners and professionals on how to incorporate evidence into their decision making. See www.barnardos.org.uk/resources/research_and_publications/theevidenceguide

Competition, conflict and controversy in the making of UK drug classification policy

> Drug misuse is associated with a wide range of potential consequences for individual drug users, their families, communities and the rest of society. Debates about drug policy choices are frequent both in the general media and the research literature. Much of this debate is influenced more by opinion and implicit values than scientific evidence. (Godfrey, 2006, p 563)

Chapter Three focused on the problematic nature of developing evidence-based politics in heavily politicised policy areas like drug policy. One significant aspect of this related to problems of data gathering in such contexts. Quite often, although not solely, this relates to the way the activity, event, behaviour, person, group or policy being researched is stigmatised (Goffman, 1963). As a consequence, the phenomenon is often hidden or the topic is 'sensitive' (Lee, 1993). Heavily politicised areas, to recap, are those characterised by the three Cs of competition, conflict and controversy. Here, the political stakes are high and there is intense media scrutiny of policy. Further characteristics of politicisation relate to the frequent lack of consensus on policy direction, and prolonged conflict between competing interest groups.

In essence, then, politicised areas are adversarial domains, located at the crossroads of autonomous department boundaries. Holistically – particularly in the UK – drug policy lies at the interface between public health and criminal justice. It is not unique in spanning different policy precincts. Indeed, UK penal policies and those from elsewhere have flirted with both social welfare impulses of rehabilitation and more criminal justice-oriented goals of discipline and control. In addition, the main legal drugs (alcohol and tobacco) policies straddle a difficult chasm between health and economic policy. Climate change policy straddles economics, ecology and issues of bio-diversity among others. Ultimately this has a bearing on the potential evidence base as in such instances debates over the evidence base for policies become heavily contested, with different interest groups declaiming the significance of quite different bodies of research. As Scharpf (1986, p 180) famously observed, 'similar policies may be produced by different institutional structures, and a given institutional structure is capable of producing different policy responses'.

The significance of contested evidence cannot be underestimated. Not only can it undermine or obfuscate attempts to bridge the gap between the research and policy groups, it also underpins what have been referred to as 'zero-sum' views of the evidence and policy connection. These accounts of the evidence and policy connection are misleading, and the case study of the UK drug classification policy is used to highlight why this is so. The issue of drug classification became a prominent theme in drug policy in the years of the New Labour government. New Labour came to power with a huge parliamentary majority offering the potential platform for sweeping reform in many areas of social and public policy. Toynbee and Walker (2001, p 17), for example, claimed that in the field of welfare reform, policy advisers such as Frank Field were given the mandate 'to think the unthinkable' (Barton, 2003, p 138). It soon became clear, however, that thinking the unthinkable in drug policy was itself unthinkable. In essence, New Labour's approach to drug policy constituted no significant departure from that of the previous Conservative administration, until the attention of the former turned towards cannabis and the classification system.

This chapter is, then, concerned with providing the background to the case study through which the tumultuous nature of evidence-based policy making is explored. With this in mind, the chapter is organised in the following way. The first section charts the origins of the implementation of the MDA 1971. It demonstrates how the passing of this Act brought into fruition the current drug classification system and how this has remained relatively stable despite being the subject of much criticism and despite significant developments in the UK drug situation from the 1980s onwards. Another feature of the passing of the MDA 1971 was how it created the first UK government drugs advisory board in the shape of the ACMD. The next section focuses on recent developments in the UK drug situation and wider policy arena in light of the election of the New Labour government in 1997. The centrality of drug classification issues in contemporary drug debates and how this ties into the evidence-based policy movement is then discussed. The chapter concludes with a summary.

The making and legacy of the Misuse of Drugs Act 1971

Histories of UK drug policy, legislation and prevalence have been undertaken by numerous authors (see, for example, Berridge and Edwards, 1981; Barton, 2003; Blackman, 2004; Bennett and Holloway, 2005; Seddon, 2010).[1] Blackman (2004), for example, offers a global historical overview of the nature of prohibition, his primary concern resting with drug legislation. By contrast, Bennett and Holloway (2005) focus more on significant UK policy developments, assigning particular policies to particular eras. Thus, the 1980s are seen as a time when policy focused on reducing supply, the 1990s when demand reduction was the goal and the 2000s placing more emphasis on harm reduction. The following account charts key developments linked to the emergence of evidence-based policy making and the efficacy of the UK drug classification system.

Drug policy, as indicated, is an adversarial domain, and in the UK, conflict in this area is long-standing. It stems from competing coalitions claiming 'ownership' of the 'drug problem'. Although it is not unique in this regard, the UK serves as a critical case in this respect as a result of its historical development. In effect, drugs have been regulated by both the criminal justice system and the medical profession, in what has been termed the 'British system' of drug control. There has, therefore, been a power struggle between the medical- and the criminal justice-related professions (Berridge and Edwards, 1981; Berridge, 1984). Around the time of the First World War it was the Home Office that had most control over drug use policy. Strang and Gossop (1994, p 343) contend that the Home Office 'used its influence' to try to push the UK towards a similar system as the US and 'a reliance upon an entirely penal approach with criminal sanctions against both users and prescribing doctors'. At this time, the prevalence of drugs in society was low, and what problems there were concerned the use of opiates such as heroin and morphine.

Although the medical profession had been involved in the regulation of drugs prior to this, the origins of the British system of drug control can be traced to the meeting of the Rolleston Committee in 1926. Named after its chair, Sir Humphrey Rolleston, President of the Royal College of Physicians, this committee sought to make a distinction between drug addiction and drug abuse. By emphasising that addiction differed from abuse, the problem was 'medicalised' as addicts and their addictions can be treated and so should not be punished. A defining feature of the meeting was the recommendation that certain drug users should be prescribed heroin or morphine either to enable gradual withdrawal or to 'maintain' a regulated supply to those judged unable to break their dependence and whose lives would otherwise suffer serious disruption (South, 1997, pp 927-8). The outcome of this was the consolidation of the medical profession's involvement in drug regulation. For certain commentators, this created a 'British system' of drug control as opposed to the US stance of outright criminal prohibition (Stimson and Lart, 1994; Barton, 2003; Shiner, 2003).

The extent to which there are two 'competing' sides is, however, open to some debate. Barton (2003) and South (1999) have argued that the relationship between the relevant constituencies is something of an asymmetric conflict. Although the medical profession, in whatever guise, has had a prominent position in UK drug policy making, its relationship with the criminal justice system is fundamentally not one of equality. Overall, in the field of illicit drug use, public health, treatment-focused initiatives increasingly operate within a framework overseen by the punishment and enforcement-oriented Home Office (Stevens, 2007b; Seddon et al, 2008). Blackman (2004, p 23), likewise, argues that the Rolleston philosophy did not constitute a 'British system' per se as the report's framework was 'ultimately regulated by the Home Office and the police' and 'its parameters if not its everyday practice were, at the end of the day, marked out by controls not treatment'. Only licensed doctors could prescribe the drugs and they had to register with the Home Office. This has led him and others (Lart,

1998; Berridge, 2005) to suggest that the British system is a 'myth' as the medical profession and criminal justice system are different sides of the same regulatory coin, both conceiving drug use to be a deviation from the norm. In turn, these perspectives have silenced – especially within political and academic discourse – a more marginal and 'politically challenging position' that drug use is, *sui generis*, a 'largely unproblematic – not deviant' phenomenon (Stevens, 2007b, p 86).

For the next 40 years UK drug policy remained relatively stable. It was not until the 1960s that the issues reappeared on the policy agenda as a raft of legislation was passed to deal with what was perceived to be an increasingly global social problem. In the UK, the Brain Committee, named after its chairman, Sir Russell Brain, was initially convened to look at the policy advocated by the Rolleston Committee. Seddon (2010, p 82) demonstrates how there were actually two interdepartmental committees – which he terms Brain I and Brain II – reporting in 1961 and 1965, respectively. Brain I, according to Seddon, effectively concluded that at the start of the 1960s, there was little evidence of a significant drug problem to warrant any change in policy or legislation. By contrast, Brain II expressed concerns over lax prescribing practices by certain doctors and recommended a tightening of drug controls. The Dangerous Drugs Act 1967 was, thus, implemented to curb the power of ordinary general practitioners (GPs) to prescribe heroin. As of April 1968 when the Act came into force, GPs wishing to prescribe heroin to addicts needed a special licence from the Home Office.

It must be stressed, however, that overall drug prevalence at this time remained low. Drug legislation enacted throughout the 1960s prior to the MDA 1971 emerged from, and was influenced by, these events, but also events occurring on the international stage. Central to the latter was the UN Single Convention on Narcotic Drugs 1961, otherwise referred to as the Geneva Convention 1961. This proffered a now classically hard-line approach to drug use in a bid to create a drug-free society. It aimed to standardise the control of narcotics across nations so that certain drugs could be used only for scientific, medical, and in some cases, industrial purposes. This was achieved by arranging drugs into schedules and applying appropriate controls based on their harm and toxicity. Possessing any article in contravention of the Convention was a punishable offence, with a custodial term for serious breaches (Fortson, 2005). Crucially this meant that possession of what later came to be called 'recreational' drugs, such as cannabis and amphetamines (substances seen to be less harmful than 'hard' drugs such as heroin and cocaine), almost invariably became a criminal offence within the signatory states.

The MDA 1971 signalled the UK commitment to the Geneva Convention 1961. It replaced the various drug control Acts of the 1960s: the Drugs (Prevention of Misuse) Act 1964 and the Dangerous Drugs Acts 1965 and 1967. A central aspect of the legislation was that it established the UK's first legal advisory body on illicit drugs. The Advisory Council on the Misuse of Drugs (ACMD) has since assumed a central role in reviewing British drug policy. According to Levitt et al (2006, p 2), the ACMD 'carries out in-depth inquiries into aspects of drug use that are causing particular concern in the UK, with the aim of producing considered reports that will be helpful to policy-makers, practitioners, service providers and others'. The ACMD has been pivotal in terms of developing an evidence base for drug policy, thus embedding science and research into the decision-making process in this domain. It has, furthermore, been common practice that the government responds to the recommendations made by the ACMD. The statute states that it is the purpose of the council:

> ... to keep under review the situation in the UK with respect to drugs which are being or appear to them likely to be misused and of which the misuse is having or appears to them capable of having harmful effects sufficient to constitute a social problem, and to give to any one or more of the Ministers, where either Council consider it expedient to do so or they are consulted by the Minister or Ministers in question, advice on measures (whether or not involving alteration of the law) which in the opinion of the Council ought to be taken for preventing the misuse of such drugs or dealing with social problems connected with their misuse, and in particular on measures which in the opinion of the Council, ought to be taken. (cited in Science and Technology Select Committee, 2006b, p 13)

Although consultation must take place between the government and the ACMD, the former is still able to act unilaterally if it wishes. The work of the ACMD is primarily based on clinical expertise and, where possible, it is driven by the clinical evidence base; its work is often subcontracted to various subcommittees made up of agents with relevant know-how. Although individuals representing the whole gamut of the sciences are on the council, the emphasis on clinical evidence is reflected in its membership:

> Under the terms of the MDA 1971 the ACMD is required to include representatives of the practices of medicine, dentistry, veterinary medicine and pharmacy, the pharmaceutical industry, and chemistry (other than pharmaceutical chemistry); and members who have a wide and relevant experience of social problems connected with the misuse of drugs. (cited in Science and Technology Select Committee, 2006b, p 17)

The creation of the ACMD was widely praised, but on implementation most aspects of the MDA 1971 were denounced by critics as being consistent with the US-inspired prohibitionist 'drug war' rhetoric (see, for example, Young, 1971). Consistent with the Geneva Convention 1961, for current purposes, the defining tenet of the MDA 1971 was its instigation of a strict classification system. Drugs were now placed in one of three categories: A, B or C. The category into which each particular drug is placed is determined by the extent of harm its misuse inflicts. Section 1.2 of the Act states that drugs are divided between classes based on: (a) whether the drug is being misused; (b) whether it is likely to be misused; and (c) whether the misuse in either case is having or could have harmful effects sufficient to constitute a social problem (cited in Levitt et al, 2006, p 15).

For reasons primarily relating to measurement, these issues are difficult to quantify and there is, therefore, an in-built ambiguity in the Act, which has heroin and cocaine in class A along with ecstasy. Cannabis is in class B along with amphetamines (when not prepared for injection) and barbiturates. Anabolic steroids are in class C. The MDA 1971 facilitates a policy where drug treatment is possible although it has also placed a certain stock in punishment, compounding in law the continuing prohibition of drugs. It is pertinent to stress at this stage that it was a widely held view that prior to, and in the immediate aftermath of, the enactment of the MDA 1971, the UK did not really have a drug problem per se. Although the numbers of known drug users are widely thought to represent the tip of the iceberg of all known users, Webster (2007, p 151) illustrates how at the start of the 1970s the 'addict' population known to the authorities was stable, numbering 4,067 and mainly centred in London. Newcombe (2007, p 26) suggests that the numbers were lower, with 927 addicts presenting for treatment in 1965, rising sharply to 2,881 in 1969 and then falling to 1,406 in 1973. The overarching point is that the number of registered addicts of heroin or morphine was low. Also, at this time the notion of widespread recreational drug use was not established. Cannabis use was restricted to certain sections of the population, for example, students and mainly black minority ethnic groups. Consequently, Downes (1977, p 89) has characterised British drug policy at this time as a period of 'masterly inactivity', referring to the fact that draconian policies were implemented to combat what was a relatively minor problem.

Through time, the MDA 1971 has remained stable, although new substances have been added when perceived to be necessary. These often relate to an upturn in use and an associated moral panic (Cohen, 1972) over the dangers of the drug. Some of the most high-profile additions to the Act since 1971 have been: ecstasy (Methylenedioxymethamphetamine, or MDMA), included as a class A substance in 1977 (although somewhat unusually this predated its assimilation into the drug-taking repertoires of certain sections of society and its widespread predominance in dance culture); ketamine was included as a class C drug in 2006; and mephedrone was scheduled as a class B drug in 2010 after being linked mainly in the media to a number of deaths. Until relatively recently it has been rare for any substance to be downgraded. This changed in 2004 when cannabis was reclassified from a class B to a class C drug. To contextualise this change, it is necessary to consider some key developments occurring in the UK drug scene and the responses to this in the 1980s.

The drug situation at the start of the 1980s can be characterised as a time of rapidly rising drug use. Buchanan and Young (2000, p 410) state of the 1980s that 'it was during this period that de-industrialisation ravaged labour-intensive industries, as factories and shipyards closed down'. Whole communities were destabilised by mass long-term unemployment. For the first time in the post-war period, a generation of school leavers who would otherwise have found secure employment in apprenticeships, factories or semi-skilled positions found themselves surplus to requirement. Work was not available and the long-standing concept of 'a job for life' was being rapidly eroded. Heroin, for many, provided a means of escape (Buchanan and Young, 2000, p 410).

Heroin use thus became a more high-profile social issue at this time (Dorn and South, 1987; Pearson, 1987; ACMD, 1988; Parker et al, 1988). Shiner (2003, p 773) contends that from the 1980s onwards, 'central government took on a more active role', as the debate about drugs became politicised. Increased emphasis was placed on law enforcement, prevention and supply reduction. Other key features of the 1980s drug situation were: (a) its size and scale – there was a fourfold increase in the number of registered addicts, arguably a conservative reflection on the total number of drug users as most, more than likely, were unregistered with agencies; (b) the spread of serious drug use from its base in London to include large Scottish cities and mainly large urban areas west of the Pennines; (c) the fact that, unlike in the US, most heroin users were white and not from minority ethnic groups; and (d) the development of global trafficking patterns as heroin was imported from the 'golden triangle' of South West Asia, Afghanistan, Pakistan and Iran (Pearson, 1987, p 67; Seddon, 2007).

All of these factors contributed to what was seen as a heroin 'epidemic'. The initial policy response was renewed vigour for the 'war on drugs' policy, with an emphasis on supply reduction. Closely related to the heroin epidemic of the 1980s was the outbreak of HIV/AIDS among many intravenous users. According to Buchanan and Young (2000, p 411), this seriously called into question the policy of strict enforcement. The medical and public health professions were particularly vociferous in this respect, claiming that draconian enforcement of the drug laws was making drug taking more risky. A report by the ACMD (1988) stressed that the threat of HIV/AIDS was more of a social problem than heroin use and that a pragmatic shift in policy should be made. This entailed incorporating a public health-inspired 'harm reduction' approach designed to establish contact with the hidden drug-using population. A pivotal feature of this was the desire to create and promote a culture of controlled and safe use of heroin. Needle exchange programmes were developed to this end. Allied to this was the roll out of heroin substitute programmes (often referred to as methadone maintenance programmes) to try and curtail the threat of HIV/AIDS.

This policy was pragmatic in that it was intended to 'protect the non drug-using society from the risk of HIV infection', yet the harm reduction approach, closely monitored by the Home Office, initially sat uneasily with its crime reduction ideology of punishment and enforcement (Buchanan and Young, 2000, p 411). In terms of the current debate, it highlights the ongoing conflict between the medical and criminal justice approaches to dealing with the drug problem. It further reflects the ambiguity built into the MDA 1971, which is not solely about prohibition. Needle exchange programmes and heroin substitute programmes have been referred to as harm reduction policies. 'Harm reduction' is a hugely contested term, but in this sense it is based on the realist principle of containment as opposed to the idealism of outright prohibition and the utopia of a 'drug-free society'.

Throughout the 1990s, these harm reduction measures were embraced on a scale never before witnessed. Although the numbers of known heroin users continued to rise, overall prevalence rates remained low. Towards the turn of the millennium, one per cent of 16- to 29-year-olds reported using heroin within the year 1999–2000 (Ramsay et al, 2001). For Barton (2003, p 136), another key policy development occurred around this time. This stemmed from the publication of an independent report commissioned by the Department of Health (Howard et al, 1993) calling for a 'greater level of co-operation across all agencies involved with illicit drug policy and practice' (Barton, 2003, p 137). This, in turn, led to the fulfilment of the Conservative election promise to make sure that action aimed at tackling drug misuse was effectively coordinated. The upshot of these developments was the Conservative Party's 1995 drug strategy entitled *Tackling drugs together* (DH, 1995); this had a profound influence on the thinking surrounding UK drug policy, which continues to this day, which is despite the fact that the document only related to policy in England. The Conservative Party, the majority of whose members have been traditionally inclined towards more draconian solutions to drug problems, amended their drug policy so that it attempted to take effective action via law enforcement, accessible treatment and a new emphasis on education and prevention. It was the aim of the *Tackling drugs together* strategy to: (a) increase the safety of communities from drug-related crime; (b) reduce the acceptability of drugs to young people; and (c) reduce the health risks and other damage related to drug misuse (DH, 1995, p 1).

This initiative received support across the political spectrum and, according to Barton (2003, p 138), by focusing on problems associated with communities, the Conservative government was able to pursue the aforementioned two-pronged approach to tackling the problem through an attempt to foster 'joint working' between the public health and law and order constituencies. This multi-agency coordination, both at local and national levels, would focus on problems associated with crime and public health with particular regard to young people (DH, 1995, p 1). In the spirit of joint working, a ministerial Subcommittee on Drug Misuse was created, comprised of figures from interested departments. Also in the spirit of togetherness, the strategy set up Drug Action Teams, the remit of which was to tackle drug-related issues at the local level. These were also multi-agency arenas comprising 'senior representatives from the police, probation services, local authorities (including education and social services) and health authorities' (DH, 1995, p 5). The intention was to foster links with voluntary sector organisations with a vested interest in drug issues. In terms of organisation, the policy arena had opened up, becoming less concentrated in central government and thus more horizontal and less top down. This created a more nuanced approach to the problem. Ultimately, this allowed for greater 'outside' involvement as more agents became embroiled within the policy process.

Although the change was more than cosmetic, overall the emphasis of policy remained firmly on supply reduction, but 'police forces, probation services and prisons, were all required to develop their own drug misuse strategies' (Barton, 2003, p 138). The health initiative was one that ensured that drug users, primarily those whose use was chaotic or problematic, had 'easy access' to services. This was facilitated by the establishment of the National Drugs Helpline in April 1995 (DH, 1995, p 3). According to Barton (2003, p 138), these harm reduction policies were, however, couched in terms of a step towards the 'somewhat unrealistic' goal of 'drug-free states', with drug abstinence 'the ultimate aim'. Indeed, the twin goals of abstinence and resistance, especially for young people, were the messages sent by the drug education literature. This was boosted by the allocation of an extra £5.9 million for training programmes for teachers to enrol on 'innovative drug education programmes' (Barton, 2003, p 138).

As a useful summary, Barton (2003, pp 138-9) highlights five main issues significant to the approach of *Tackling drugs together*. First and foremost, it transferred the government's drug policy from the Home Office to the Cabinet Office. This was symbolic as the Cabinet Office does not have the same ideological commitment to law and order. Second, it 'acted as a catalyst' for a policy explosion in the field of illicit drug policy and practice. Drugs came to be identified as a 'major problem' thus further politicising the issue. Third, it began to 'create a climate' where law and order and medical approaches could be combined to operate together under a banner of harm reduction. Fourth, this placed joint working at the forefront of policy, forcing previously unilateral agencies into collaboration. Finally, it gave guarded recognition to the fact that isolated law and order approaches based on supply reduction alone were failing and there needed to be education-based demand reduction approaches to tackling drug misuse (Barton, 2003, pp 138-9).

The Conservative strategy was something of a hotchpotch of ideas. In his detailed critique of the strategy, Howard (1997, pp 8-13) highlighted numerous positive and negative aspects. On the desirable side, it provided national leadership and coordination. The leader of the ministerial subcommittee was the Lord President of the Council, thus ensuring some semblance of neutrality in that no department could, in theory, dominate proceedings. The formation of the Drug Action Teams also served to cement joint working in areas where it was already established, providing a model of good practice for elsewhere. In addition, it gave recognition to the work of specialist drug service providers and highlighted the value of the demand reduction paradigm. In this sense, 'harm reduction' became associated with 'demand reduction' within a hitherto supply reduction-dominated paradigm. The approach also catered for the provision of additional resources and countenanced a more realistic approach to the drug scene. This was viewed as providing a counter-balance to the more sensationalising and demonising deluges from the press and its associated 'drug war' rhetoric (Barton, 2003, pp 138-9).

There were, however, in turn, a number of problems and criticisms voiced about the strategy, not least, the various problems associated with joint working stemming from institutional animosity and suspicion. Allied to this, there was still concern over the power struggle between law and order and public health, this time over the allocation of resources. Indeed, Howard (1997) indicates that the allocation of resources for supply reduction, that is, the cause of the law and order lobby, outnumbered by two to one those allocated to the demand reduction initiatives of treatment and prevention. Barton (2003, p 139) suggests that this was probably related to the fact that the strategy placed greater emphasis on the protection of communities from harm rather than the protection of the individual and, in doing so, maintained the ascendancy of law and order responses to drug problems.

Overall, the framework provided by *Tackling drugs together* was successful in recognising that, until this point, there had been a lack of coherency in UK drug policy. By association, as the goal of a drug-free society was proving elusive, the aim was to create a new philosophy with which to deal with the drug problem. In this respect, it was successful, but only to a point. By reorganising local services, the strategy provided a green light for some pioneering means of addressing the problems of illicit drug use, thus opening the door for other voices to be heard in the debate. This process continued with the election of New Labour in 1997.

New Labour, the modernising agenda and evidence-based drug policy?

New Labour came to power on the back of a huge majority, offering the potential platform for sweeping reform in many areas of social and public policy. As far as domestic drug policy was concerned, however, there seemed to be a tide of continuity flowing from the Conservative approach to drug policy to that of New Labour. Indeed, Bean (2002, p 56) observed that the New Labour approach, laid out in *Tackling drugs to build a better Britain* (Cabinet Office, 1998), 'largely reiterated the themes of the 1995 document whilst adding performance indicators for drug reduction in the next decade'. Barton (2003, p 141), however, points out that this claim is something of an over-simplification and, while conceding that the New Labour approach carried many similarities with what had gone before, it did also offer some new initiatives.

The New Labour administration was able to address some of the more noticeable shortcomings in the 1995 document. For Barton (2003, p 142), this meant that multi-agency work started to become more 'meaningful' as more 'concrete projects' were put in place. In terms of substance, the main policy areas were concerned to: (a) help young people resist drug misuse in order to achieve their full potential in society; (b) protect communities from drug-related anti-social behaviour; (c) enable people with drug problems to overcome them through drug treatment and to live healthy and crime-free lives; and (d) stifle the availability of illegal drugs on the streets. This was consistent with the Conservative approach.

One change related to the organisation of the drug issue within government rather than the substance of the policy itself. As regards administrative organisation, at the national level the organisational structure remained intact, with the continuation of the ministerial Subcommittee on Drug Misuse. This kept its brief to ensure that individual departments with an interest in illicit drug use contributed to the overall vision and strategy. The appointment of Keith Hellawell, former Chief Constable of West Yorkshire Police, as a new 'anti-drug coordinator', or 'drug tsar', with Mike Trace as his deputy, was a noticeable development. Barton (2003, p 141) suggests that both were seen as being 'prepared to think radically about drug policy', and part of Hellawell's remit was to head up the UK Anti-Drugs Strategic Steering Group, a new body comprised of government officials, local government representatives, representatives of independent bodies and voluntary sector agencies (Barton, 2003, p 141). In addition, the drug tsar was required to:

> ... scrutinise rigorously the performance of departments and agencies – individually and collectively – against the actions, objectives and performance indicators set out in this report; and produce a National Anti-Drugs Plan for implementation in each succeeding year. (Cabinet Office, 1998, p 2)

In this way UK drug policy making was opened up even further. A more inclusive consultation process between key stakeholders was a key aspect of this process. In addition, policy appraisal and monitoring, as we have seen, is also consistent with other aspects of New Labour policy making and is tied into the modernising agenda and NPM governance.

Although the Conservative and Labour strategies did signal a slight shift in policy, the treatment/punishment dichotomy still shaped the boundaries of the debate, although subsequent developments have made this characterisation somewhat fuzzier. Since the 1980s, but gaining momentum in the 1990s through to the present, a new direction for drug policy can be witnessed as much social policy has been enlisted in the fight against crime. This increasing criminalisation of social policy has resulted in the light of a perceived loss of confidence in liberal welfare policy models by the powerful middle classes (see, for example, Garland, 2001; Rodger, 2008). Although widely accepted, there is actually little agreement on the causes of the criminalisation of UK drug policy (Stevens, 2007b; Seddon et al, 2008). Such debates have been preoccupied with heroin misuse and to a lesser degree with (crack) cocaine. One by-product of this has been the resultant confusion surrounding the concepts of 'harm reduction' and drug treatment (Webster, 2007). This is because there is little agreement over what 'harm' actually is. Who or what is being harmed by drugs? How is this harm being manifested? And with what consequences? Any attempt to answer such questions depends on a particular ideological standpoint. As we shall see in subsequent chapters, this also raises significant issues when trying to decipher the nature of 'evidence'.

For Barton (2003, p 142), the New Labour approach did, however, recognise that a unilateral law and order enforcement approach was not deemed to be the sole solution to the 'drug problem'. In doing so, it kept open the door for harm reduction to play a key role in the drug strategy. The upshot of such developments was the perception of more proactive policies that could address the realities of the drug situation in the 21st century. While heroin remained a political problem, in the 1990s the UK drug situation began to change markedly. It became apparent that drug use was not restricted to problem users of hard substances and that the current drug situation was radically different from anything that had preceded it (Parker et al, 1998). Cannabis use remained popular but the onset of the 'Acid House' movement and the subsequent expansion of dance culture (Collin, 1997; Hammersley et al, 2002) established recreational drug use as a key component of leisure activities. This development contributed to the notion that drug use among certain sections of the population had, in fact, become 'normalised' and culturally accommodated (Parker et al, 1998, 2002; Aldridge et al, 1999). The 'normalisation' of drug use is anathema to those who support the 'war on drugs', as the rhetoric associated with the 'drug war' and the perceived dangers of drugs did not correspond with many young people's experiences of illicit drugs (MacCoun and Reuter, 2001).

The issue of drug-related harm has become entwined with another key debate in UK policy – the emotive and controversial issue of whether the current classification system is 'fit for purpose' (The Police Foundation, 2000). It was cannabis and not heroin that took centre stage. The issue of the relative harms of cannabis were central in the decision to reclassify the drug in 2004. Issues relating to the legal status of drugs and the wider drug classification legislation have been at the forefront of contemporary drug policy developments in the UK and elsewhere. In Portugal, the flagship decriminalisation of the use and possession of drugs is indicative of this (van het Loo et al, 2002), and current British drug policy cannot be fully comprehended without benchmarking it against changes occurring elsewhere.

According to Blackman (2004, pp 183-4), in various European countries more relaxed policies towards cannabis possession were implemented towards the start of the 21st century. Although prohibition still remains the overarching strategy, consistent with UN regulations, new ways of monitoring the problem are now apparent. For some time the Netherlands has pursued a policy of 'normalisation' for soft drugs, such as cannabis. Although there have been amendments to Dutch drug policy over recent years, and cannabis is still illegal under the Opium Act 1976, there is now great emphasis on keeping drug users away from the criminal justice system and within the 'socio-medical field'. In terms of the substances themselves, this meant that licensed premises, which morphed into the coffee shop system, sprang up in many Dutch towns where cannabis could be consumed in a controlled environment. These premises prohibited the sale of harder drugs on site as well as alcohol.

As noted by Bergeron and Griffiths (2006), there has been a steady shift to convergence as many nations have grappled with rising levels of the use of recreational drugs and heroin. This is signalled, for instance, in a general movement away from custodial sentences for non-problematic possession and a movement towards diverting drug users towards public health treatment, whether compulsory or not. Blackman (2004, p 184) states that non-enforcement policies have been 'taken up in a variety of ways by Switzerland, Portugal, Italy, Spain and certain states within Germany'. Belgium has also recently altered its legislation, as have Canada and certain states in Australia. Drugs are still illegal in these countries, as legalisation is not an option for signatory states to the UN conventions. Thus, they remain within a prohibitionist framework.

According to Blackman (2004, pp 184-5), this 'normalisation' approach constitutes a new 'paradigm' in understanding contemporary drug use in a cross-national context. It presents a new package of ideas and beliefs, which become influential as they structure and determine the terms of the political discourse. It is apt to point out, however, that the convergence of policy described above masks significant divergence of policy that still exists within the EU. For instance, the Dutch approach contrasts markedly with that of Sweden – they are often held up as examples of more liberal and conservative approaches respectively (Chatwin, 2003). This divergence of policy has an impact on the nature of evidence cited in support of each policy stance. Indeed, national differences in drug policy and its associated evidence base have been recognised for some time. A snapshot of this is revealed in an inquiry into the Dutch policy on illicit drugs conducted in the 1990s:

> People generally perceive reality by filtering it through some preconceived model.... Appraisals of the drug problem also involve such constructions, and it seems that the ways of viewing drugs and of defining the underlying causes of the drug problem often differ sharply from one country to another.... In the Netherlands sociologists have been instrumental in defining the drug problem, whilst in France the psychiatrists have played a prominent role. (Boekhout van Solinge, 1999, pp 518-19)

The end result is a mixed picture. All member states have developed specific drug strategies to tackle the problem within their borders. These are developed by using up-to-date epidemiological information on drug prevalence and they also have in-built evaluation and monitoring apparatus to gauge their achievements and effectiveness. And yet differences in substantive policy, of course, remain (EMCDDA, 2009). Nowhere is this more apparent than divergent philosophies marking the Portuguese preference for an approach decriminalising all drug possession in a bid to tackle the public health effects of drugs (van het Loo et al, 2002) and the Swedish inclination towards drug prevention and a zero-tolerance approach to drug possession (Lenke and Olson, 2002). The evidence supporting these stances is, therefore, inevitably contested. It is interesting to note how a repeat of these issues was played out in the UK in debates over the evidence base for the current classification system, as subsequent chapters show.

The move towards informal warnings and/or civil fines to deal with possession for small amounts of cannabis on the continent – increasingly commonplace around this time – were deemed to be a 'proportionate response' to the problem (Blackman, 2004, p 185). It was in this international context that David Blunkett's decision to reclassify cannabis can be seen, but this was not the determining factor. Indeed, the UK has not gone as far as some of its European cousins. The reclassification of cannabis from class B to class C did herald a subtle, but significant, change in UK drug policy. Although a relatively minor substantive change, symbolically, the impact of cannabis reclassification has been wide-ranging. It represents the first instance in the UK whereby an extensively used illicit substance has had penal sanctions lightened. This is, however, an over-simplification of the situation, as the amendment of the Police and Criminal Evidence Act 1984 – so that cannabis assumed a unique status as a class C drug – contradicted any perception of liberalisation, as did the draconian punishments associated with drug supply introduced by the Criminal Justice Act 2003.

Although around this time there was renewed interest in the use of cannabis-based substances in the treatment of certain illnesses, this did not form part of the justification for the initial reclassification. There were two initial stimuli for this change. First, a number of high-profile inquiries into drug policy and legislation which occurred in and around this time, both domestically and internationally (Boister, 2001; Dorn and Jamieson, 2001), highlighted the relatively benign nature of cannabis *vis-à-vis* other prohibited substances. As regards the domestic situation, The Police Foundation (2000) inquiry into the MDA 1971, also known as the Runciman Report, suggested that in terms of its toxicity or harmfulness, it was not comparable with either class A or class B drugs. This was supported by the subsequent inquiries of the Home Affairs Select Committee (2002) and the ACMD (2002).

The second trigger related to the New Labour government's concern with efficient public service delivery. The Police Foundation report (2000) also recommended that cannabis be reclassified from a class B to a class C drug, making cannabis possession a non-arrestable offence (except in aggravated circumstances). It was perceived that this would reduce the number of 'otherwise law abiding, mainly young people' being criminalised and potentially receiving a custodial sentence to the detriment of their futures (The Police Foundation, 2000, p 7). It was also perceived that this could remove a considerable source of friction between the police and the wider community of cannabis smokers, freeing up police time to enable them to concentrate on problems posed by class A drugs such as (crack) cocaine and heroin, in line with the drug strategy (Home Office, 2002). In the UK, throughout the 1990s, for the most part cannabis-related offences had increased as a result of stop-and-search policies. This was combined with a general upturn in the prevalence of frequent use (May et al, 2002, p 14), which placed significant pressure on the police in terms of time and resources.

Running contemporaneously to the political deliberations of the legal status of cannabis was a pilot project of policing cannabis in Brixton, South London. The 'Brixton Experiment', or 'Lambeth Experiment' as it became known, effectively replaced the threat of arrest with informal disposal and a formal on–the–spot warning for those caught in possession. This would not form part of a national record. There is some debate as to the origins of this initiative (Crowther-Dowey, 2007) and to its success in reducing bureaucracy (PSS Consultancy Group, 2002). It was, however, subsequently evaluated and judged a success by both the Metropolitan Police Authority (MPA, 2002) and the local community (MORI, 2002). On the back of these findings, the then Home Secretary, David Blunkett, told the Home Affairs Select Committee in October 2001 that he was 'minded' to downgrade cannabis and would seek advice from the ACMD on the possibility of reclassification. Both parties reported back in early 2002 that cannabis should be reclassified (May et al, 2002). In July 2003 it was announced that cannabis would be reclassified to a class C drug, coming into force in January 2004.

For some commentators, the cannabis reclassification has been heralded as one of the first examples of UK drug classification policy being developed with specific recourse to significant evidence (Levitt et al, 2006). Hence the episode can be considered as an explicit conjoining of UK drug policy with the principles of evidence-based policy making. As subsequent chapters will demonstrate, this is not universally accepted, nor is it straightforward. The two main spurs for the policy change constitute and require different evidence bases. They are, in turn, linked to the two main traditions in the UK drug policy debate with both medical and criminal justice-related reasoning given for the policy amendment. This adds to the confusion about what counts as evidence in policy. Although the change was considered in light of the movement towards evidence-based policy making, it also needs to be stressed that no in-built evaluation of the impact of reclassification was ordered by the Home Office and no key performance indicators (KPIs) were identified through which to gauge its impact. Ultimately this resulted in confusion as to the purpose of the policy change and opened up the possibility of continuing debate as to the efficacy of UK drug policy and its associated evidence base. Subsequent developments have buttressed this.

In the months following the reclassification, there was increasing concern about the potential links between cannabis and mental illness. This association has been long, but uncertain (Mills, 2003). A study by New Zealand-based scientists (Fergusson et al, 2005) suggested that smoking particularly virulent strains of cannabis ('skunk') virtually doubled the risk of developing mental illnesses, such as schizophrenia, for those with a family history, and significantly increased the risk for those without. These findings were supported in studies from the Netherlands (Henquet et al, 2004) and the UK (Arseneault et al, 2004). This received significant public and media attention. In March 2005, the then Home Secretary, Charles Clarke, announced that the reclassification, undertaken by his predecessor David Blunkett, would be placed 'under review', urging the ACMD to reassess the evidence. Justifying this move, Clarke cited further evidence from Europe to back up his proposals. He stated that the Dutch government was recently looking into the issue of whether 'skunk' above a certain strength should be given a higher classification. In January 2006, the ACMD (2005) published its review, stating that the initial reclassification should remain, thus maintaining cannabis as a class C substance.

What this reveals is further confusion over the 'evidence'. Not only was there uncertainty over the evidence for the initial reclassification, but both Blunkett and Clarke had different understandings over what 'evidence' could trigger potential policy changes, the former being convinced by the public management issue of streamlining police activities and the latter expressing concerns over the health implications of cannabis. The complex history of ownership of the UK drug problem was also distilled in this debate and as a consequence casts doubt as to whether this could be considered an evidence-based decision, as it is unclear what evidence was or should have been used. This is, of course, not to say that the reclassification of cannabis was evidence-free.

With the benefit of hindsight, it is clear that the cannabis reclassification was the trigger for the developing interest in the evidence base for UK drug classification and the debates of evidence thereon. In the aftermath of cannabis reclassification and review several other significant events occurred relating to debates over the evidence base of the UK drug classification system. This process started with the parliamentary debate over the passing of the Drugs Act 2005. This Act was subsequently the subject of much criticism, in particular, the inclusion of derivatives of 'magic mushrooms' as class A substances. The primary significance, however, was the wider interest in the drug classification system that this fostered. Towards the end of 2006 and into 2007, the debate between various constituencies concerning the efficacy of current UK drug policy and legislation, specifically relating to the evidence for the efficacy of the MDA 1971, became widespread (see, for example, Levitt et al, 2006; Science and Technology Select Committee, 2006b; Nutt et al, 2007; Reuter and Stevens, 2007; RSA, 2007). The publication of the Science and Technology Select Committee's report (2006b) was particularly significant. Running alongside these, senior members of the ACMD also conducted research into the tri-partite system of the MDA 1971, developing a matrix on which they claimed the dangers of drugs could be more accurately measured and from which appropriate punishments should be ascertained (Nutt et al, 2007). Additionally, an Academy of Medical Sciences (2008) report recommended that new measures of harm be developed to inform the classification of drugs. These studies are to varying degrees concerned about the evidence base for the current classification system.

Within weeks of assuming office, the policy landscape changed again as the then Prime Minister, Gordon Brown, announced that, in the light of continuing interest in the link between cannabis use and mental health (see, for example, Moore et al, 2007), and as part of the run-up to the review of the 2008 drug strategy, the classification of cannabis would be referred back to the ACMD. The same week, erstwhile Home Secretary, Jacqui Smith, announced – along with five Cabinet colleagues – that she too had tried cannabis as a student but welcomed the call to revisit the classification. In May 2008, against the prevailing advice from the ACMD (2008), the government signalled its intention to reclassify cannabis back up to a class B drug. The ACMD concluded that although the Council was still 'very concerned' that cannabis use was widespread and a genuine health threat to users, it pointed out that it was a 'public health' problem requiring a public health solution. In this sense, although the 'criminal justice and classification systems have a role to play – especially in reducing supply – the major emphasis must be directed at ways that drastically reduce demand' (ACMD, 2008, p 33). The accompanying recommendation was that cannabis should remain a class C drug. The report also stated that decisions about classification were ultimately 'based on the Council's collective judgement of substances within and between classes' (ACMD, 2008, p 34).

The decision to maintain cannabis as a class C drug was based on the fact that although there is recognition of a 'consistent (although weak) association from longitudinal studies between cannabis use and the development of psychotic illness', little evidence exists of the social harms associated with cannabis use, particularly its association with 'acquisitive crime and anti-social behaviour' (ACMD, 2008, p 34). As this is the case, the report suggested that cannabis currently resides in the correct class, class C, as the harms caused by cannabis are 'not considered to be as serious as those of drugs in class B' (ACMD, 2008, p 34). It was one further conclusion of this latest ACMD study that the cannabis classification issue should, however, remain under review in the light of potential new evidence emerging. This reflects the dynamic nature of this particular policy area. In 2009 it was announced, however, that cannabis would be reclassified back up to class B. This was the origin of the dispute between Professor Nutt and the New Labour government. One outcome of this was round condemnation of the government by the majority of the policy community over its claims to evidence use in drug classification policy. This episode re-emphasises the point about the inherent fluid nature of politicised policy areas and the connection therein between evidence and policy, which is likewise unpredictable and non-linear. The implications of this are returned to in Chapter Eight, when an attempt to model the evidence and policy connection is undertaken.

Summary

This chapter has provided the background to the case study through which the tumultuous nature of evidence-based policy making will be explored and explained in later chapters. It has charted the origins of the implementation of the MDA 1971, illustrating how the passing of this Act brought into fruition the current drug classification system and how this has remained relatively stable despite being the subject of much criticism and despite significant developments in the UK drug situation from the 1980s onwards, when drug policy became a political concern. Another feature of the passing of the MDA 1971 was how it created the first UK government drugs advisory board in the shape of the ACMD. From the 1980s and into the 1990s we have also witnessed an 'opening up' of the drug policy process, stemming from various government policies that have tried to foster joint working between the two main constituencies involved in drug control: the criminal justice and medical professions. There has been a long history of conflict and mutual suspicion between these groups.

This serves as a good example of how, because politicised policy areas lie at the intersection of autonomous department boundaries, they are characterised by adversity and instability. This stems from competing beliefs about the nature of these policies, and the direction in which they should move. Relating to the current concern, this has a knock-on effect for the production and utilisation of evidence. The debates over the struggle for ownership of the policy have shaped different accounts of what does or should count as evidence in drug classification decision making. In such instances, debates over the evidence base for policies are heavily contested, with different interest groups declaiming the significance of quite different bodies of research. Unpicking the various ways that evidence is understood in policy is significant if the concept of evidence-based policy is to have any currency. Before embarking on the task of further highlighting the complex nature of evidence utilisation in heavily politicised areas, it is worth pausing to discuss the tools appropriate for this task. It is to this that the discussion now turns.

Note

[1] Although the MDA 1971 applies across all of England, Northern Ireland, Scotland and Wales, it is worth pointing out that there are actually differences within this political entity in the way that drug policy is put into practice. Although most commentaries refer to the 'UK situation', what is actually being discussed is the situation in England and Wales.

FIVE

Developing tools for exploring 'evidence' in politicised policy areas

> "Information" in public policy is rarely "objective". Indeed virtually every think tank, interest group, or government organization seeks power and influence in the political marketplace and in the battle of ideas. This is not said to discredit any given source, but rather to assert the fact the "policy game" is a serious one, often played for the highest stakes. In this game, setting the agenda and controlling the dialogue are the primary ingredients of success. (Caldwell, 2002, p 1)

Chapter Four outlined how the history of UK drug policy is characterised by a continuing power struggle over ownership of the drug problem. The legacy of these debates has been felt in recent developments in UK drug policy making, more specifically issues relating to the legal status of drugs and the evidence used to buttress decisions in this area. It was suggested in Chapter Four that the cannabis reclassification and the interest in drug classification that this engendered represents a useful case study for analysing the relationship between evidence and the political machinery in the policy process. It was stated that it is plausible to suggest that evidence is embedded in policy making, but that its use remains opaque. This is because there are differing claims to ownership of the policy and the evidence used to inform it. Drug classification policy is not unique in this respect; indeed, it is likely that similar themes can be identified in various adversarial domains.

This chapter turns its attention to how evidence use in politicised areas can be explored and explained, so that the subtleties in the relationship between evidence and policy making can be revealed. In doing so, it considers some theoretical and methodological tools that can be used to explore the nature of evidence in politicised policy areas. A guiding principle of the evidence-based policy movement is that it has entailed an initial 'opening up' of government (Solesbury, 2001). This suggests that the policy process is characterised by diffused decision making stemming from the interactions, negotiations and deliberations of a wide range of stakeholders. By concentrating on the input of various individuals and groups, the horizontal model is consistent with Dahl's (1961) pluralist perspective of the policy process and various similar theories that this gave rise to, many of which have, or can be, employed in drug research (Ritter and Bammer, 2010). As we shall see, pluralist models are, in turn, consistent with what Colebatch (2002) has termed the 'horizontal model' of policy. This is not without some semblance of hierarchy, however, as the starting point is often the 'pronouncement of authorised decision-makers' (Colebatch, 2002, p 42).

The first part of this chapter, then, offers an overview of some of the main options of pluralist analysis covering the literature on multiple streams, policy networks and the Advocacy Coalition Framework (ACF). Of all the available theories and methods, a modified version of the ACF offers the most potential for exploring and explaining the evidence and policy connection in heavily politicised areas because of its specific focus on conflict in the policy arena. We have already witnessed how a key component of politicisation is that such policies involve often fractious debates between adversaries. The ACF is, therefore, selected for further critical discussion. Ultimately, it is maintained that to make it fit for purpose as a method for analysing the turbulent nature of evidence in policy, some modification of the method is needed. These adaptations are therefore brought to attention. The remainder of the chapter connects the history of UK drug policy with the modified version of the ACF. Drawing on the author's own research, it introduces the interested coalitions or 'perspectives' engaged in UK drug classification debates, setting up the analysis for the subsequent chapters. A summary is then provided.

Pluralist accounts of the policy process

What is policy? This is not an easy question to answer. According to Lindblom (1968, pp 1-2):

> Most people – even poets and ballet dancers – know a good deal about policy making. They know, for example, that the immediate responsibility for policy making has to be delegated to officials, that interest-group and party leaders greatly influence these officials, and that the rest of us play less active (though not insignificant) roles in the policy making drama. Yet many aspects of policy still need explaining, because almost no one is satisfied with his [*sic*] understanding of how policy is made.

Policy is a complex and multi-faceted phenomenon. Comprehending its nature is, therefore, a troublesome enterprise that has taxed many analysts for many years (see, for example, Lasswell and Kaplan, 1950; Friedrich, 1963; Jenkins, 1978; Hill and Bramley, 1986; Gordon et al, 1993; Colebatch, 2002). Gordon et al (1993) contend that it is misleading to view policy analysis as the study of identifiable things called 'policies', which are produced, or crystallise, at a particular stage in the decision process. Hill and Bramley (1986) also suggest that policy should not be treated as a self-evident or motionless phenomenon and that any attempt to define policy will be artificial in that what is being defined is inherently contested. For these thinkers, viewing policy as an artefact created by policy makers is misleading.

Bridgman and Davis (2000, p 6) offer a broader account. They define policy as 'a course of action by government designed to achieve certain results'. This definition, however, neglects the notion that policy making is not always the sole domain of the government or state and could involve various external actors and stakeholders. In this sense, Jenkins (1978, p 15) suggests that key to deciphering the nature of public policy is to view the phenomenon as 'a set of interrelated decisions taken by a political actor or a group of actors concerning the selection of goals and the means of achieving them'. This occurs within specified situations and 'where these decisions should, in principle, be within the powers of these actors to achieve'. The debate continues.

Ultimately, there is little agreement on its characteristics, which raises significant issues for how policy is to be analysed. In their analysis of comparative prison policy making in the US and the UK, Jones and Newburn (2005, p 60) comment that 'there is a large body of work within political science that has analysed policy making by dividing it up into distinct stages' and has then proceeded by 'undertaking detailed examinations of each'. This is taken as a 'commonsense' approach to the analysis of policy. This is a rigid process involving 'problem definition, formulation of alternative solutions, consideration of implications of alternatives, to experimentation with the preferred choice' (Jones and Newburn, 2005, p 60). This is frequently referred to as a 'policy cycle' model, illustrated in Figure 5.1.

Figure 5.1: A policy cycle model

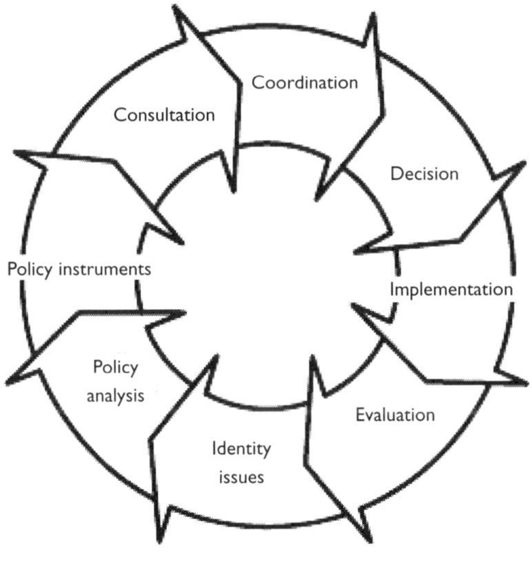

Source: Bridgman and Davis (2000)

Colebatch (2002) uses different terminology to describe policy. He makes a distinction between a 'vertical' model of policy making, where decision making is top down, and a 'horizontal' model, where it is characterised by a 'process of structured interaction' (Colebatch, 2002, p 23). The vertical model shares some similarities with the policy cycle approach. The horizontal model, by contrast, suggests that policy cannot be reduced to a stages approach because this is an over-simplistic, mechanistic and sequential outlook and that the process is, in reality, much more arbitrary. The vertical and horizontal models represent, for Colebatch, the 'two great models' of policy making.

Influenced by thinkers such as Lasswell (1951) and Easton (1965), and often referred to as the 'Westminster model', the vertical model divides the policy process into neatly packaged and logically ordered stages. Such depictions have been described as the 'stages model', 'stages heuristic' and the 'textbook approach' (Nakamura, 1987). The stages approach has enjoyed significant longevity as an explanation of the policy-making process because of its resemblance to how the public and powerful decision makers understand the policy process. This is based on a rational division of labour between the 'executive and legislative institutions of the government', which serves to legitimise 'the role of bureaucracy within representative systems' (Sabatier and Jenkins-Smith, 1993a, pp 2-3). Additionally, policy makers view the stages model as being consistent with democratic theory as it draws on the inputs of the broader society to make policy, which is, in turn, handed over to other government actors for implementation. This 'commonsense' understanding of the way that policy is made rests on a number of assumptions. Foremost among them is that policy making involves a specialised division of labour and a 'single chain of authority'.

For detractors, the 'top-down' view of policy making from the vertical model represents an idealist explanation of the process, which is in reality much more piecemeal or 'muddled through' (Lindblom, 1959). In most instances, and particularly in politicised areas, policies transcend a number of disciplines, areas or government departments and thus it is not always transparent where the top is or which actors occupy this position. Additionally, it is not consistent with the process of policy formulation and analysis in supranational bodies, like the EU, which operate within a 'complex political and bureaucratic process' that 'involves a plethora of actors' in the Council, Commission and Parliament (Bache and George, 2006, p 351).

As indicated, the horizontal model suggests that policy making is not characterised by direct diffusion from the top. This view has gained currency in recent years (see, for example, Kingdon, 1984; Ostrom, 1990; Baumgartner and Jones, 1993; Hill, 1997). It involves negotiation and the 'dispersal of authority' through various spheres of the political arena. As emphasis is placed on the nature of negotiation, the horizontal model allows further consideration of other agents' roles in the process. These could be agents of the state such as the police or those of civil society such as NGOs and think-tanks. This is, of course, not an exhaustive list.

This view of the policy process is consistent with aspects of both March and Olsen's (1976) notion of the 'garbage can model' and the widely referenced 'incremental model'. Both cast doubt on rational views of the policy-making process (Dahl and Lindblom, 1953; Lindblom, 1959; Braybrooke and Lindblom, 1963). Advocates of incrementalism focus on how multiple interests impact on the policy-making process via 'a process of mutual adjustment to achieve consensus'

(Nutley and Webb, 2000, p 27). In its extreme versions, incrementalism defies analysis as policy making is viewed as primarily an ad hoc activity. Although the horizontal approach does not perceive the policy-making process as a closed system, it does recognise that there are certain recognisable and even consistent features to it.

A useful rallying cry for advocates of the horizontal model would be Lindblom's (1968) assertion that policy making is an extremely complex process without beginning or end, whose boundaries remain most uncertain. Somehow a complex set of forces, including unintended consequences, produce effects called 'policies'. Consequently, the horizontal model takes as its starting point the 'pronouncements of authorised decision-makers' (Colebatch, 2002, p 42), but suggests that these can only be understood with recourse to the ongoing interaction which makes them achievable. To extend the analysis of the process to constitute a broader area for interaction and by focusing on who actually participates means that it offers a more diverse view of the policy process than the vertical model and accounts for the mobilisation of actors both inside and outside government who potentially or actually come to engage with policy. It therefore has its origins in Dahl's (1961) pluralist account of the policy process and various other similar manifestations of these that have since been developed; for instance, epistemic communities (Haas, 1992; Dunlop, 2007); issue networks (Heclo, 1978); policy networks (Kingdon, 1984); policy communities (Rhodes and Marsh, 1992); and the ACF (Sabatier and Jenkins-Smith, 1993b, 1999).

It is suffice to say that pluralist accounts of the policy process are consistent with the model of policy that underpins the evidence movement. Both allow for the input of a range of often interdependent actors in the decision-making process. In essence, the process of policy making now incorporates a greater range of players than those that constitute the 'iron triangle' of administrative agencies (government), legislative committees and interest groups. As suggested in Chapter Two, pluralist policy models are also linked to recent changes in governance. On the one hand, this relates to changes and adaptations to and of the state under the conditions of late modernity; on the other, it also refers to the way the state still plays a role in the coordination of social systems and the theoretical representation of this (Pierre, 2000, p 3). As has been stressed, the governance of any advanced capitalist society now entails coordination between various layers of agents and structures of control. This means that there are numerous levels of decision making that take place and these have to be consistently and coherently managed (Pierre and Stoker, 2000). In terms of policy analysis, the list of key policy personnel swells under the conditions of governance. In other words, pressure from different groups involved in setting agendas and proposing solutions to policy problems becomes embedded in the process, as does the evidence that they bring to the table. The following examples all testify how this can happen.

Multiple streams and policy communities

The multiple streams model, developed by Kingdon (1984), is a useful example of what Colebatch is referring to when he suggests that policy making is characterised by structured interaction. For Kingdon, policies have two constituent parts: the 'policy process' (the 'how') and the 'substantive level' of policy (the 'what'). The current concern is with the process, which is, in turn, split into three distinct elements or 'streams': the problem stream, the policy stream and the political stream. The 'problem stream' refers to the ways in which particular problems or issues emerge that concentrate the thoughts of policy makers. These are issues that require action. It is in this area that the nature of the problem is decided or 'categorised', for instance, whether drug policy should be a public health concern or a matter for the criminal justice system. The 'policy stream' refers to the process of deciphering 'compelling' problems that require responses from policy makers and politicians, and deciding what the most efficacious solution may be among the list of alternatives. The evidence community may be prominent here acting as advocates for their own solutions. For Kingdon, policy ideas and proposals are rarely new and many float around continuously, in what Kingdon (1984) terms the 'policy primeval soup', waiting to be attached to a problem. Finally, there is the 'political stream', where decisions are ultimately taken. These decisions are contingent on issues such as the outcome of general or other elections, fluctuations in the 'public mood' and interest or advocacy group campaigning, among other things.

The streams are largely independent from one another but can and do converge at certain times. At such junctures, solutions become joined to problems and, when political forces allow, 'a policy window' is created. Of particular note here is the interaction between the problem, policy and political streams and the way that the political considerations impact on policy possibilities. Although researchers play a role in all streams it is in the policy stream where they are arguably most active. Yet research alone is not likely, in this model, to be a key driving force of policy and requires a vehicle through which to achieve impact. The promotion of certain ideas often stems from advocacy by policy communities. Policy communities refer to a group of actors with a significant degree of specialism who may or may not be part of a governing administration. Academics and evaluators may play a role here, as may practitioners, 'street-level' bureaucrats and other interested stakeholders:

> They may have diverse orientations and interests, but all share specialist knowledge and experience of a particular policy domain.... Policy communities play a key role in developing, testing out, selecting and refining those policy ideas and proposals that make it on to the policy agenda. (Nutley et al, 2007, pp 106-7)

A key strength of Kingdon's analyses lies in the recognition that by its very nature, policy formation is not always a 'rational' process. The choices and decisions that governments make are a product of issues becoming categorised as a 'problem'; they are in turn influenced by the activities of policy communities, but are ultimately bound by what is feasible at certain times and in certain contexts.

Kingdon's (1984) multiple streams analysis is one that shares many similarities with the model of policy making that underpins the evidence-based policy agenda. For current purposes, it does have particular drawbacks. Ultimately, little attention is given to the way that there are often competing assertions and accounts – particularly within the policy stream – of the nature of problems. Allied to this, the mechanisms by which one approach assumes the status of a workable solution to a problem requires further elaboration. In effect, more attention is required to the conflict that occurs in the arena of agenda setting. These are particularly noticeable shortcomings when we consider that heavily politicised policy areas are ones that precisely involve significant degrees of conflict.

Policy networks

Networks are an increasingly prominent and fashionable concept in the analysis of social, political and economic life (Castells, 1996). According to Duke (2003, p 10), policy networks are one of three levels of association (along with the 'policy universe' and 'policy community') visible within the wider policy process. The policy universe refers to the large population of actors or potential actors who share a direct or indirect interest in a particular policy area, and interact with one another to shape policy. Policy communities are more disaggregated systems of actors drawn from the policy universe, who share a common interest in a particular area and interact with one another to shape policy. The policy network is the linking process or the outcome of the interaction within a policy community or between a number of policy communities over particular policy issues, problems or functions. In essence, policy issues, problems and functions provide the platform on which a policy network emerges.

The policy networks approach has been frequently, if not uniformly, employed in political science, and is entrenched in this discipline (Knoke, 1990; Marsh and Rhodes, 1992; Rhodes and Marsh, 1992; Smith, 1993; Marsh and Smith, 2000). A particular fruitful area of policy network analysis has been in the area of criminal justice-related policy (Ryan et al, 2001; Savage and Charman, 2001; Duke, 2002, 2003). Policy networks are heterogeneous. They vary across policy domains and jurisdictions. Their impact on policy formulation is contingent on their make-up and relationship with governing administrations. They operate on the principle of cooperation stemming from the shared interests of members. In this respect, a contrast can be drawn between the concept of network and those of hierarchy and markets which are based on command and competition, respectively (Cope, 2001, p 1).

Rhodes and Marsh (1992) equate policy networks with the 'meso-level' of policy, providing a link between the micro-level concerning the role of interests and the macro-level corridors of power, with a typical focus on the way that power is distributed. It is Rhodes and Marsh's terminology that has now become common currency. The policy networks concept has received a significant amount of criticism, however. A primary area of concern relates to the nature of policy networks in the context of debates over the ontology, epistemology and methodology of political science (see, for example, Dowding, 1995, 2001; Marsh and Smith, 2000, 2001). For Dowding (1995, p 137), policy networks are 'essentially metaphorical', premised on non-formal models and are therefore not consistent with the principles of scientific inquiry. Non-formal models are fortified with numerous 'unstated assumptions', making them impossible to evaluate and from which it is difficult to draw out any definitive predictions. In effect, they are not scientifically sound. Unstated assumptions are, for Dowding, those that remain opaque within the model and consequently defy empirical test. Dowding (2001, p 93) suggests that one main problem of a model premised on a number of unstated assumptions is that it becomes difficult, if not impossible, to tell it apart from other models, and therefore its utility as an explanatory tool has to be called into question. In response, advocates of policy networks have questioned Dowding's views of 'science', dismissing his claims as 'positivist' (Marsh and Smith, 2001).

These debates need not concern us at this juncture, but Duke (2003, p 11) highlights a further problem and this is one that does resonate with current themes. For her, the network approach fails to provide an account of why these networks and relationships form, how, if at all, they change and how power is exercised. This neglect of power is significant in the current context as power differentials are central to advocacy and promoting evidence (Caldwell, 2002). Ultimately, policy networks, like policy communities, offer significant potential for studying the policy process when research questions focus on an area of policy characterised more by consensus than conflict. Heavily politicised policy areas cannot be considered in such terms.

Advocacy Coalition Framework

Initially developed by Sabatier (Sabatier, 1987, 1988; Sabatier and Jenkins-Smith, 1993b), the ACF is one of the most widely discussed theories of the policy process. By focusing on the interdependencies between actors in a bid to ascertain how policy decision making functions, the ACF shares similarities with the policy community and network literature. The ACF can also be read as addressing many of the problems raised regarding the utility of policy networks. In particular, it promotes to the fore a consideration of the role of conflict and power differentials within a policy arena and also how policy analysis is utilised in policy decision making.

Central to the ACF, indeed its main unit of analysis, is the 'subsystem'. This is made up of identifiable 'advocacy coalitions' actively concerned with a specific policy issue. There are usually between one and four identifiable coalitions in any given subsystem. Subsystems emerge out of significant dissatisfaction with the policy status quo and attempt to foster policy change as a result (Sabatier, 1993). Advocacy coalitions, meanwhile, are:

> ... people from a variety of positions (elected and agency officials, interest group leaders, researchers etc) who share a particular belief system – that is, a set of basic values, causal assumptions and problem perceptions – and who show a nontrivial degree of co-ordinated activity over time. (Sabatier and Jenkins-Smith, 1999, p 120)

Coalitions are dynamic. Sabatier and Pelkey (1987) have pointed out that it is an extremely complex task to develop a model that could involve changes in the positions and patterns of association of the many units involved over the time span of a decade, the minimum time in which the policy cycle is completed. Coalitions form as a result of a commitment to a particular belief system. Over the course of the last few decades, the impact of beliefs on policy making has received greater attention (see, for example, Heclo, 1978; Majone, 1989). For Sabatier, the ACF is ultimately a tool for highlighting how these ideas or beliefs shape a coalition's views of the policies with which they are concerned (Sabatier, 1988, p 132). Echoing Lakatos (1970), by and large coalitions are based around a hierarchical tri-partite structure of 'deep core', 'policy core' and 'secondary aspects'.

Within this framework, the higher levels (deep core) constrain the more specific (secondary) beliefs. For Sabatier and Jenkins-Smith (1999, pp 191-2), the deep core refers to an ontological perspective or 'worldview'. These shape the 'perceptual filters' through which coalitions and individuals view the social world. At the opposite end, the secondary aspects are a large set of narrowly held beliefs. These are often not held by all members of the coalition, manifested in the way that administrative agents (politicians) or agencies (political parties) within a coalition often hold 'less extreme' positions than a campaigning NGO, for instance. This could be a product of institutional constraints, such as a politician's need to be re-elected. In the middle range lies the 'policy core'. This concerns the particular policy issues in question. It contains various dimensions including the coalition's 'basic normative commitments and causal perceptions of the problem', as well as its perceived seriousness (Sabatier and Jenkins-Smith, 1999, p 122).

The more deeply held the belief, the less resistant it is to change. Indeed, a change in deep core beliefs is considered to be akin to a religious conversion. Changes in the policy core are also unlikely. Thus, where change does occur, it is usually in the secondary aspects of a coalition's belief system (Sabatier and Jenkins-Smith, 1999, p 122). One way of attempting to change an opposing view or to reaffirm a core belief occurs through the process of policy-oriented learning. Members of particular coalitions seek to show those in others, including those in positions of power, that their evidence or knowledge is the most applicable and should be called on to formulate, alter or continue the direction of policy. The ACF is, then, a theory that considers the role played by technical information, especially that detailing the scale and nature of the problem, its causes and the likely impact of potential solutions. Sabatier and Jenkins-Smith suggest, however, that policy-oriented learning is unlikely to be the major driver of policy change. Instead, changes or 'perturbations' in the real world, for example in related socio-economic conditions, also have a direct impact on policy. These are exogenous factors impacting on the policy subsystem. Furthermore, changes internal to the subsystem can also have a direct bearing on the nature of policy change. For example, the death or retirement of a significant policy actor 'can substantially alter the political resources of various coalitions and thus policy decisions' (Sabatier and Jenkins-Smith, 1999, p 123).

The ACF has also been the subject of significant criticism. Fischer (2003) and Hajer (1995) suggest that the framework is inherently positivist. The crux of this critique rests on the way that Sabatier and colleagues highlight the causal prowess of the ACF as a means for explaining and predicting change. By focusing on causal statements in the form of empirical hypotheses much of the minutiae of policy deliberation is missing from the analysis. In effect, it neglects the social and historical context in which policy change happens and as a result it is missing an interpretive dimension. It is, therefore, a 'black box' theory (Fischer, 2003, p 101). Schlager (1995) also questions the rational nature of the policy-making process the ACF depicts, casting doubt on the feasibility of coordinated activity and its potential, and deeming it to be the exception not the rule. A related significant point of contention is the extent to which the ACF has been empirically tested, that is, whether coalitions actually share similar beliefs and engage in meaningful, coordinated behaviour. Logically, it follows that if there is no such commitment to the belief system then coalition membership cannot be sustained and, ultimately, the framework becomes redundant.

In response, Sabatier and Jenkins-Smith (1999) point out how the costs of 'coordination' are smaller than Schlager (1995) conceives. Whereas Schlager draws on Ostrom's (1990) theory of institutional analysis and development, to show that individuals can be rational and 'self-interested', the ACF is premised on bounded rationality. This views the agent as being not altogether focused on maximising his or her material self-interest (Jenkins-Smith and St Clair, 1993). In emphasising the bounded nature of rationality, Zafonte and Sabatier (1998) make a distinction between 'strong' and 'weak' types of coordination. Strong coordination requires a 'common plan of action, the communication of that plan to potential coalition members, the monitoring of member compliance, and the imposition of sanctions for non-compliance' (Zafonte and Sabatier, 1998, p 480). By contrast, weak coordination simply requires organisational actors to monitor each other's political behaviour and then alter their actions 'to make their political strategies complementary with respect to a common goal' (Zafonte and Sabatier, 1998, p 480). At its most basic level, weak coordination presupposes that actors share policy core beliefs.

In light of the criticisms and subsequent rebuttals, the ACF has been remodelled. It no longer assumes that 'beliefs' are identical across entire coalitions and that the boundaries between them are more fluid than earlier iterations suggested.

By reviewing a significant proportion of their own work and others' (Sabatier and Jenkins-Smith, 1993b; Sabatier and Zafonte, 1995; Zafonte and Sabatier, 1998), Sabatier and Jenkins-Smith (1999, p 128) suggest that by developing a range of techniques such as systematic coding of testimonies given to legislative hearings, they have been able to 'confirm the existence of advocacy coalitions'. This debate also remains unresolved. What is clear is that in recent years the ACF has maintained its popularity in the light of strong criticism (Weible et al, 2009).

Modifying the ACF

With its emphasis on the nature of conflict and power in the policy process, of the available theories and methods, the ACF offers the most potential for exploring and explaining the evidence and policy connection in heavily politicised areas, that is, how zero-sum views are prevalent, but inaccurate. There is some precedent for discussing drug-related issues in terms of competing perspectives. Stevens (2007b), for example, uses a 'discourse coalition approach' to show how the construction of the concept of 'drug-related crime' materialised and came to the fore in UK drug policy. Likewise, Kübler (2001) employs a version of the ACF to explain changes in the philosophy of Swiss drug policy in the 1990s away from a prohibitionist model towards a harm reduction model. Although there are key differences between Stevens' and Kübler's approaches, both examples illustrate how drug policy debates can be analysed from a starting point of conflict between various actors.

As was demonstrated in Chapter Four, the debate over the evidence base for the UK drug classification system is characterised by competing perspectives with recognisable adherents. Despite this, to analyse the relationship between evidence and policy in politicised areas, some modification of the framework is required for two main reasons. First, the criticisms of the ACF documented above are compelling and cannot be ignored, particularly the rigid view of the policy process that the conventional ACF approach employs. Second, the ACF was developed as a way of explaining policy change, but this is not the current goal. Here the aim is to demonstrate issues surrounding the nature of evidence in policy and the implications this has for evidence-based decision making. As this is the case, the current use of the ACF departs from the original in one key way.

Although there are 'distinct groupings' or configurations in UK drug policy, with different takes on the nature and purpose of the drug classification system, these do not correspond to 'coalitions' in the sense maintained by Sabatier and colleagues. In the ACF, 'coalitions' assume a significant degree of coordinated activity with the aim of working towards the end goal of policy change. Here, groups coalesce around a shared understanding of what 'evidence' is or should be, in the context of UK drug classification policy. As an alternative, then, the term 'perspectives' is favoured over 'coalitions'. Perspectives do not presuppose the same amount of coordinated activity from actors. The notion of perspectives is informed by what Vickers (1965) has termed 'appreciative systems'. These generally refer to the process of attaching meaning to communications, and involve:

> … making a judgment of fact about the "state of the system", both internally and in its external relations. I will call these reality judgments. These include judgments about what the state will be or might be on various hypotheses as well as judgments of what it is and has been. They may be thus actual or hypothetical, past, present or future. It also involves making judgments about the significance of these facts to the appreciator or to the body for whom the appreciator is made. These judgments I will call value judgments. Reality judgments and value judgments are inseparable constituents of appreciation…. (Vickers, 1965, p 40)

The incorporation of appreciations can pacify critics of the ACF who are troubled by its rationalist assumptions. Appreciations and perspectives build into the analysis the notion that there are 'fuzzy' boundaries between groups in the policy subsystem. In essence, an actor could be located in a certain perspective in terms of deep and policy core beliefs but secondary aspects may be consistent with other groups. Appreciations also temper the excesses of advocates of incrementalist views of policy. To recap, these state that the process defies analysis and that policy is characterised by its ad hoc nature. Appreciations, meanwhile, suggest that there are recognisable features and processes at work in decision making that require explanation. It is, then, to illustrate the nuances of 'evidence' that 'appreciations' and 'perspectives' form the basis of the reworking of the ACF in the spirit of what Layder (1998) refers to as 'adaptive theory'. The three-tier belief system structure of the ACF is maintained. The advantage of pursuing this path is that it helps incorporate the inevitable spectrum of views within and between perspectives on what does and should count as evidence in UK drug classification decision making. As a result, the ACF is utilised here as a middle range theory (Merton, 1957) explaining the role of conflict in policy debates, in this case about evidence and drug classification.

The organisation of the drug classification policy subsystem

The research into appreciations of the evidence base for UK drug classification decision making that informs the analysis in the remainder of this book primarily used qualitative methods. These included documentary analysis of relevant parliamentary reports and 'elite' interviews with a wide range of key policy actors involved in the decision-making process (for more details on the methodology, see Monaghan, 2008). MPs, civil servants, directors and senior figures of drug agencies and NGOs, and representatives of law enforcement agencies were among those interviewed. Different participants had differing degrees of involvement in policy formulation. None were involved in direct decision making but most were involved in the consultation process, either directly or via their organisation. Selection was made on the grounds of their knowledge of the evidence and policy relationship regarding the MDA 1971.

As will become clear, debates over UK drug classification involve numerous interested constituencies. These made up the different 'perspectives'. Adapting the work of Goddard (1997), the various actors in this particular policy subsystem can be split into two identifiable parts: 'interest groups' and 'official organisations' (see Tables 5.1, 5.3 and 5.5). Goddard's study on belief systems in post-war criminal justice policy making also incorporated political parties into the analysis. One paradox of the UK drug classification debate, however, is that although it is highly politicised, the stances of political parties are primarily non-partisan and differences within them are frequently greater than those between them. In the subsequent discussion, mention is given to how certain perspectives have an affinity with 'traditional' party political stances, although this is not straightforward.

For the purposes of this research, 'interest groups' refers to any organisations (usually not-for-profit) – ranging from the tightly to the loosely organised – that are determined to impact on policy through advocacy, while remaining independent of the political arena. An 'official organisation' shares many of the same traits but is answerable to, or linked with, certain agencies of the 'state' in some manner, most obviously through being the beneficiary of central funding. It is accepted that this distinction in and of itself is somewhat problematic as certain organisations may be recipients of government funding, but may also have a critical stance towards certain aspects of government policy.

Membership to particular groups was assigned to respondents initially from statements (both written and oral) given to previous UK parliamentary select committee reports. At the outset, an appropriate respondent from each perspective was initially identified from submissions given to House of Commons select committees closely related to this area (see, for example, Home Affairs Select Committee, 2002; Science and Technology Select Committee, 2006b), and then other respondents were snowballed from the initial contact. This does not necessarily mean that the initial contact was part of the final sample, however. Also, not all the groups or organisations listed in Tables 5.1, 5.3 and 5.5 were represented in the interviews and likewise not all interviewees were members of these organisations. In all, 24 semi-structured interviews were carried out between June 2006 and April 2007, 22 face-to-face and two telephone-based. A question guide was used to structure discussions. All interviews were recorded on audiotape and transcribed verbatim by the author. They were then analysed using thematic coding assisted by an NVivo computer software package. To protect anonymity, a pseudonym and broad job description were assigned to each respondent in line with the key ethical commitments of the original research.

All perspectives start from the premise that the relationship between evidence and policy in this area is disorderly because alcohol and tobacco, the most widely used substances (along with caffeine) and generally regarded as the two substances which cause the most harm (for example, by causing drug-related deaths), are absent from the MDA 1971. This skews the messages it gives out. In this regard, all perspectives were, to varying degrees, critical of the 'official' government line of the time with regard to the efficacy of the UK drug classification system and its associated evidence base.

This position was expressed by Vernon Coaker MP, one-time Parliamentary Under-Secretary at the Home Office and holder of the drugs brief, who suggested that:

> The Government maintain that the classification system has withstood the test of time and that it continues to discharge its function fully and effectively. Its single purpose is to provide a legal framework in which criminal penalties are set by reference to the harmfulness of a drug to the individual and to society, and to the type of illegal activity undertaken…. Our tri-partite classification system allows clear and meaningful distinctions to be made between drugs. Its familiarity and brand recognition should not be dismissed. (*Hansard*, 2007, 14 June)

This position – that the current system is fit for purpose – is understandable and to be expected in that countenancing any radical change to drug legislation, in the current climate, is, for a politician, not conducive to furthering their career.

All the perspectives, then, are founded on general ontological or philosophical ideas and beliefs about the nature of the drug problem and what it is that the classification system is supposed to do. These ideas and beliefs can be described as the deep core or 'ideological' beliefs. They relate to how policies would look, that is, what the policy outcomes would be if all the evidence were taken into account in the decision-making process. This impacts on the policy core and secondary aspects. To reiterate, the policy core relates to specific policies under the microscope. Eagle-eyed readers will notice that there are two substantive aspects to all perspectives' policy core views. In what follows, the policy issue of the evidence base for the reclassification of cannabis (Chapter Six) and the evidence base for the wider drug classification system (Chapter Seven) will be discussed. The deep and policy core beliefs of each perspective are presented in table form (see Tables 5.2, 5.4 and 5.6). Each perspective, as indicated, also has a range of opinions or appreciations (secondary aspects) on the kinds of evidence that were or ought to have been used in the cannabis and wider drug classification decisions. An illustration of these is considered throughout the analysis of the relevant chapters. The titles given to each group emerged from the research process. These were descriptions given by respondents in the course of the interviews. Although the labels could be seen to be value-loaded, they are, in effect, mainly an organisational tool. As this is the case, although one is described as 'rational', this does not mean that the other perspectives are somehow 'irrational'. Bearing this in mind, it is to each perspective that we now turn.

Radical perspective

The radical perspective is comprised of various NGOs and supporters concerned with significantly reforming UK drug legislation. Their aim is the abandonment of the prohibition of illegal substances. Table 5.1 highlights the key players in this group, which is typically smaller than other groups. Some of the core beliefs of each perspective can be highlighted by statements given to parliamentary reports into the drug problem. Release is an independent UK-based charity that provides free legal advice for young people about drugs and drug-related issues. In written evidence to the Home Affairs Select Committee, they stated:

> We believe that in the long term the use and supply of all drugs be controlled and regulated within the law, using different and appropriate supply models for different drugs. This is the only way to assure effective drugs education and harm minimisation across the board and also the only way to eliminate the involvement of criminal gangs and terrorist networks in the supply of drugs. (Home Affairs Select Committee, 2002, memorandum 56)

Transform is a leading UK-based organisation campaigning for a 'just and effective drug policy'. They exist to 'minimise drug-related harm to individuals and communities and believe that this is best achieved by legalising drugs' (Home Affairs Select Committee, 2002, memorandum 66). In their written evidence to the Home Affairs Select Committee, they commented:

> In Transform's view prohibition has caused or created many of the problems associated with the use and misuse of drugs. As with alcohol prohibition in the US in the twenties and thirties, drugs prohibition effectively hands the trade over to organised crime and unregulated dealers. Government abrogates all responsibility for the management of the supply side of the market and chaos prevails. The illicit drugs market is probably the most free and deregulated commodity market on the planet, constituting nearly 10 per cent of international trade and valued at £300 billion a year....Whilst Transform ultimately calls for the legalisation of drugs, that can only happen in conjunction with other countries and after the rewriting of the international treaties. In the meantime, decriminalisation would remove criminal sanctions from users and enable resources to be focused in more useful areas. (Home Affairs Select Committee, 2002, memorandum 66)

In terms of the sample, four respondents were located in this perspective, with one respondent (Noel) leaning towards the rational position. The appreciations of this perspective are consistent with the smaller political parties in the UK such as the Green Party and, in a partial way, the Liberal Democrats, with fringe support in the main parties. No 'official organisation' is located in this perspective as, historically, advocating the legalisation of drugs has precluded organisations from receiving large sums of public money, a product of the politics of electoral anxiety. Conversely, it has traditionally been the way to achieve widespread vilification in the media.

The radical perspective occupies a position in the drug policy debate that was at one time considered extreme. Consequently, its adherents occupied a pariah status and this stance is still unpalatable for most decision makers in positions of power. In recent years, there are signs that this is changing, typified by the increasing media profile of members of the group and a space opening up for informed debate as to the opportunity to deregulate certain illicit substances, both domestically (Home Affairs Select Committee, 2002) and internationally. This is compounded by the fact that, as of August 2007, Transform was granted consultative status at the UN. Sharing a similar outlook towards the drug problem, it was the view of one MP, Phil, that the origins of the problem with the current drug legislation were clear:

Table 5.1: Radical perspective composition

Interest groups	Official organisations
Transform, Release	None

Table 5.2: Radical perspective belief system structure

Deep core	Policy core
Minimise drug-related harm via a humane and useful regulatory system of drug control culminating with the abolition of prohibition. Less emphasis on enforcement as drugs are an inevitable feature of daily life for many	Cannabis reclassification not 'evidence-based' but broadly a step in the right direction for UK drug classification; wider classification (MDA 1971) system primarily not evidence-based

> One thing you can guarantee in politics is that when all parties agree on something they are almost certainly wrong....They did agree in 1971 that they needed to have a crackdown on the use of illegal drugs.... In Britain, we tackled this by producing a classification of illegal drugs and that was irrational and omitted the dangerous legal drugs. The classification was an abject failure and was counterproductive. When it was introduced in 1971, there were a thousand addicts of heroin and cocaine and after 35 years of the classification, the number had grown to 280,000 and there was certainly a causal link between those two events.

The respondent went on to say:

> At the moment all the United Nations countries are signed up to a policy set in 1998, that we will work towards the elimination of the

use, or a very substantial reduction in the use, of illegal drugs and this was a 10-year strategy. Those 10 years are up in 2008 and we haven't made an inch of progress towards that aim. Let alone eliminating drugs, we haven't reduced them in any way. The situation is very much the same, if anything slightly worse than it was in 1998, so the United Nations and all the countries that are signed up to its policies are on a course that is completely impossible.

The starting point of their analysis is that drug use is an inevitable part of existence for certain individuals predisposed to this activity. This has the outcome that there is some inevitability about the place of drugs in society. This is an interesting point of comparison between the perspectives. Much of the core beliefs of the radical perspective relate to the futility of the current MDA 1971 framework, stemming from the view that the current system does not effectively carry out its deterrent function. The radical group are not alone in surmising this, but are unique in their suggestion that the cause of this state of affairs relates to the ineffectiveness of using a criminal justice mechanism to control what is, essentially, a public health issue. For thinkers in this perspective, this is the epitome of a prohibitionist paradigm, which is itself an 'evidence-free zone' (Rolles et al, 2006, p 6). With this in mind, the deep core beliefs of this perspective are expressed by James, a journalist and writer with a long-standing interest in the drugs debate:

> I think it is a curious warping effect that the health debate has because, as far as I am concerned, it is not about arguing that drugs should be legal because they are safe, that is kind of back-to-front. If there are more concentrated and different forms of cannabis on the street, that is precisely because we have an illegal market in which we can't intervene and which is driven by, in the case of skunk, those people who are growing a dozen plants in their back bedroom. And you get five times as much money out of a very strong skunk plant than you do out of a mellow old-school weed, and that is why we have got stronger stuff on the street.

For the radical perspective, a new framework is required, enabling state regulation of the currently illicit drugs market. This equates to a policy position that states that not only is the current system an ineffective deterrent, but it actually causes many problems associated with drugs. Consequently, policy reformulations that involve existing tweaks to the legislation, such as cannabis reclassification, do not radically alter the problematic framework of the MDA 1971. Ultimately, this means that the current system cannot be 'evidence-based'. Again, this is linked to the evidence surrounding the deterrent effect. James continues:

> As regards questions about what is the evidence base for the classification system acting as a deterrent, the answer is there is no

evidence base for that. But the government response was "yes we are a bit short of evidence for that and we will go out and get some evidence supporting that view and we will get back to you" so, you know, I think it is difficult for drug policy to be evidence-based if it is not prepared to countenance a profound rethink.

Overall, the philosophy underpinning the radical perspective is that prohibition has failed and needs to be replaced by a different system of regulation.

Rational perspective

Comprising actors from a range of backgrounds and disciplines, the rational perspective is the broadest group in this subsystem. This is reflected in the sample, with 13 respondents affiliated to this group, one of whom (Michael) had many secondary beliefs that were consistent with the 'conservative' position outlined below. In the words of a senior figure in a leading drug treatment NGO (Noel), it constitutes, although not solely, the drug policy 'establishment' and 'critical friends' of government. The philosophy of this group is consistent with the premise of the MDA 1971. This maintains that criminal penalties should apply to drug offences and that these should be proportionate to the perceived harm the substance causes. The rational group do claim, however, that as it stands there are clear anomalies within this legislation that undermine its credibility. Table 5.3 indicates how it includes many members of the ACMD and a number of official organisations and other NGOs, often the recipients of central funding. These include DrugScope, the National Treatment Agency and the Association of Chief Police Officers, among others. Additionally, more independent bodies such as the newly formed UK Drug Policy Commission and the Royal Society of Arts share, to a degree, the same philosophical standpoint. Many members of this perspective also come from 'academic scientific' backgrounds.

It is necessary to say that although there are many similarities between the work of the ACMD as typified by Nutt et al (2007) and the Royal Society of Arts (RSA, 2007) report, there are also numerous differences. Indeed, the former operates within the broader substantive framework of the MDA 1971 but suggests that it needs amending, whereas the latter is more explicit in advocating its repeal and replacement with a Misuse of Substances Act. The Royal Society of Arts report also offers some novel suggestions for the direction of UK drug policy such as 'requiring ministers to take into account the best available scientific evidence relating to drugs and their use', and if this is not done, then for ministers to 'state formally and publicly' their reasons (RSA, 2007, p 15). Both reports are, however, consistent with the rational perspective, in that evidence is linked to the working out of the toxicological properties of certain substances, which are then calibrated against other ones to show where they should fit into a system of drug control legislation that maintains the prohibition of drugs.

A snapshot of the core beliefs of this group can also be witnessed from evidence given to parliamentary select committees. In written evidence to the Home Affairs Select Committee, the National Treatment Agency stressed that:

> Recreational drug use has become normalised amongst young people, that isn't to say that all young people use drugs, about half never will, but that recreational drug use is now regarded as part of a normal repertoire of behaviours. Most people use drugs because they enjoy them, and for the vast majority of users this experience remains pleasurable and under their control…. For a minority of drug misusers their pattern of use comes to include opiates and cocaine and escalates beyond their control developing into dependency. Associated with this will be a range of other harms and risks impacting on the individual's health and welfare, the health of the wider public, and the safety of the communities within which they live…. Improving the accessibility and effectiveness of treatment for this minority is at the core of the drug strategy. Despite much effort the evidence base to take forward a prevention strategy is at best patchy, similarly the success of attempts to restrict availability fluctuates but it is generally acknowledged that the best we can do is restrict the market, not eliminate it. Treatment on the other hand is beginning to build up a convincing evidence-base of what works best. (Home Affairs Select Committee, 2002, memorandum 46)

To take another example, according to its website, DrugScope is:

> [T]he UK's leading independent centre of expertise on drugs and the national membership organisation for the drug field. Our aim is to inform policy development and reduce drug-related harms – to individuals, families and communities. We provide quality drug information, promote effective responses to drug taking, undertake research, advise on policy-making, encourage informed debate. (www.drugscope.org.uk)

In written evidence to the Science and Technology Select Committee, it stated:

> While accepting that some problems caused by illegal drug use are actually a product of drug prohibition itself, neither DrugScope nor its members supports the blanket legalisation of drugs. We have seen no examples of an alternative control regime which would both substantially undermine the fortunes of international organised crime while safeguarding public health interests…. (Science and Technology Select Committee, 2006b, Evidence 89)

The conclusion to its evidence neatly summarises further the core beliefs of the rational perspective:

> 1. As signatories to international conventions, the UK is obliged to have in place laws to restrict a range of specified drugs.
>
> 2. However, the Misuse of Drugs Act is quite a flexible instrument and the UK is not obliged to either classify drugs or penalise their distribution within any rigid international framework.
>
> 3. This means that there is plenty of opportunity for an overall review of the whole classification of drugs in the light of current best evidence.
>
> 4. This is necessary because DrugScope would contend that the evidence base for the current classification of drugs such as ecstasy and magic mushrooms is weak. There also needs to be more clarity over the penalty tariff between classes.
>
> 5. DrugScope feels that when dealing with such an emotional and highly charged subject, it is most important that the government continues to make best possible use of the expert advice enshrined in the legislation. (Science and Technology Select Committee, 2006b, Evidence 89)

As Table 5.4 illustrates, the rational perspective therefore has a deep core view that primarily non-coercive drug treatment is also central to managing the drug problem. In party politics, support for this stance has usually been linked with Liberal Democrat policy, but has also been shared by some of the Labour Party and not so many from the Conservative Party. Within most administrations, before and since 1971, this has been the favoured policy direction of the Department of Health. Table 5.4 also indicates a set of policy core beliefs, focusing on anomalies in the location of certain drugs within the MDA 1971, which undermines its credibility.

Table 5.3: Rational perspective composition

Interest groups	Official organisations
UK Harm Reduction Alliance, International Harm Reduction Association, The Beckley Foundation, UK Drug Policy Commission	ACMD,[a] National Treatment Agency, Association of Chief Police Officers, traditionally the Department of Health, DrugScope

Note: It is accepted that there is always a range of views represented by the ACMD. As this research points out, however, a prevailing view or philosophy can also be identified.

Table 5.4: Rational perspective belief system structure

Deep core	Policy core
Promotion of human rights and public health placing treatment at the centre of the drug strategy as drug use is an inevitable part of everyday life for many. Using evidence to inform policy by ironing out anomalies of existing framework	Cannabis reclassification primarily 'evidence-based' as a step towards ironing out MDA 1971's anomalies; wider classification system increasingly evidence-based

The core beliefs of this perspective reflect its composition of leading figures in the drug policy establishment, such as the ACMD and the National Treatment Agency. In this sense, the starting point for what constitutes the 'drug problem' demarcates them from their conservative counterparts, and links them to the radical perspective, in that drug use is inevitable for certain individuals. According to Henry, a member of a drugs charity:

> We start from a position that ... the reality is that as a species we have got a very long history of a desire to alter consciousness and take mood-enhancing drugs whatever they are, and you ain't never going to stop that from happening. Therefore, if you are never going to stop it from happening, what's the next thing that you do? Well, you try and mitigate the risks and dangers that people will be putting themselves through, as a result of using drugs both as individuals and for communities and society at large. In the process of doing that you have to weigh up all sorts of different things. Community safety against human rights, and all of that kind of stuff, which is why we sign up to a harm reduction agenda, so that is where we come from.

So the main difference between the radical and rational groups is precisely how the risks associated with drugs should be mitigated. For the former, this should be achieved via the abandonment of prohibition and the creation of a system of licensed regulation. For the latter, it can be achieved in two ways that do not require a radical altering of the current legislative framework. First, it involves increasing the role of public health agencies in the form of drug treatment, while simultaneously maintaining the criminal justice framework, as we have seen. The second point is to make the system on which the current criminal justice controls are based (that is, the MDA 1971) internally valid. This means accurately measuring the harms and risks associated with certain substances. The DrugScope evidence cited above raised concerns about this in relation to ecstasy and magic mushrooms. Similarly, it was the view of one scientist and member of an ACMD committee, Rod, that:

> ... one of the problems is the historic drug classification system is riddled with anomalies. So there are two aspects to it; one is looking at the evidence which surrounds any particular drug which is being considered at the moment, to establish the degree of harm or potential harm. But then you have got to calibrate that against, a not quite random, but a good scatter in terms of where the existing classified drugs actually sit in a harm classification status spectrum. One initiative ... is to take a root and branch look at how classifications look. To start to build up a firm evidence base because the classification system came through a whole raft of historical issues. And when you take a cold, hard look at it, there are some spectacular anomalies in there.

Why is something a class A? Why is something else only a class C? It just doesn't seem to fit. So one of Professor Nutt's initiatives when he took over the role of chairman was to say "we really need to start looking at this and can we get some kind of more structured approach as to how drugs are classified?".

The reference to the work of Professor Nutt relates to the Nutt et al matrix. To recap – but at the risk of being repetitive – all legal drugs, along with tobacco and alcohol, would be placed in a scale according to the harm they cause drug users. This would, in turn, be decoupled from the associated penalties. Nutt et al (2007) identified three main categories of harm. These include:

- *Physical*, which is an assessment of the propensity of the drug to cause physical harm, for example, damage to organs and systems. There are three separate aspects to this: first, acute physical harm – the immediate effects linked to the notion of overdose; second, chronic physical harm – this is the health consequences of repeated use, such as the link between cannabis and psychosis; and, finally, specific problems associated with intravenous drug use.
- *Dependence*, which entails the relationship between the pleasurable effects of the drug and its propensity to induce dependent behaviour both psychologically and physically.
- *Social harms*, which occur in various ways, for example with intoxication impacting on family, community and social life through costs to systems of health and social care and the police.

As a brief snapshot, the Nutt et al matrix provides a contrast to the current location of certain drugs in the ABC system of the MDA 1971. According to another scientist and member of the ACMD technical committee, Joe:

From the work we did in this risk assessment exercise, starting in 2000, what we did was we looked at 20 substances over a period of a couple of years; we usually examine a few substances at each meeting. This process was presented as evidence to the [Science and Technology] Select Committee.... Without going into the details we came out with the conclusion that the rank order had no correlation with the status of the 1971 Misuse of Drugs Act.... That didn't come as too great a surprise to us as we knew that the original classifications were not really evidence-based we also have to say that the evidence on the toxicology, pharmacology and all the rest of it of these drugs has built up over the years.

The terrain marked out by the rational perspective differs, then, in many respects from the radical one, even though there is an acceptance by both that drug use is an inevitable feature of contemporary society. The primary difference is that the rational perspective operates within the current prohibitionist MDA 1971 framework, whereas the radical perspective wishes to transcend this. An alternative perspective is provided by the conservative contingent, who stress that more emphasis on drug prevention is a desirable policy direction.

Conservative perspective

The conservative perspective – so-called as it advocates a back-to-basics approach to drug policy that mirrors that of Sweden – consists primarily of actors advocating drug prevention education messages. They also have a strong emphasis on determined law enforcement as the most effective means of dealing with the drug problem. In effect, they recommend both a preventative and punitive approach. With this in mind, they support the continued prohibition of substances, but are sceptical of the purpose of the drug classification system and the operation of the MDA 1971. Table 5.5 illustrates that members include the former National Drug Prevention Alliance[1] and the seemingly short-lived Coalition Against Cannabis, among others. In terms of the fieldwork sample, seven respondents were allied to this perspective, one of whom had leanings towards the rational perspective (Gary).

Again testimonials to the aforementioned select committees highlight the core beliefs of this group. The National Drug Prevention Alliance is:

> A network of professional and lay groups and individuals who seek to improve the quality and application of primary prevention, set appropriately within the context of the whole range of drug services and wider social policy. (Home Affairs Select Committee, 2002, memorandum 44)

As will become apparent, the National Drug Prevention Alliance was against the reclassification of cannabis on the grounds, among others, that it was contrary to the principles of New Labour's drug strategy of which they were generally supportive in theory, if not practice:

> The core value of the UK drug strategy is that drug misuse has a negative effect on the user, on those around him/her, and on society at large; it is therefore to be discouraged, whilst those who have become involved are encouraged and helped, with least harm, to cease. (Home Affairs Select Committee, 2002, memorandum 44)

Responding to a question of whether existing drugs policy works, their statement says:

> Yes, as an adequate definition of goals and the means to achieve them. It suffers in the delivery, both by lack of commitment in some aspects as well as by assault from those who prefer a more libertarian approach.

It seeks to engage all of the relevant community and government elements around a common purpose, but the delivery of it is ceded to local choice. (Home Affairs Select Committee, 2002, memorandum 44)

Likewise, the Maranatha Community had similar misgivings about UK drug policy in the light of the initial reclassification. This organisation is a:

… Christian movement with many thousands of members throughout the country active in all the main churches. Its membership includes a substantial number of people involved in the health and caring professions and in a wide range of voluntary work. Since its formation 25 years ago, it has been deeply involved in work amongst those with drug and alcohol problems…. (Science and Technology Select Committee, 2006b, Evidence 82)

In their conclusions to the Science and Technology Select Committee, they point out that in relation to the initial decision to reclassify cannabis:

It appears that political considerations took precedence over scientific evidence and over the precautionary principle. This is shown by the determination of the then Home Secretary, David Blunkett, to request an assessment of downgrading from the ACMD, and by the refusal of the Home Office to meet leading researchers on cannabis and mental health just before the vote was taken in Parliament…. The current classification system based on the Misuse of Drugs Act 1971 needs to be replaced with a simpler and more effective system, such as the Swedish model. Sweden has among the lowest rates of drug misuse among European countries…. It is futile to pursue discredited policies of so-called 'harm-reduction' and vital that the Government and the nation are totally committed to the ideal of a drug-free society. (Science and Technology Select Committee, 2006b, Evidence 82)

Table 5.5: Conservative perspective composition

Interest groups	Official organisations
Coalition Against Cannabis, National Drug Prevention Alliance, Europe Against Drugs, The Maranatha Community	(Traditionally) Home Office

Table 5.6: Conservative perspective belief system structure

Deep core	Policy core
To promote drug-free healthy and wholesome lifestyles through drug enforcement/ prevention and education. Drug use not an inevitable aspect of daily life	Reclassification of cannabis fundamentally not evidence-based nor a step in the right direction; classification system not evidence-based

The first point to note about the conservative perspective is that, unlike the other groups, there is a reluctance to accept that drug use is an inevitable aspect of social life. Drug use is preventable and therefore drug prevention should be the overall, and most desirable, direction for drug policy. This, in their own words, puts them at odds with the rest of the policy subsystem and even with the parliamentary process that is, they claim, increasingly sympathetic to this view. The deep core beliefs of this perspective are best illustrated in the following quotation from Donald, a retired senior law enforcement officer and member of a drug prevention NGO:

> I have a feeling that drugs are harmful, illegal drugs are harmful, so government, ACMD and senior police officers, indeed everyone, ought to be very careful about what they say and do less they make the situation worse and Blunkett made the situation worse. [Reclassifying cannabis f]rom B to C was damaging.

This is supported by data from Stuart, a former high-ranking police officer, who stated:

> ... you have got to ask the question in the first place, why are we classifying drugs, what is the purpose of classifying them? Is it by the nature of their harm? Is it by their ingredients? Is it by the commonality of their use? Is it by the way that they are marketed? ... Maybe I am being simplistic but I don't know why in enforcement terms, which is what we are talking about primarily ... why you need to classify drugs because police officers don't go out and say 'right, today I am going to investigate class A drugs'. You go out saying that you suspect somebody is trafficking drugs so let's see what they are up to. And if it turns out to be a class C drug or a class A drug, the procedures and the consequences and penalties are very similar. Maybe the classification influences judges and they say that this is a particularly horrible drug and you get an extra two years in jail but I don't think so and I don't think it matters. I think each case needs to be considered individually and the judge and the jury are capable of deciding the nature of the harm in the context of the case.

As a result, it is a commonly held view that the understanding of 'evidence' related to this position is not considered in debates about UK drug policy that occur at central government level. This is reflected in their deep core views. According to Kenneth, a committee member of a drug prevention campaigning group, with the current system:

> You end up with endless debates about whether cannabis is more dangerous than amphetamines or amphetamines are more dangerous than cannabis. And I think it also leads to confusion and in the end

you need to give a clear message that drugs are dangerous. If you have a certain amount of drugs, a small amount is for personal use and if you have a large amount then you are a potential drug dealer and have penalties associated with that. That is the approach they use in Sweden and looking at the data it seems to work.

Another key concern for the conservative perspective, then, is that the current system has the propensity to send out misleading messages to drug users about the dangers of drugs. This is a particularly acute issue when there are calls for a reclassification downwards of drugs within the existing framework. Donald states:

> I was against it because I thought the downgrading was going to send mixed messages to young people and indeed the government accepted that when they did their review and went back to the ACMD, you have got Charles Clarke effectively saying 'we fucked up'. We made a mistake. He wasn't in sympathy with it. The intelligence that reaches me is that it was sold to [Tony] Blair on the basis of a package of things, one of which would be reducing crime through more prescription of heroin…. I don't have any particularly strong views about the drug classification system, I don't think it is that important. I think it is much more important about clear messages. Moving things up or down does send a signal.

The problem of down-classifying drugs within the MDA 1971, from the conservative perspective, is that it is contrary to the emerging evidence base relating to the substances themselves. This is a key distinction that marks this perspective out from the radical group, for example. For the conservatives, the harm of drugs stems from the innate properties of the substances themselves. For the radical group, the main dangers of drugs are a product of their (il)legal status. According to Anne, a representative of an international drug prevention NGO:

> The government just don't take the evidence on board. I mean I wish they would just do what Sweden does. All drugs are the same because cannabis, for somebody with one of these genes, is more dangerous than probably even heroin. Heroin can be prescribed safely in a hospital. You are never going to get a proper hierarchy of harms…. It would just be so simple if you said that all drugs are the same.

This relates to the point mentioned previously concerning how this position is frequently neglected in recent drug policy debates. On the whole, there are many more differences and conflicts that have been made visible here. From the overview of the structure of the subsystem, it is apparent that central to each perspective is a range of views about the nature of evidence in this particular area. It must be stressed, however, that although lines of demarcation between the perspectives have been illustrated in the above discussion, there are also lines of consensus within the subsystem over the role and nature of evidence-based policy making. These issues are explored in the following chapters.

Summary

This chapter started out by consolidating the link between pluralist models of policy analysis and the evidence-based policy agenda. It suggested that any analysis of evidence-based policy making should use a pluralist model as such models are consistent with the aforementioned opening up of government. Politicised policy areas represent another challenge, however. We have witnessed how they are characterised by a non-trivial degree of adversity, between various protagonists, about how the policy agenda should be shaped. In the current study, this has manifested itself in a debate over what should count as evidence in debates over UK drug classification policy decision making. As this is so, the ACF, with its particular emphasis on conflict in policy making, provides a useful means of exploring appreciations of evidence in politicised areas. This is a result of its focus on conflict in the policy arena. The ACF has, however, been the subject of much criticism, primarily along the lines that there is uncertainty over the nature of coordinated activity in the policy process that is implied by the ACF.

It is worth pointing out that the ACF was designed as a model to explain policy change. The current concern is on highlighting the nature and role of evidence in evidence-based policy. With this in mind, and also as a means of addressing the issue of coordinated activity, a reworking of the ACF has been necessary, replacing coalitions with 'appreciative' perspectives. The remainder of the chapter indicated how this can work in practice, using debates over the evidence base of the UK drug classification system as a case study. Based on primary research conducted by the author, three recognisable perspectives in drug classification debates were introduced, each with their own take on evidence-based policy making in this context: radical, rational and conservative perspectives. The central thesis of this book is that for the evidence-based movement to maintain any currency, clarity over the concept of evidence is required. This can help avoid the pitfall of reducing evidence down to zero-sum views (Monaghan, 2008) where it directly impacts on policy or more frequently where evidence is absent from the decision-making framework. This often involves a juxtaposition of evidence with politics, with the latter trumping the former. When appreciations of evidence are looked at in closer detail, it is clear that such accounts do not stack up. The following chapters undertake the task of showing how this is so, beginning with an analysis of the nature of evidence in the decision of the UK government of the time to amend the legislation regulating cannabis in the UK in 2004 and the impact this had on the wider drug classification system.

Note

[1] According to the organisation's website this organisation has since merged with its sister charity Positive Prevention Plus to form one charity, National Drug Prevention Alliance (http://drugprevent.org.uk/ppp/).

SIX

The nature of evidence in a politicised policy area

> At one extreme it might be argued that all evidence must conform to certain scientific rules of proof…. In other circumstances, any observation on an issue (whether informed or not) might be considered evidence…. However, perhaps the unifying theme in all the definitions is that the evidence (however construed) can be independently observed and verified, and that there is broad consensus as to its contents (if not its interpretation). (Davies et al, 2000b, p 2)

Previous chapters have contributed towards exploring the way in which in heavily politicised areas the utilisation of evidence is often boiled down to a case of present (evidence-based) or absent (evidence-free). The origins of this lie in entrenched positions adopted by those involved in the policy process and those offering some commentary thereon. This chapter aims to explore how these appreciations occur in more detail and questions whether these are an accurate portrayal of the way that evidence is or is not embraced by decision makers. This involves an ACF-inspired analysis of the way that 'evidence' was understood by key players in the policy process in relation to recent policy changes in the UK drug classification arena. Drawing on the platform of the previous chapters to do this, it turns specifically to debates over the nature of the evidence base for the initial cannabis reclassification in 2004, the first review of this policy in 2005 and the wider interest in UK drug classification that this stimulated. Readers wishing to familiarise themselves with the complete back story here should revisit Chapter Four.

With the benefit of hindsight, it is clear that the cannabis reclassification was the trigger for the developing interest in the evidence base for UK drug classification. In the aftermath of the 2004 cannabis reclassification and review, several significant events occurred relating to debates over the evidence base of the UK drug classification system. The parliamentary deliberations over the passing of the Drugs Act 2005 were significant. This Act was controversial due to the inclusion of derivatives of 'magic mushrooms' as class A substances. The primary significance, however, was the wider interest in the drug classification system that this fostered. Towards the end of 2006 and into 2007, the debate between various constituencies concerning the efficacy of current UK drug policy and legislation, specifically relating to the evidence for the efficacy of the MDA 1971, became widespread (see, for example, Levitt et al, 2006; Science and Technology Select Committee, 2006b; Nutt et al, 2007; Reuter and Stevens, 2007; RSA, 2007).

To fully understand the complexities of debates over the evidence base in politicised policies, it is worth being reminded of how differing appreciations of what counts as evidence can be easily identified in politicised policies, precisely because they are often located at the intersection of autonomous disciplines. This is illustrated succinctly in the following quotation from a former senior government adviser, Nick, who stated that:

> ... because it is a complex field and it cuts across health policy, crime policy, education policy and ideology, it is not a field where you can assemble the evidence to prove the case.... I don't think we will ever be able to say 'the evidence clearly says we should do this'. And in that situation you never have something strong enough that you can plonk in front of a minister or the public and say 'we are following the evidence-base'. It is always open to question.

Consequently, this chapter takes the following format. The opening discussion focuses on the appreciations of evidence from the radical, rational and conservative perspectives identified in Chapter Five in relation to drug classification. This is followed by a summary of evidence utilisation in this particular subsystem. It is suggested that a plurality of different accounts of evidence can be ascertained. This is interesting in the light of the zero-sum conclusions that are drawn by the various groups documenting whether or not the decision to reclassify cannabis was evidence-based. The next section looks at how to explain the various accounts of evidence. The existence of a hierarchy of evidence is put forward here as a possible explanation, but ultimately ruled out on the grounds that appreciations of differing evidence are ideological as opposed to methodological. The chapter concludes with a summary.

Perspectives of the nature of evidence in UK drug classification decision making

Political pronouncements relating to the initial reclassification of cannabis in 2004 and the first review of this in 2005 illustrate the point that understandings of evidence in this area are varied. Instigating the reclassification, the then Home Secretary, David Blunkett, had suggested that downgrading the substance would, among other things, free up time for the police to enable them to concentrate on problematic behaviours associated with class A drug use. In short, this was a public management call related to more efficient public service delivery. In 2005 Blunkett's successor, Charles Clarke, suggested that this policy change needed revisiting. His main concern was that certain strains of cannabis were responsible for, or at least linked to, the onset of certain kinds of mental illness. For Clarke this was, in essence, a public health issue. The hypothesis at this stage is that the different appreciations exist precisely because of the different core beliefs of each perspective in relation to the issue. The nuance of evidence is explored by ascertaining from each respondent appreciations of whether the reclassification was 'evidence-based' (policy core) and what evidence was used in the decision-making process (secondary aspects). The secondary aspects range from the very abstract to the more definitive. This data are presented in table form (see Tables 6.1, 6.2 and 6.3). These also detail the deep core beliefs of each group.

Radical perspective

To recap, the deep core view of the radical perspective is that the most effective way to regulate drug use is through the abolition of prohibition. This places less emphasis on the enforcement of unworkable laws. Applying this directly to the debate in hand, this underscores a wish for the abandonment of the MDA 1971 and its system of classifying drugs with a hierarchy of harms. It was maintained in Chapter Five that the radical perspective is particularly sceptical as to whether the prohibition of drugs has any deterrent effect on their use. This criticism is actually taken further, with the claim that prohibition not only fails to solve the drug problem but actually makes the problem more acute, as it serves to concede control of the market to 'illegal syndicates' (Rolles et al, 2006, p 6). Even though this is the case, there is still recognition in this group that some evidence may have been drawn on in the decision to reclassify cannabis. This does not, however, constitute 'evidence-based' policy making. An overview of the radical position of evidence is illustrated in Table 6.1.

Table 6.1: Radical perspective's view of the nature of evidence in the cannabis reclassification

Deep core	Policy core	Selected secondary aspects/ appreciations
Minimise drug-related harm via a humane and useful regulatory system of drug control culminating with the abolition of prohibition. Less emphasis on enforcement as drugs an inevitable feature of daily life for many	Cannabis reclassification not 'evidence-based' but broadly a step in right direction for UK drug classification; wider classification (MDA 1971) system primarily not evidence-based	• Appreciation of the risks and harms of substances (toxicological and social) and the weak link to mental health problems • Appreciation of anecdotal evidence from parents of drug users • Appreciation of the role of high-profile reports in the drug legislation field • Appreciation of public management issues, with the saving of police time

For members of the radical perspective, the maintenance of the existing legislative framework means that the policy cannot be providing value for money and thus cannot be evidence-based. On these grounds, it is possible to anticipate the answer this group offered as to whether the cannabis reclassification was evidence-based. According to Dave, a senior figure in a drug policy NGO:

> If you accept the [premise of the] classification system, clearly cannabis was misclassified…. I'd refer you to the ACMD report on cannabis which was really a high-quality meta-analysis of a load of research concluding that cannabis is not without risks, of course. And for a small number of people those risks are very significant. But for the majority of people – in terms of relative harms compared with other drug-using populations with other drugs – it was relatively less harmful than other class B drugs and should therefore go to class C which is, within the classification paradigm, perfectly sensible.

The 'high-quality meta-analysis' refers to aforementioned work carried out by the ACMD (2002, 2005) detailing risks associated with cannabis by looking at epidemiology, acute and long-term risks to human health (physical and mental), and issues of potency in the form of a systematic review of the available research. The operative phrase is, however, 'within the classification paradigm'. Although there is a hint here that some form of evidence did have a role to play in this policy decision, this does not translate into evidence-based policy making, Dave continues:

> Whether that was an evidence-based policy, I would argue clearly not, clearly not. The fact is that cannabis was criminalised in the first place as a political decision back in whenever it was…. The ACMD was calling for cannabis to be reclassified for more than 20 years…. It has systematically been ignored, ignored and ignored. Not because they were wrong or the evidence wasn't good enough, but because it wasn't politically the moment to do it. It wasn't that they suddenly went 'oh look! there is all this new evidence and cannabis is misclassified', that had been known for years…. It was always political.

What can again be witnessed here is the juxtaposition of evidence and politics and a reoccurrence of the view that evidence is not the only driver of policy decision making. The politicised nature of drug policy making is a theme that resonates with the radical perspective. Politics in the form of expediency and opportunism is viewed as inherently detrimental to the nature of evidence-based policy making. In the words of one MP, Phil, regarding the initial reclassification:

> David Blunkett was impressed by a group of parents that he saw who said to him that their children, having taken cannabis, decided that the warnings that they had were baseless…. The warnings they had were [that cannabis was] a wicked, dangerous drug. But having tried cannabis, they realised it was nothing of the sort and it was just like having a couple of pints of beer. They stopped believing those warnings and they also stopped believing the warnings about heroin as well.

> They thought that if someone is deceiving us on cannabis they are
> probably deceiving us on heroin.

Here, the evidence is more anecdotal. There is some discrepancy in the literature
as to whether this constitutes 'evidence' at all. For current purposes, anecdotal
evidence serves as an appreciation of the kind of evidence that was used in the
cannabis reclassification according to the radical perspective.

Up to this point, a prevailing zero-sum position on the nature of evidence in
the cannabis classification can be seen. For adherents of the radical perspective,
this is illustrated in the way that they do not perceive the policy change to be
evidence-based. A more moderate view is put forward by Noel, director of a
UK-based drug treatment NGO. In response to a question detailing why the
conditions were right for a change in the cannabis legislation in 2004, he stated:

> You had got a change in society where more and more people are
> smoking cannabis and general trends are in that direction and the
> government reciprocated with a series of reports – Runciman and
> so forth – that were all pointing in the same direction. This allowed
> them to more strongly assert that they were just following "expert
> guidance". So, obviously we have had that sort of thing before. There
> is a strong history to this sort of stuff and, I think, this time the voices
> were clearer, stronger and included the establishment – ACMD and
> the Runciman Report [The Police Foundation, 2000] – and I think
> that made it easy for the government.

Noel suggests that the cannabis reclassification was not made in an evidence
vacuum, hinting that various high-profile studies had contributed to the legal
change. Two key aspects of The Police Foundation report (2000) were that
reclassifying cannabis would free up police time and that in terms of harms
and toxicity, cannabis was not comparable with other class B substances. This
appreciation of evidence is summed up as a 'public management issue', and is
therefore included in the radical perspective's appreciation of evidence used in
the cannabis reclassification.

As mentioned, although it is acknowledged that some form of 'evidence' played
a role in the government's decision, the overriding feeling is that this is not enough
for the policy to be considered 'evidence-based'. This line of argument can be
seen from another respondent, James, a journalist and writer, and frequent expert
witness in court proceedings concerning MDA 1971 offences:

> I think there has been an enormous accretion of evidence supporting
> the contention that the prohibition of cannabis is ineffective and
> unjustified and Commission after Commission from the '60s onwards
> has found relatively little evidence of harm.... So I think for those who

wanted to say that the evidence is now that cannabis is less harmful than we thought, there was an enormous amount of evidence to point to.

As a consequence, in respect of whether the cannabis reclassification was an evidence-based change, James goes on to suggest that:

> … some bits of evidence get much more media play and public debate than others. A good example in the cannabis debate is the question of evidence as to whether cannabis is stronger now than it used to be in the 1960s. This is complete 'non-evidence' really. Who is comparing what with what? Are people altering their doses? So if it is stronger they use less of it…. So that whole body of evidence has been given an enormous amount of publicity and airplay and I would argue that that is not evidence at all.

Ultimately, this is the crux of a zero-sum view. The appreciation here is that the evidence that shows the futility of prohibition is left out of the decision-making process in favour of evidence that is more politically expedient. Consequently, the decision was not evidence-based, but evidence of some kind was not entirely absent from the policy discussion, as the final column of Table 6.1 illustrates. Overall, however, for the radical perspective cannabis reclassification, although nominally a step in the right direction (in terms of the reduction of criminal penalties relating to drug offences) ultimately changes little. No matter what research, scientific or otherwise, is produced to support a policy change, this is not the defining tenet of what it means for a policy to be 'evidence-based' if this occurs within the existing paradigm, which is perceived to be problematic. In this context, the maintenance and futility of prohibition means that until this changes, UK drug policy remains 'evidence-free' despite being made with recourse to some evidence.

Rational perspective

As indicated in Table 6.2, the deep core beliefs of this group relate to a public health-inspired approach that operates within the wider criminal justice paradigm of the MDA 1971. For the rational perspective there is great emphasis on the nature of substances themselves in terms of scientifically assessing their risks. The increasing significance of risk assessment, as a key aspect of the evidence base in this area, was augmented by the publication of the Nutt et al matrix (2007). This, it was claimed, would more accurately reflect the relative harms and dangers of substances. It is suggested by its creators, furthermore, that the matrix should be used as the basis for criminal justice responses to the drug problem, in effect determining the extent of the criminal sanctions with regard to offences relating to particular substances. In this sense, the rational perspective operates with a similar philosophical outlook to that of the government and indeed most of the political establishment.

Table 6.2: Rational perspective's view of the nature of evidence in the cannabis reclassification

Deep core	Policy core	Selected main secondary aspects/ appreciations
Promotion of human rights and public health placing treatment at the centre of the drug strategy as drug use is an inevitable part of everyday life for many. Using evidence to inform policy by ironing out anomalies of existing framework	Cannabis reclassification primarily 'evidence-based' as a step towards ironing out MDA 1971's anomalies; classification system increasingly evidence-based	• Appreciation of risks and harms of substances (toxicological and social) and the unproven link to mental health • Appreciation of the potency issue and the lack of data to prove contemporary cannabis is stronger • Appreciation of wider policy outcomes, with policies providing value for money (ironing out anomalies of MDA 1971) • Appreciation of the role of influential reports in the drug legislation field • Appreciation of public management issues, with the saving of police time

For the purposes of this discussion, it is the maintenance of a hierarchy of drug harms allied to the continuing prohibition of substances that shapes the rational perspective's understanding of evidence. Thus, in response to whether the cannabis reclassification was an evidence-based decision, it was the view of a one-time government adviser, Nick, that:

> If you are going to invest taxpayer's money in enforcing drug laws, you should target that investment at the most harmful behaviours. And we weren't targeting that investment at all but by proxy, all that investment was going on very minor people who shouldn't be in the criminal justice system in the first place. So, in that sense, it was evidence-based.

There was a clear consensus among many members of the rational perspective that the evidence base for efficient management of public services, in this case, policing, was pivotal. A senior member of the ACMD, Richard, suggested that:

> I think Blunkett thought the law was stupid and was being flouted widely. The Brixton Experiment had shown that, in practice, you could save a lot of police time by not arresting people for smoking or dealing in small amounts and, I think, he thought it was a sensible policy, and I respected him for it.

The conclusion that the cannabis decision was evidence-based, in terms of targeting investment of taxpayers' money to ensure policies provide value for money, relates to the appreciation of evidence as policy evaluation, and this is consistent with the appreciations of the radical perspective. These similar understandings, however, lead to different conclusions. For the radical perspective, the cannabis reclassification was, fundamentally, not evidence-based. By contrast, for the rationalist perspective, it was, by highlighting how cannabis is not as harmful as other substances that the overall drug policy is rationalised. The reclassification of cannabis was intended to direct criminal justice resources towards the drugs that do the most damage. A similar sentiment was expressed by Rod, a co-opted member of the ACMD technical committee:

> The evidence was very closely examined....There was a groundswell building up … particularly highlighted in south London [Brixton] where the issues had come up with local policing priorities and that had brought things to the fore. The police had been signalling for a long time that given the broad range of things they are supposed to be responsible for, policing cannabis, was increasingly coming to be seen as a bit of an embarrassment. So I think the time was right to look at it and the Home Secretary was right as well.

Further schisms between the radical and rational perspectives can be seen in the nature of evidence used to rationalise the current system. Another member of the ACMD technical committee, Joe, stated of the cannabis reclassification that:

> We had a couple of days reviewing cannabis, [it] was almost entirely on the work done … on cannabis potency. That work … published in 2004 was done for the European Agency in Lisbon who saw at that stage the need to review the information because of a lot of conflicting information in the press on what high-strength cannabis actually meant and what were the facts. So that was quite timely.... It was 2005 when ACMD were asked to review cannabis again and one of the areas of concern was the appearance of high potency cannabis. One of the other ones, of course, was the mental health issues.

The published work referred to in the above quotation relates to that carried out by the European Monitoring Centre for Drugs and Drug Addiction (EMCDDA, 2004). This study concluded that, based on the available evidence, contemporary cannabis is no more potent than in previous times. There is the suggestion here that the potency issue – the lack of evidence that contemporary cannabis is of a higher strength than in previous years – was a major aspect of the evidence base for the eventual reclassification. As we have seen, this appreciation contrasts with that of the radical perspective, where this was referred to as 'non-evidence', and as we shall see, the conservative perspective's interpretation of this particular aspect of the evidence base is different again.

The health issue surrounding cannabis potency is another contested area. According to a one-time ACMD member, Claire, it was the consideration given to such issues that typified why the cannabis reclassification was evidence-based:

> I think that there was a lot of assessment in terms of the relative health harms. We were fully aware of some of the stuff around the mental health problems so there was no discounting that. One looked at the relative risk, the known risk assessment across the harm domains. One looked at those – had what material was available – and in that sense used that to weigh up a proportionate response of which seemed to suggest that its alignment was not right in class B.

Similarly, a former senior ministerial adviser, Nick, questioned rhetorically:

> Does the science around an issue such as cannabis use indicate that its potential risk to individuals is of a lower class C order?... I think that that is evidence-based as well. The sorts of things you need to look at are acute neurological effects. In which case, in the global evidence on cannabis, it is hard to find any trend or body of evidence showing the harmful impact of cannabis. 160 million people use cannabis world-wide and nobody has ever died from an overdose. There is not an acute reaction in the brain that could cause an immediate dysfunction and it doesn't cause violence and all that sort of thing. So clearly it can't be called a dangerous drug on these fronts.

This appreciation is the epitome of the deep and policy core views of the rational perspective. There is clearly an acceptance that a plethora of evidence was included in the debate over cannabis reclassification, although there was also clear recognition that this takes place in a heavily politicised context. When asked if the cannabis reclassification was an evidence-based decision, Pat, chief executive of a leading drug policy NGO, stated:

> Oh, very much so on the grounds of the Ruth Runciman work, the Home Affairs Committee and I know, being a member of ACMD, we looked through the evidence base. I think, there was a ... collision of opportunities and windows and doors opening and it provided a match between the evidence and the policy aspiration of the Home Secretary. In that sense, the planets were aligned temporarily.

This is reminiscent of Kingdon's (1984) policy windows thesis and also reveals the importance of high-profile reports to the government in its decision-making process. The reference to the 'collision of opportunities' also stresses that, for the rational perspective too, evidence is not the sole determining factor influencing decision making.

To sum up, there is a clear stress for the rational perspective that the most up-to-date research should direct the framework of the MDA 1971. In this context, the key distinction between members of the rational perspective and those of the radical perspective is that the former advocate modifying the existing legislative mechanism but, ultimately, criminal sanctions should still apply to certain drug offences. For the radical perspective, this is precisely the cause of the problem. In addition, the rational perspective has misgivings over the operation of the current classification system. This is because there are anomalies in the location of certain drugs, which distort the messages it gives out. The solution is that evidence should inform policy to create an holistic drug policy that promotes public health and human rights by accurately assessing the risks of all drugs and coordinating criminal justice responses accordingly. The key feature of the policy core reveals that the cannabis reclassification was broadly an 'evidence-based' decision in that it signalled an attempt to do precisely this. The significance of this is that there is some recognition of the role that evidence can play in policy even when the policy is heavily politicised.

Conservative perspective

The deep core view of the conservative perspective is that more rigorous drug prevention and enforcement can result in drug-free lifestyles. To recap, unlike the radical and rational perspectives, there is no assumption from the conservative group that drug use is an inevitable aspect of social life for many people. For the conservative perspective, then, the decision to reclassify cannabis was devoid of evidence on the grounds that it compromised the goal of more rigorous enforcement of the drug laws as a means of addressing the drug problem, and therefore sent out the wrong messages regarding the dangers of the substance. In addition, where cannabis is concerned, there is a major preoccupation with the medical issue, in particular, the potential harm cannabis use can cause. For this perspective, this moves beyond effects on the brain to encapsulate a range of medical dangers associated with the substance. A summary of the conservative perspective's appreciations of the cannabis reclassification subsystem is provided in Table 6.3.

Table 6.3: Conservative perspective's view of the nature of evidence in the cannabis reclassification

Deep core	Policy core	Selected main secondary aspects
To promote drug-free healthy and wholesome lifestyles through drug enforcement/prevention and education. Drug use not an inevitable aspect of daily life	Reclassification of cannabis fundamentally not evidence-based nor a step in the right direction; classification system not evidence-based	None

For this perspective, there is some recognition of the evidence that should have been, but was not, used in the episode of cannabis reclassification. On these grounds, for this group, the cannabis reclassification was primarily evidence-free. As will become clear, there is a sense that 'cherry-picking' evidence is a significant issue. Regarding whether the reclassification was evidence-based, it was the view of one member of a campaigning NGO, Kenneth, that:

> The policy issue, I think is not evidence-based.... You have the entire issue of the health effects of cannabis; the issue of the adverse effect on the respiratory system; the increase in cancer rates; the increase in chronic lung disease. Then there is the entire issue of mental health, with a number of studies linking cannabis to schizophrenia, depression, anxiety and other mental health issues and all this evidence was there. And I thought it extremely problematic for them [the government] to say that it is actually less dangerous.

The view here is that there was evidence relating to the negative impact of cannabis on human health, but that this was ignored. Of all the medical issues, the subject of mental illness was fundamental. The submission by the Maranatha Community to the Science and Technology Select Committee also illustrates this point:

> When the downgrading of cannabis from a Class B to a Class C drug was debated in both Houses of Parliament in October and November 2003, strong scientific evidence was available linking cannabis to serious mental illness including schizophrenia, psychosis and depression. This link between cannabis and serious mental illness has prompted the current Home Secretary, Charles Clarke, to review the classification of cannabis. (cited in Science and Technology Select Committee, 2006b, Evidence 76)

In a similar vein, in response to whether the cannabis decision was evidence-based, Anne, a UK representative of an international drug prevention organisation, stated:

> No. The worst thing with cannabis is the mental illness and there have been papers around on that since the '60s and '70s and even before, warning about this. So it goes back in history that people were warned, so the government didn't look at the evidence, they really didn't.

The absence of evaluative research into the harms of cannabis and its potential to cause schizophrenia was problematic. This belief is compounded further in relation to a question detailing why a political decision was taken, by Charles Clarke, to review the initial reclassification of cannabis made by David Blunkett. Anne continues:

> [It was] about mental illness because people like Robin Murray then started really campaigning. This is the trouble with research scientists, they are not campaigners, but Robin Murray is. He is not an out and out table thumping campaigner, but he has spoken out a lot more than a lot of the others have. And he started saying things in the press and on the radio and got through to people about the problems. And then there were lots of people who wrote in to papers. There was a great flood of things like 'My son's life was destroyed by cannabis' or 'My son has schizophrenia'. Loads and loads of articles came out there and I think all that had an influence, even journalists.

Likewise, the significance of the health issue is reinforced in the views of a retired senior law enforcement officer, Donald:

> Certainly, the downgrading sent a signal to potential users … that cannabis was less harmful than when the list had been drawn up, pre-'71 and that isn't the case. We now know that it is actually more harmful, all the evidence is there and the evidence was there in the 1997 World Health Organization report.… All the thing about schizophrenia is in there, couched in strong language about whether it is causative or causal.… All the evidence coming out was that some people are genetically disposed to be damaged by cannabis. So it was all there and the government ignored that at the time the classification was being thought through.

There is again a shared understanding of what the evidence should be in regard to cannabis reclassification, between the conservative and rational perspectives, that is, that the decision should have been based with recourse to the mental health evidence. The conclusions reached, however, are diametrically opposed. For the rational group, this formed a key part of the decision-making process with the conclusion that cannabis was not as harmful as other drugs. For the conservative perspective, this evidence was not taken into consideration, because if it had been, the reclassification would have been impossible, especially if the precautionary principle is to play a role in policy. All the evidence, for the conservative perspective, pointed to increasing medical harms linked to cannabis use.

A similar line of argument can be seen with the potency issue. Already considered as either 'non-evidence' (radical perspective) or a key aspect of the evidence base, in that there was no evidence for increased potency (rational perspective), the conservative perspective had a different take on this part of the evidence:

> Now you have fairly high concentration cannabis available that wasn't available 20 years ago or so. The genetically modified cannabis and hydroponic cannabis that can have THC contents of 13, 14, maybe even 20 per cent. In the '60s it would have been maybe a maximum

of five per cent average so it is much stronger now than it has been in the past. (Kenneth)

The conclusion is that this aspect of the evidence base was also ignored. In the words of a one-time high-ranking police officer, Stuart:

> I can point to lots of research that was not taken into account when that decision was arrived at. The ACMD went into a great deal of explanation as to why they had reclassified cannabis. But they were anxious that people would not get the impression that other drugs in class B were not of a similar nature to cannabis. By that I mean that you can smoke a joint and it can have absolutely no effect whatever but, you know as well as I do, that the modern forms of cannabis are significantly more potent than they were 30 years ago, and the average strength now is around eleven and a half per cent THC and the Skunk and Nederweed is as much as 35 per cent. So the UN world drug report and the head of the UNODC [United Nations Office of Drug Control] has said that they regard cannabis as being as dangerous as the other botanically based drugs, cocaine and heroin.

That cannabis potency and mental illness issues were not given due weight in the discussion was not the sole reason as to why the decision was seen, by the conservative perspective, to be evidence-free. One other body of evidence linked to the cannabis reclassification was the public management variety, relating to the freeing up of police time. For the conservative perspective, this was also problematic:

> The result in Brixton was catastrophic because you had an increase of drug misuse and an increase in hard drug misuse. There was an increase in drug dealers there. And so, I think the experiment in Brixton was a disaster. It led to more police time being saved and blah, blah, blah but I'm not really convinced. (Kenneth)

Additionally, a director of a leading NGO in the drug prevention field, Malcolm, suggested that:

> We were told from Westminster sources…. Blunkett bought the idea that if he gave the Libertarian camp something, they would back off and stay quiet. But as a politician, this was absolutely crass because it was completely obvious to us, having lived in that atmosphere for 20 years, that if you give these guys something that will encourage them to ask for the next thing and the next thing, which is exactly what has happened.

The critique of politics triumphing over the evidence is again apparent here as is the view that evidence is not the sole driver of policy making. The overall conclusions drawn from this are, like those of the radical perspective, of the negative zero-sum variety that the cannabis reclassification was evidence-free. The rationale, however, is very different. There is no appreciation here that any relevant evidence was used when the decision was taken to reclassify cannabis because all the existing evidence that should have been used would have made the policy change unworkable.

A summary of evidence utilisation in the cannabis subsystem

The above section has demonstrated how the label 'evidence-based policy making' is problematic when the minutiae of the concept is explored, particularly the evidence component. In effect, evidence never speaks for itself. To a lesser extent within and to a greater extent between perspectives, there are clear discrepancies over what constitutes evidence in this particular subsystem, but at the same time there are clear crossovers. Cross-referencing these findings with the deep and policy core views of each perspective, in terms of whether the decision to reclassify cannabis was evidence-based, provides some intriguing data. To recap, for the radical and conservative perspectives, the answer was negative, but for the rationalist perspective it was affirmative. It is possible to summarise the nature of evidence in the cannabis reclassification subsystem in relation to what each perspective deems was present, but to highlight the complex nature of evidence, appreciations of evidence deemed to be absent are also identified. This is particularly revealing when it is remembered that all perspectives adhere to a zero-sum position, in one way or another.

By way of an overview, a summary of each perspective's view of the cannabis reclassification is presented in Table 6.4. It is suggested that descending the ladder of abstraction in relation to the concept of evidence reveals some interesting issues. On one level, the perspectives have a general understanding of the same kinds of evidence, but offer different interpretations of this, as seen in the slightly different wording of some of the appreciations in Table 6.4. The cannabis potency issue and the (perceived) links with mental health are indicative of this. All perspectives recognise the significance of these debates, but there were clear differences in the way that this was construed. For the radical and rational perspectives, there is a weak correlation between cannabis use and mental illness. For the conservative perspective, there is a strong causal link between cannabis and schizophrenia. These subtleties are not always clear when debate concerns the abstract concept of 'evidence'. Other debates about evidence-based policy making do not always account for the different ways that evidence is contextualised.

Developing this example from those listed above, a key aspect of evidence cited by the then Home Secretary for this decision was that in respect of toxicity, cannabis was less harmful than other class B drugs such as amphetamines (May et al, 2002). This calculation related to the purity of the substance and the levels of

Tetrahydrocannabinol (THC), the main psychoactive ingredient found in cannabis. Such a benchmark, however, soon became hotly contested. For supporters of the policy change (the rational perspective), evidence was referenced pointing to the fact that the purity and potency of 2004 cannabis obtained on the street was much the same as 20 years previously. For detractors of the policy change this was a misreading of the science, which discovered levels of THC in genetically modified and hydroponic cannabis some four times higher than the strains previously used (conservative perspective). A third significant voice in the debate (radical perspective) claimed that this 'evidence' was actually 'non-evidence' on the grounds that to understand the effects of drugs on human subjects, data are not only required on the properties of the drug itself, but also on supply, uptake, modes and means of ingestion. From this it can be stated that evidence in a politicised subsystem is inevitably contested.

Despite this, the radical perspective shares with the rational perspective many of the same appreciations of evidence in terms of what was and should have been used in this policy area. Both recognised the significance of debates about the toxicological properties of the substance and the evidence concerning efficient service delivery and acknowledged the role of high-profile inquiries into drug policy. For the radical group, anecdotal evidence was also prominent, for instance, the way that David Blunkett's views were influenced by concerned members of the public. The crux of the reason as to why the decision to reclassify cannabis was not evidence-based, for the radical perspective, related to the absence of evidence about the futility of prohibition. It is this perspective which typifies the paradoxical nature of zero-sum assertions (Monaghan, 2008). Their conclusion that the cannabis reclassification was not evidence-based was made in spite of the recognition that the government did draw on and utilise a range of evidence in its decision making. Because there is no appreciation given in this instance to the futility of prohibition (their deep core belief) as a means of regulating the drug problem, the cannabis decision ultimately achieves little in terms of the bigger picture of UK drug policy. The change cannot be evidence-based as, in their appreciation, the evidence points to the legalisation of cannabis and all other substances as the most effective means of dealing with the drug problem.

The rational perspective conclusion is different. For this group the government did utilise a range of relevant evidence in reaching its decision. Importantly, because they perceived the high-profile reports as being a key aspect of the evidence base, this included some account of the significance of ironing out the anomalies of the existing framework (their deep core belief). The conservative perspective, like the radical one, departs from the government and rationalist view by stating fundamentally that the cannabis reclassification was not evidence-based. This is primarily because the reclassification sent out the wrong signals. In their eyes, for a policy change to be evidence-based it would have to move in the opposite direction. This would entail more emphasis on prevention (their deep core belief) and not something that tacitly suggests that certain drugs are less harmful than others. Unlike the radical position, there is no paradox here, as in their eyes no appreciations of evidence were used in the decision. There are, however, clear similarities between the conservative perspective and the other perspectives over what general kinds of evidence should have been used in the decision-making process in this scenario.

Table 6.4: Summary of evidence utilisation in the cannabis subsystem

Perspective	Present evidence	Absent evidence
Radical	• Appreciation of the risks and harms of substances (toxicological and social) and the weak link to mental health • Appreciation of anecdotal evidence from parents of drug users • Appreciation of the role of high-profile reports (for example, The Police Foundation, 2000; Home Affairs Select Committee, 2002) in the drug legislation field • Appreciation of public management issues, with the saving of police time	Appreciation of wider policy outcomes (efficacy of prohibition)
Rational	• Appreciation of risks and harms of substances (toxicological and social) and the weak link to mental health • Appreciation of the potency issue and the lack of data to prove contemporary cannabis is stronger • Appreciation of the role of high-profile reports (for example, The Police Foundation, 2000; Home Affairs Select Committee, 2002) in the drug legislation field • Appreciation of public management issues, with the saving of police time • Appreciation of wider policy outcomes (ironing out anomalies of MDA 1971)	None
Conservative	None	• Appreciation of medical risks and harms of substances (general health effects) • Appreciation of the risks and harms of substances (toxicological and social) and the strong link with mental health • Appreciation of the potency issue and growth of data to prove contemporary cannabis is stronger • Appreciation of wider policy outcomes that reclassifying cannabis provides a contradictory message to prevention, which 'works'

There are, then, clearly, discrepancies between the perspectives over what did count and should have counted as evidence in this subsystem. One outstanding question concerns how the plethora of appreciations of evidence, in this subsystem, is to be explained. In other words, what are the origins of the key differences between the different perspectives' understandings of what is evidence-based policy making in this context? In other policy areas (those more akin with the principles of evidence-based policy making), the concept of a hierarchy of evidence has been applied to explain the predominance of particular kinds of evidence when a plurality of evidence is apparent. This has an impact on why different accounts of the nature of evidence are visible. One question to consider, then, is whether this also serves as a plausible explanation in this scenario.

The plurality of evidence as a hierarchy of evidence?

The notion of a hierarchy of evidence has its origins in evidence-based medicine, in light of Cochrane's (1972) radical critique of medical procedures. It refers to how a shift in medical practice based on 'expert opinions' of doctors and clinicians should be replaced with research from experiments and demonstrations. In effect, a scale is proposed with the findings from valid research at the top end and opinion-based evidence towards the bottom, with various steps in between. This view of evidence is now firmly established in the mind-set of both the policy-making and evidence-producing communities, and is typically constructed as in Table 6.5 below.

This hierarchy has not been accepted uncritically, particularly in terms of whether meta-analysis and systematic review should be the gold standard, although these debates need not concern us here. As indicated previously, it is clear that appreciations of evidence (secondary aspects) are heavily influenced by deep and policy core views. The hierarchy of evidence, meanwhile, offers an account of the pluralism of evidence that is primarily methodological. This only broadly explains what kind of evidence is used in the subsystem and not why. In UK drug classification, issues surrounding the methodology of evidence were not the sole concern of those in the subsystem. Because the cannabis reclassification and its aftermath represent a politicised area, they are, in effect, an untypical example of the traditional remit of evidence-based policy making.

As this is the case, it is questionable as to whether the hierarchy is a comprehensive explanation for the plurality of appreciations of the nature of evidence, in this particular scenario. Selectivity is certainly an issue, however, and this starts with how organisations manoeuvre themselves into a position to supply evidence to policy. This can occur in the process of consultation. The expectation of consultation with key stakeholders is increasingly commonplace

Table 6.5: A hierarchy of evidence

Level	Methodology	Brief description
1	Systematic reviews and meta-analyses	Systematic reviews of a body of data of all the existing research of a particular kind of intervention Meta-analysis is the sum-total of analysis, the analysis of all previous analysis. It goes through stages of: (a) hypothesis formation, proposing a relationship between an implementation (I) and an outcome (O); (b) data collection, collecting data from all studies that have investigated I and O relationships; (c) pooling together findings from all previous analyses of the relationship between I and O; (d) hypothesis appraisal, stating the confidence in the causal relationship between I and O
2	Randomised controlled trials (RCTs) (with concealed allocation)	In the social science format individuals are randomly allocated to a control group and a group who receive a specific intervention (experiment group). Otherwise the two groups are thought to be identical for any significant variables. They are followed up for specific end points
3	Quasi-experimental studies (using matches)	Used in situations when it is impossible to randomly apply subjects to experiment and control groups, based on the same principles as the RCT but lacking in equivocal internal validity
4	Before and after comparisons	'Cases' with the condition are matched with 'controls' without, and a retrospective analysis used to look for differences between the two groups
5	Cross-sectional, random sample studies	Survey or interview of a sample of the population selected purely by chance at one point in time
6	Process evaluation, formative studies and action research	Process evaluation/formative studies are often built into the design of any implementation. They struggle to inform policy because they are retrospective Action research is a process whereby the researcher and client collaborate in the diagnosis of a social problem and come to a mutual agreement in the development of a solution based on the diagnosis
7	Qualitative case study and ethnographic research	Qualitative case study is research based on a detailed examination of a single case or small number of cases. They are beset with problems of generalisation Ethnographic research is where the researcher immerses him/herself in the social setting for an extended period of time and refers to both the method of research (usually qualitative) and also the written output (narrative)
8	Descriptive guides and examples of good practice	Evidence taken from similar interventions seen as a beacon for other similar future interventions
9	Professional and expert opinion	A consensus of experience from key figures in the field (the good and the great)
10	User opinion	Primarily anecdotal based on reflections of those usually the recipient of any given intervention

Source: Adapted from Pawson (2006a); School of Health and Related Research, University of Sheffield (no date)

in the development of policies in many areas, including the drugs field. According to Noel:

> A consultation is often just an expediency thing. You have got to consult; you are committed to consulting. How do you decide between 50 or 60 or whatever the number is of possible groups you want to consult? Or do you say: 'well, who do we think are the main ones?'. And approach them. There is a bit of a judgement made there and sometimes they get it wrong. But I do think it can have a bearing and that is the way it happens.

The general idea here is that the cherry-picking of evidence is widespread, but in this particular subsystem this is not based on methodological considerations. A similar sentiment is expressed by members of the rational perspective. When asked whether there was a hierarchy of evidence in this subsystem, one experienced denizen of the bar, with expertise in criminal drug trials, Andre, commented that:

> My impression is that government has called for a great deal of evidence about all kinds of matters relating to drugs. What happens to that evidence is another matter. My belief is that some of it is 'lost' (given that there is so much of it) and that other information simply does not speak loudly enough. The Runciman Inquiry [The Police Foundation, 2000] was highly influential…. It had the advantage of collating a wealth of material and then authoritatively speaking its recommendations. This led to intense public debate during the course of which some issues (more than others) were brought into sharp focus. I am not convinced that there exists a structured 'hierarchy of evidence'. I have no doubt that the voice of the law enforcement agencies carries much weight with government, particularly if it appears to chime with public opinion.

Likewise, the conservative perspective proved equally sceptical as to whether the widely accepted cherry-picking of evidence was based on a preference for a certain kind of methodological evidence. One researcher for a leading NGO in the drug prevention field, Ben, commented:

> I wouldn't say that, I wouldn't say there was a hierarchy based on those [methodological] things…. If you look at other debates going on, for example, sexual orientation discrimination, all those regulations that are being proposed are based upon very, very small-scale incidences of what is deemed to be homophobia so they have drawn up far-reaching regulations based on a handful of instances when a homosexual couple have not been able to get a hotel room together or something like

> that…. I think there is an ideology that is determining the cherry-picking as opposed to any other kind of idea that it is methodological.

Unlike the hierarchy of evidence shown above, it is suggested that in this circumstance the bases of selection are not methodological but more a product of the deep core standpoints of each perspective. Therefore, although there is a perceived significant degree of selectivity in the use of evidence in this area, the origins of this are as much ideological as methodological and relate to the government's preference for particular kinds of evidence in this manner.

Summary

The aim of this chapter has been to shed some light on the problematic nature of evidence-based policy making, particularly in politicised areas. Drawing on the platform of previous chapters, a modified version of the ACF has been used to indicate how evidence, broadly conceived, is embedded in the decision-making process, regardless of negative zero-sum views that may suggest otherwise. The problematic nature of evidence has been uncovered by concentrating on different takes on what constitutes the 'evidence base'. In essence, the episode of cannabis reclassification constituted only a minor perturbation in the oscillation of UK drug legislation, but it indicates the ever-present potential for contention over what counts as legitimate evidence in any given domain. This chapter has explored the different appreciations of evidence in the cannabis episode. All perspectives draw zero-sum conclusions while recognising the diversity of evidence. It is interesting to note how these conclusions are reached despite a plethora of understandings over what constitutes evidence in this particular scenario.

Zero-sum appreciations of evidence utilisation are logically problematic. They emerge from deeply held views about the desired direction of policy. These are often normative assertions about what the policy should be like. For instance, the rational group were supportive of the cannabis classification and its associated evidence use because it was consistent with their appreciation of what the policy should be and how it should be formulated. By the same token, the discontent felt by the radical and conservative positions stems from their departure from this. Although this is the case, it has been demonstrated that claims stating that policies are evidence-free are often made while simultaneously accepting that some form of evidence played a role in the decision-making process. Conversely, the other side of the argument claims the policy to be evidence-based, while accepting that certain kinds of evidence were not considered in the decision-making process.

It can be concluded from the above discussion that evidence means different things to the different perspectives. This broad account of what does and should count as evidence in policy making will be returned to in Chapter Nine, when an attempt to model the use of evidence in a politicised area is undertaken. One aspect to be factored into this is the widespread acceptance that evidence is not the only influence on policy formulation. It should also be pointed out, however, that although diverse, evidence is not completely contested. There was a clear crossover in the perspectives' accounts of what does or should count as evidence in UK drug classification policy. The following chapter picks up the theme that there is some consistency in appreciations of evidence, despite the widespread disagreement over its nature. This is illustrated by considering the different perspectives' accounts of where evidence should play a role in the decision-making process, that is, how evidence is utilised.

SEVEN

The utilisation of evidence in a politicised policy area

> New Labour proclaims the need for evidence-based policy, which we must take to mean that policy initiatives are to be supported by research evidence and that policies introduced on a trial basis are to be evaluated in as rigorous a way as possible. (Plewis, 2000, p 96)

In Chapter Six the episode of cannabis reclassification was used as a case study through which to explore how evidence is not considered homogeneously by those embroiled in the policy process. This has a significant knock-on effect for applications of the label 'evidence-based policy' because it can lead to zero-sum understandings of the connection where evidence is frequently deemed to be absent from the process, or conversely, where the policy is considered to be wholly evidence-based. Neither account, it is maintained, is an accurate reflection on the utilisation of evidence. This chapter broadens the substantive focus to consider appreciations of evidence in relation to the wider drug classification system. With the benefit of hindsight, it is clear that the cannabis reclassification was the trigger for the developing interest in the evidence base for UK drug classification. Readers wishing to familiarise themselves with the back story here should again consult Chapter Four.

Central to the issue of cannabis reclassification and its first review were debates over the nature and extent of the potential harm that the drug causes. The concept of drug harm is again a central feature of the current discussion and is a significant, even defining, feature of the radical, rational and conservative perspectives' positions on the efficacy of the MDA 1971. Although this chapter reveals further discrepancies in the applications of the nature of evidence, in a departure from the previous discussion, attention also turns to appreciations of the role of evidence in policy decision making (Monaghan, 2010). Drawing on the distinction made by Gordon et al (1993, p 5), the issue of whether evidence should be used to analyse policy outcomes ('analysis of policy') or whether it should be used in the process of decision making ('analysis for policy') or both reveals an interesting point of comparison.

A further significance of exploring the location of evidence relates to the fact that although there is a degree of contestation surrounding the concept, there are also traces of consistency. This chapter starts with a brief introduction of the significance of drug-related harm before moving on to consider in detail the radical, rational and conservative perspectives' appreciations of the role of evidence in debates over UK drug classification policy (highlighted with recourse to different understandings of the nature of drug harm). Here a paradox is revealed in that although evidence is generally confused and contested, there is a simultaneous correlation among rival groups in the way that its use is understood. Finally, some extended summarising remarks are documented that suggest that to fully comprehend the nature of evidence utilisation in heavily politicised areas it is necessary to view evidence as both contested, but with elements of certitude. The implications of this are taken up in Chapter Eight, when an attempt to model the evidence and policy connection in the context of heavy politicisation is undertaken.

Appreciations of the causes of 'drug harm' and the impact on 'evidence' in the UK drug classification system

The government and the majority of Parliament were alone in arguing that the MDA 1971 had withstood the test of time and that the tri-partite structure is currently fit for purpose. As was the case with the initial cannabis reclassification (see Chapter Six), there are noticeable differences between the different perspectives and their view of evidence in this area. The deep core beliefs of the radical, rational and conservative perspectives also make for an interesting comparison about the issue of what constitutes evidence 'utilisation'. To illustrate this, the focus is primarily placed on their appreciations of what constitutes drug harm in the context of discussions about the drug classification system. The definition of the causes of drug harm is an issue that has been continuously fought over. This can provide the prism through which to explore further appreciations of evidence in politicised areas, focusing particularly on the issue of where evidence is thought to be located in the decision-making process.

Radical perspective

For the radical perspective, as we have witnessed, the cannabis reclassification was not an evidence-based change. This was in spite of the fact that it did involve the use of some particular bodies of evidence. To recap, central to this perspective is the view that it is not the intrinsic properties of the substances themselves that produce the greatest harm, but the manner in which they are prohibited (deep core). Moving the debate on to consider the wider drug classification system, the radical appreciation of drug harms explains why the current system is not evidence-based.

For the radical perspective, then, for the policy to be considered to be evidence-based, it must transcend the wider paradigm of prohibition. This is illustrated by James, an author and journalist:

> If your policy really is evidence-based, then I think it really all points one way, and you can't include the evidence that says the system of classification and prohibition works and exclude the evidence which

shows abundantly that it doesn't work. So I think that they [the government] have made themselves a bit of a problem by declaring that they are going to have an evidence-based drug policy because they obviously haven't got one and we saw that quite clearly in the Science and Technology Committee hearings.

A snapshot of what James is referring to can be seen in relation to the following excerpt from this Committee's evidence hearings, between the then Liberal Democrat Committee member, Dr Evan Harris, and the then chairman of the ACMD, Sir Michael Rawlins, in relation to the Nutt et al matrix, which was at the time unpublished:

> **Q188 Dr Harris:** In this matrix you include under 'social harms' intoxication, health care costs, and other social harms. Included under 'other social harms' do you include the harm that stems from criminalisation itself?

> **Professor Sir Michael Rawlins:** Yes.

> **Q189 Dr Harris:** You do not spell that out but that is understood?

> **Professor Sir Michael Rawlins:** Yes and whether this leads to acquisitive crime.... (Science and Technology Select Committee, 2006, Evidence 10)

For the radical perspective, this is the crux of the reason as to why the current classification system is not evidence-based. According to Dave, a respondent from a leading NGO advocating drug law reform:

> There is this bizarre ... circularity and [the next question] basically said 'well, why don't you classify alcohol? It's a dangerous drug that kills loads of people'. The response was 'well, the problem is we tried that in America and loads of gangsters took over and everyone was selling hokey moonshine and people were dying of it'. And the chairman [Phil Willis] was going, 'isn't that what happened with all the other drugs?'. And Rawlins (sheepishly) goes 'well, now you mention it, yeah it is'. Honestly, some of those responses from Rawlins, respect to the guy for being really straight and honest and I don't think they [ACMD] are unprincipled scum bags or anything; they are doing their job within a system. Their failing on my part is that they haven't challenged the system that I think they deep down know is flawed.... Our role is to be that voice that challenges by asking those difficult questions and

saying, 'hang on, if the system that you are advocating is creating the harms that you then use to define the system, is that not a bit weird?'.

This passage gets to the crux of the problem as to why the classification system cannot be evidence-based. Here, as with the cannabis issue, drug harms are caused primarily by the legal status of the drugs themselves. Dave continues:

> The classification system is incredibly vague. If you look at the various vectors of drug harms, in terms of different types of users, different drugs, different drug using patterns, modes of administration, different users' predispositions, different doses, it's actually incredibly complex and there is a whole series of variables which are translated into a whole series of short, medium and long-term harms for the individual, or for the community. To boil all that down for an individual drug into A, B, C, I really do think is almost completely meaningless. If you're a potential drug user or a current drug user, if you want proper, useful information on drugs, about how harmful they are, or about how to reduce risk or anything like that, ABC gives you no information at all. None!

This has a knock-on effect for how the radical perspective views the efficacy of the overall system and also for the science underpinning the current system, particularly when trying to accurately depict what is meant by drug harm:

> Something … said in one of the Select Committee sessions was that for some people ABC becomes a sort of quality guide. So, it's like A is only for special occasions, the good stuff, and B is for week days and C. But a class A drug, something like cocaine … used occasionally in small doses its relatively unharmful. People who have a line of coke at a party … it's not always a problem for them, it doesn't do them any harm, they enjoy it, it's not giving any physical, personal or community harm, really aside from the argument about illegal markets which are intrinsically harmful, but again that is a factor of prohibition. (Dave)

Looking at the bigger picture, for the radical perspective the framework is rendered meaningless by what is excluded: alcohol and tobacco. There is a lack of clarity about harm because of the spectre of alcohol and its uneasy legislative relationship with currently illicit substances:

> People don't distinguish between the harm caused by prohibition and the harm caused by drugs and I think this is skewed rather by alcohol.… In terms of drug harm, what most people see in real life is alcohol, leery people fighting in the street, but because the assumption is that alcohol is safe because it is legal and all other drugs are worse than

> alcohol.... There is an assumption that all these other drugs are very
> dangerous and harmful in the way that alcohol is, except worse. And
> in public health terms, alcohol is really quite conspicuously harmful
> and the harm caused by cocaine, for example, is really hard to identify
> ... cocaine deaths are pretty low. Most people go through a period
> of cocaine use where they make arse-holes of themselves and come
> out the other end with their wallets a bit lighter, but not much harm
> done otherwise. So I think that drug harms are radically misperceived
> because of the illegal activities associated with them. (James)

There is a clear indication here of what constitutes drug harm and, by association,
what constitutes 'harm reduction'. The concept of harm reduction, for this
perspective, involves removing the damage caused by the (il)legal status of drugs.
This renders the current system 'evidence-free' because it is doing the exact
opposite of its original intention. The introduction of a hierarchical system of drug
regulation with associated punishments, as in the MDA 1971, has not only failed
to solve the drug problem, but is actually a contributory factor to the problem
which has made it worse. Dave continues:

> It's methodologically flawed and the evidence for it is that it has
> achieved the exact opposite of what it's supposed to. [For] any scientist
> coming at this objectively, it would be laughed out of town. It fails every
> single test, and yet ... we just waltz blithely on. I think in a way the
> debate about the classification of cannabis and the scientific evidence
> for that really suits the government because we've been arguing this
> boring bullshit debate about cannabis classification for years now. It
> dominates the media.... Any drug, if you use it the wrong way, is going
> to harm you. But in the meantime, whilst we have been arguing over
> this, the tiniest policy tweak – ie, the reclassification of cannabis – hasn't
> made much difference at all, or not a particularly significant one. The
> bigger picture ... is the apocalyptic failure of prohibition and all the
> harm it causes and the fact that the classification system is ridiculous,
> scientifically laughable.

The understanding of 'science' here is particularly illuminating. It sheds light on
how, for the radical group, the MDA 1971 is not so much viewed as a policy but
as an 'intervention'. For current purposes, this has significant implications for
where evidence should play a role in the decision-making process. It is worth
dwelling on what, ultimately, evidence-based policy means for this perspective:

> Basing policy on science rather than ideology. It's about having effective
> evaluation procedures in place.... You decide what you want your
> policy to achieve, you assign a series of key performance indicators to
> measure whether it is achieving that, you look at evidence from other

countries or other regions to see which policies have been effective there. Then, you come up with a balanced scientific view on which is going to be the most effective policy for achieving the aims that you want as measured by your indicators. Then once a policy is put in place you evaluate, measure and monitor it properly in a scientific and consistent way to see whether it is doing what it is supposed to do, and if it isn't either change it or abandon it altogether and try something else entirely. (Dave)

In the above quotation 'evidence' is equated with policy evaluation and appraisal. The implementation of the MDA 1971 is viewed as an intervention, making the Act an independent variable. The desired outcome is the eradication of the drug problem, which is the dependent variable. For the radical perspective, the intervention has not only failed to achieve the desired outcome and so must be considered to have not worked, it has actually made the problem worse, hence the previous reference to the 'apocalyptic failure of prohibition and all the harm it causes'. For now, the key point is that for the radical perspective evidence-based policy making is ultimately contextualised in terms of evaluations. The role of evidence is restricted to an analysis of policy outcomes. It will be argued later that this is a short-term, narrow and linear view of the relationship between evidence and policy where evidence relates directly to policy. This is returned to in Chapter Eight.

Rational perspective

For the rational perspective, the cannabis reclassification was broadly conceived as an 'evidence-based' decision. It signalled an attempt to apply a scientific understanding to, or to 'rationalise', the MDA 1971. Relating to current concerns, the thorny issue of drug harm focuses more on the properties of the drugs themselves and not on their legal status, as the radical group implies. This, however, masks a complex set of issues. According to Harry, director of a leading drug treatment NGO:

> I think one of the problems is how we decide what the harms are and what causes the harms. Because if you take an argument that I imagine would be put forward from Transform, that a lot of the harms stem from the control mechanisms themselves, so you take some of the control mechanisms away and regulate the market.... So, at one level, you can say what are the inherent harms. And I suppose on a health basis that would be pretty easy to do. Once you start looking at social harms you are then in a bit of a circle because it is hard to decide where the social harms originate, whether they are inherent in the drug itself. Well, certain drugs possibly, yes, because certain drugs have a deleterious effect on behaviour and very often culture mediates

those behaviours and very often there is a risk environment, which is a whole constellation of things coming together which determines whether people suffer harms.

There is recognition here that harm is multi-faceted, the causes of which are difficult to pinpoint. Referring back to the belief system structure of this perspective, harm reduction is intrinsically linked to non-coercive drug treatment. This involves, among other things, catering for the most problematic drug users in a public health setting as opposed to applying criminal justice sanctions to such behaviour and making the current drug legislation internally consistent. Current problems with the overall MDA 1971 framework stem from a concatenation of causes internal to it, such as the misplacement of certain substances. Part of the rationalising process, then, involves introducing 'science' into the control of substances, thus attempting to equate levels of harm with levels of punishment. In effect, this constitutes 'evidence-based policy' for members from this perspective.

When asked about the relationship between evidence and policy with regard to the wider UK drug classification system, Pat, a one-time member of the ACMD and senior figure of a leading drug policy NGO, commented that:

> The short-hand answer to that is, if you look at David Nutt's work [Nutt et al matrix] and if you look historically, there isn't a huge relationship. I think, in a way, there is a crude relationship between these historically.... That is not to say it is hugely wrong, but rather it is a nuancing. And you look at things like ecstasy and magic mushrooms and stuff like that and there isn't the evidential base, I would suggest personally … that I wouldn't think these particular classifications are warranted in terms of the harms and the risks.

This relates to how, for the rational perspective, the system can be improved without radically altering the overarching philosophy of UK drug policy. Unlike the radical perspective, then, it is eradicating these discrepancies from the current framework that typifies the main understanding of what evidence-based policy is in this context. In oral evidence to the Science and Technology Select Committee, one-time chair of the ACMD, Professor Sir Michael Rawlins, revealed how this process ideally works:

> When we look into a particular area we usually set up a small working group. That small working group undertakes or usually commissions a systematic review of the public evidence, the chemical, the basic science and the social science evidence. That is supplemented by a search for unpublished material from all sorts of sources, not only from scientists we know are working in the field but through our national and international contacts, and then we interact with experts in the field, seeking their written evidence, seeking oral evidence from them

and seeking their views on the systematic review and whether we have left anything out. That then forms the basis of a draft report which is looked at by the Technical Committee and then finally goes to the Council for further discussion and consideration and sometimes a bit of iteration between the Council and the Technical Committee. (Science and Technology Select Committee, 2006b, Evidence 4)

An equally interesting account of the process is revealed by Joe, a government adviser and member of the ACMD technical committee, in response to a question detailing understandings of the government's favoured kind of evidence in this area. It was suggested that:

> This comes down to the sort of evidence that ACMD might collect and present and in the case of the cannabis review last year that was very much based on published academic work.... Peer-reviewed work....

This above discussion highlights the centrality of the ACMD to UK drug policy making and its use of evidence. From this we can deduce that evidence is a vital part of the process of decision making for the rational group. There are a couple of points to note about this. At this stage we get an insight into what constitutes evidence and how it should be used. Evidence ideally takes the form of systematic reviews of public evidence, the chemical, the basic science and the social science evidence. In addition, there is also an indication of where, ideally, this evidence should come from (peer review) and how it is synthesised (by the ACMD), all of which can improve on the existing framework. Overlapping with some of the themes mentioned previously, in particular the significance of the peer review process, the following exchange from the Science and Technology Select Committee (2006b) oral evidence sessions is informative. It is between Dr Evan Harris, MP, the chair of the ACMD technical committee, Professor David Nutt and the chair of the main committee, Professor Sir Michael Rawlins:

> **Q177 Dr Harris:** ... Professor Blakemore [a co-author of the Nutt et al matrix] has argued for a scientifically-based scale of harm for all drugs with alcohol and tobacco included in some form of calibration. I am curious as to your thoughts on that.
>
> **Professor Nutt:** I think it is a very sensible idea.
>
> **Professor Sir Michael Rawlins:** I think, inevitably, as David [Nutt] says, it will inform the decision but it will not determine it. These things cannot be entirely algebraic.
>
> **Q178 Dr Harris:** You have not done that. You have got this matrix that you sent us, which you did not send us originally, but you kindly

supplied it later, which is very interesting and I think it is possibly among your interesting memorandum the most interesting. If you did this scale and you put in tobacco and alcohol then that would be a useful thing. I cannot understand, since you have agreed it would be useful, why you have not done it, unless it would show that the current ABC would not….

Professor Sir Michael Rawlins: We can send to you the paper that David has been preparing.

Professor Nutt: We have done this.

Q179 Dr Harris: Has it been published?

Professor Nutt: No, it has not but the plan is to send it to *The Lancet*, get it peer-reviewed, and hopefully have it in the public domain.

Q180 Dr Harris: Has there been a delay? If you have done it, why not publish it?

Professor Nutt: Because it takes some time. It is an iterative process. There are four authors and it has taken some time. It is not trivial writing a quality paper for *The Lancet*. (Science and Technology Select Committee, 2006, Evidence 8-9)

This paper was, as stated, finally published in March 2007 and such discussions have come to dominate the ACMD understanding of requisite evidence in this field. According to Joe, a member of the ACMD technical committee:

It's only since we've taken on board the risk assessment processes in the last six years or so that we've really made any effort in changing that early policy [of the MDA 1971]. Because all the time that the Act has been in existence, very few substances have been removed and very few substances have been reclassified. Some that were removed had to go back in again later because misuse then grew once they came out of the Act and so the feeling with time was that it was dangerous to tinker with the Act because it caused all sorts of problems. So the feeling was that we should leave things where they were. Or at least other people felt that. It's only been in the last few years to say that the scientific base doesn't really support the classification we've got today. I feel that very strongly now.

It is clear that the Nutt et al matrix (2007) was a key feature of the ACMD's decision making. The matrix, as illustrated, works within the current system and seeks to make it internally valid. With this in mind, evidence is a key part of the decision-making process and is not restricted to policy evaluation, as is the case with the radical perspective (as we have seen), and as is the case with the conservative perspective (as we shall see).

There is a clear indication of a general acceptance that the ranking of drugs in some form of scale of harm is a desirable enterprise and is thus central to the general understanding of evidence. The Nutt et al matrix is an example of this. Overall, the causal explanations of the defects of the current system, via understandings of drug harm, do reveal an interesting point of comparison, which results in a broader view of the evidence and policy relationship than is identifiable in either the radical or conservative perspectives or the government's. The general understanding of the causes of drug harm relates to the substances themselves, but this has numerous dimensions and is mitigated by cultural and social factors. This need not concern us here; what is of more significance is where evidence plays a role in the decision-making process because of this. Reducing harm does not require a radical overhaul of the current framework. For those who do come into difficulties, drug treatment in its various guises is considered to be the most efficacious means of minimising the impact of drugs, instead of some form of drug legalisation or more emphasis on prevention. For certain members of the rational perspective, this is the only aspect of drug policy that is evidence-based, a point succinctly made by Angie, director of a leading drug treatment quango (quasi-autonomous non-government organisation):

> I think it is very rare that the law is based on evidence actually. I don't think we quite know what we are trying to achieve, which doesn't help. Are we trying to contain? Are we trying to punish? Are we trying to prevent harm? I think that the only bit that is evidence-based is around drug treatment actually, because if you look at the four strands of the drug strategy, the only one where there is any real coherent evidence of any quality is around drug treatment having an impact on health and crime.

A second dimension of reducing harm relates to the messages that the current system gives. Having certain substances in the wrong categories can actually cause harm. By accurately depicting the harmful nature of drugs in relation to one another, within the framework drug users should be able to make informed choices about the risks they take. Whether the emphasis is on drug treatment or on rationalising the current system, the point remains that evidence is seen to have a role in the decision-making process. This is consistent with what Weiss (1986) has described as an 'enlightenment' function, where research filters into the policy process over time. This is a more dynamic view of the policy process and the role of evidence therein than either the radical or conservative perspectives display. There is no sense here that the MDA 1971 is seen as an intervention. It is more of a framework. The knock-on effect for evidence is that the rational perspective shows how evidence is prominent in the process of policy formulation.

Conservative perspective

For the conservative perspective the cannabis reclassification was evidence-free, primarily as the necessary and relevant health research was ignored. There was also the belief that reclassification sent out the wrong message that some drugs are less harmful than others. The core belief structure shows a specific concern with the deleterious properties of the drugs themselves. These statements are consistent with the deep core beliefs of promoting wholesome and healthy lives through abstinence. In terms of drug harm, the conservative perspective demarcates itself from the radical and rational groups by suggesting that the general understanding of harm within the drug policy debate is actually too narrow. Thus, according to Malcolm, a central figure in a leading drug prevention organisation:

> In general when people talk about harm and harm reduction they tend to talk about harm to the user. They tend to talk only about physical harm and I am including brain damage in that, rather than the use of the brain cells. And they tend to think that it is only in the stages of addiction that it occurs, but this is wrong in three senses. Lots of other people are affected by drug users and you could do a bulls-eye if you like, of the drug user in the middle and you get family, friends and siblings. And then you go out to work mates and ambulance drivers, police and so on, and so any one drug user actually affects a lot of other people. That is the first of the three points. The second one is that if you are looking at health damage, it isn't just physical and these things include physical but also mental, intellectual, social, emotional, spiritual and environmental. And I didn't invent those, the World Health Organization uses those and, actually, if you look in biblical readings or in Buddhism or in Judaism you'll find pretty similar things that it is not just the physical. Thirdly, there is the issue of costs to people. This can start from day one. Using an unlikely example, but one that is easy to explain, someone uses cannabis for the first time, they are stoned and they get in their car and they wrap it around another car and bump off a number of people. I am not saying that that will happen with every cannabis user. That is patently stupid, but I am trying to illustrate that harms can happen from day one.

Additionally, for the same respondent, this has a knock-on effect for the measurement of harm and the way it is discussed in policy debates:

> People are not measuring these other harms when they are assessing or not how harmful a particular drug is. We do know, if you take, for

example, siblings and other relatives. In the drug agency work we did – face-to-face work with alcohol and street drug abusers – time and again it came up that it was the people around the user who were suffering more or were harmed more. Until the drug or alcohol user got to the real stage of addiction, then they were suffering a lot, but up until that point they were fine. They were getting all the stuff they wanted and they weren't getting 'nicked' by the police because they were lucky and they had ways of getting it or maybe they had a job.

These harms are generally considered to be social harms and, for the conservative perspective, they are downplayed. In contrast to the rational perspective, there is clear scepticism concerning the utility of basing policy on a rationally developed scale of harm. According to Donald, a one-time senior law enforcement officer:

> I think that whole thing about that new list [Nutt et al matrix] is a con job.… Where is the advantage in discussing it? I would just rather have they are legal or they are not legal and the hierarchy of harm … it is used by law enforcement and it is used by the courts but I actually think that a better determinant would be scale and size of operation and profitability and I think we have got ourselves locked in a debate splitting hairs.…

In debates about the relationship between evidence and policy as regards the drug classification system, it has been precisely the endeavours of Professor Nutt and colleagues that have come to assume a dominant status. The upshot of this is that there is a noticeable critical view of the mechanisms by which the government receives its evidence. The efficacy of the ACMD as a body capable of synthesising the evidence is called into question, particularly the extent of its objectivity. It is a commonly held view of this group that the ACMD's deliberations and reports, although for the most part significantly cerebral, are shaped by a particular philosophy. A previously high-ranking police officer, Stuart, pointed out that:

> The ACMD is not an organisation I have a particularly high regard for and I don't think it is as impartial, as independent and as professional as it could be. There are an awful lot of experts that ought to be on that committee that aren't and I mean genuine qualified people from well-established universities and the like, but nevertheless the ACMD has made some good reports.

A more damning criticism of the ACMD comes from the following respondent, Anne, a current representative of an international drug prevention organisation. She ultimately raises serious doubts about the mechanism through which the government receives its advice:

> The ACMD are not a proper scientific body. There are only a few proper scientists and even they are libertarian types….The ACMD is government-appointed, everything is skewed….There was one paper by a chap called MacLeod and others on mental illness. I think it was dated 2004 and they [the ACMD] looked at that and that bucked the trend of all the other papers that had been written.… I was asked to look at that paper and I did, and I did a criticism of it….To begin with, two of the co-authors were on the ACMD, they looked at a whole load of papers, obscure papers that I have never seen. I wrote a paper on psychosis and schizophrenia with 76 references. They included, I think it was two…. They just downplayed everything and I mean they didn't look at the main research of people who had been in the research field for years and years and years, really prominent people and they just ignored all that research and downplayed it…. It was a faulty paper.

Overall, allied to the views that the ACMD is not a completely objective organisation, and that the concept of harm has become distorted, is the assumption from this perspective that the platform on which the evidence debate takes place is misleading. For their part, when asked about the relationship between evidence and policy with regard to the current UK drug classification system, a typical response of members of the conservative perspective was to point out the futility of the current classification system. For example, one former UK government adviser, Michael, explained:

> I don't think that it is enormously shaped by evidence. I think that in certain senses it is a bit of a mystery as to why certain drugs are placed in some categories and others are in a different one. I think that one can envisage that the classification system is something that should be much more evidence-based…. I don't actually have a huge degree of sympathy with the investment of considerable effort in trying to work out where certain drugs sit within the classification system. I think it is a bit outmoded actually and I don't know that it serves any more useful function, for example, to seek to differentiate between heroin and cannabis but that is where the classification system takes you.

There is a sense here that the initial implementation of the MDA 1971 has done little to address the drugs problem. This overlaps with that of the radical perspective, albeit for different reasons. There is a view in this group that the MDA 1971 is best thought of as an intervention, although it is one that has not achieved what it set out to do, solving the 'drug problem'. For the conservative perspective, however, it is not the Act itself that produces the problem per se. The overarching philosophy is generally considered to be sound, but more enforcement is needed and more emphasis should be placed on prevention of drug use. At present, the current framework does not target the correct areas and a three-tiered ABC structure only confuses the issue.

The key point is that the intervention of the MDA 1971 unnecessarily complicates the issue, and that tweaking the mechanism internally does not get to the root of the problem. In essence, drug classification does not accurately depict that all drugs are dangerous and should be given equal weighting in the legislation. Consequently, a reworking of policy is advocated which places more emphasis on prevention mechanisms and more stringent enforcement based on the amounts of drugs involved in relation to certain offences. This is a model that mirrors, as mentioned, the Swedish approach to drug control.

In many ways, this is the antithesis of the rational model of informed choice based on receipt of accurate information about the nature of drug harms. In this regard, there is an affinity in appreciations of the location of evidence in evidence-based policy making between the conservative and radical perspectives, in that the focus is on the overall efficacy of the policy. This equates evidence with policy evaluation and is restricted to the outcomes of policy. In effect, policy outcomes are seen as the correct location for considering the role of evidence in policy making. In this sense, the conservative perspective also has a narrow appreciation of evidence utilisation.

The significance of the position of evidence in policy

There are a number of points to note from the above discussion about the location of evidence. On one level, these debates over the nature of drug harm and how this impacts on classification continue the contestation that surrounds the nature of 'evidence', for instance, whether evidence needs to be 'peer reviewed' or not. This point is related to the second issue about why zero-sum appreciations of the evidence are understandable, even if they are inaccurate. It is worth pausing here to consider this point in more detail. Elsewhere (Monaghan, 2010), it has been suggested that if evidence is going to be selected for consideration in policy making then more often than not the evidence producers will share a view of policy that is consistent with those who are making the decisions. As this is the case, it is to be expected, in this context, that there will be some consistency between the government and the rational perspective's appreciations. And this is, indeed, the reality. In oral evidence to the Science and Technology Select Committee (2006b, Evidence 43), Vernon Coaker MP, who then oversaw the drugs brief in the Home Office, highlighted the centrality of the Nutt et al matrix to the government decision-making process:

> We have a matrix which we use. That matrix is part of the way we determine which drug should be in which category. Of course, we always look at the evidence that people give us; we always look at the opinions that they give to us …we have a scientific basis for determining harm. The ACMD refer to that when they classify drugs.

As the government was committed to using the ACMD and the Nutt et al matrix in its decision making, the conceptualisation of evidence cited by the rational perspective is '*contemporaneous*' and '*consanguineous*' to the legislation. In other words, it occurs in real time, and is intrinsic to the legislation to which it refers (Monaghan, 2010, p 9). It is this issue that accounts for their view of the cannabis reclassification and the wider drug classification system as being evidence-based. Similarly, when the political winds changed and the government no longer found the matrix to be applicable in its decision making concerning cannabis and ecstasy, there was a reframing of appreciations of the evidence base for drug classification from key personnel within groups contained in the rational perspective. David Nutt's proclamation of the New Labour government's 'devaluing' of science is indicative of this.

Prior to the change back to class B, for the rational perspective the cannabis reclassification represented the first instance of an acceptance that the classification system may not be scientifically valid and it was the first attempt to iron out one of the anomalies of the existing classification system by reducing some of the regulations around the drug. Consequently, the notion of 'scientific' evidence was pushed to the fore and there were indications about how this evidence should be produced. 'Peer review' and 'published material' were mentioned as significant aspects of the evidence base by members of the rational perspective, alongside obtaining 'expert advice' from relevant bodies. Again, this conceptualisation of 'evidence' includes that used in the *process* of policy making and shares similarities with that of the government. Indeed, in the run up to the passing of the Drugs Bill 2005, the then Home Secretary, Charles Clarke, pointed out:

> Of course, when we look at the analysis of the banding classification system, it is appropriate and right to consider the advice of the professionals who make the medical assessment before coming to a view. That is precisely what we will do…. (cited in Levitt et al, 2006, p 3)

Such appreciations are again absent from both the radical and conservative perspectives, because their view of evidence, as mentioned, is restricted to a higher level of abstraction, equating evidence with the evaluation of policy outcomes. This is because the overarching strategy of UK drug policy is problematic for these groups. Research has been conducted relating to the evaluation of the successes or otherwise of prohibition and likewise for policies advocating more rigorous enforcement of the drugs laws alongside drug prevention interventions as the overarching strategy governing UK drug policy, but this is easily dismissed by decision makers as being ideologically driven and speculative (Monaghan, 2010). As this is so, peer-reviewed published data becomes less of a concern for these groups.

This brings us on to the next point that there are, then, clear schisms over the role or purpose of evidence in the decision-making process and that all the perspectives operate with a seemingly narrow understanding of the connection. For the radical and conservative perspectives, evidence is restricted to a role in policy evaluation, whereas for the rational perspective, evidence is central to the process of decision making. Yet the notion of evidence that has become widely accepted, particularly in the aftermath of the increasing popularity of systematic review, is that evidence-based policy making equates to both aspects, that is, evidence for policy and evidence of policy, as the quote by Plewis at the outset of this chapter neatly illustrates. Although there are clear differences in appreciations of the role and nature of evidence in policy, there are also areas of crossover or vestiges of consistency in the way evidence is conceived, for example, in the similarities between appreciations over the location of evidence in the policy process. With this in mind, to dismiss evidence as wholly contested would be inaccurate. There is a general consensus for all groups about what it means and entails – hence the very fact that it is possible to analyse different appreciations of the phenomenon. A central aim of this book is to produce an account of the evidence and policy relationship in politicised areas that is more nuanced than the zero-sum accounts. The fact that evidence is primarily but not wholly contested is central to this, and the following chapter turns its attention to this task.

Summary

A key theme of this book has been that no matter how vociferously they are made, and no matter how understandable, zero-sum views do not accurately describe the relationship between evidence and policy. The true picture is much more opaque and complex. This chapter and Chapter Six looked into the nature and role of evidence in a politicised policy area, the UK drug classification policy. As we saw in Chapter Six, in simple terms, the negative zero-sum account is paradoxical because it assumes policies to be evidence-free, while in some cases accepting that evidence was present in the decision-making process. The positive zero-sum account is also problematic because it assumes that favourable evidence will be used in the process, but there is always evidence that is missing. In addition, there is the possibility – particularly in heavily politicised areas – that decisions made will be reversed or renegotiated in some way, due to the dynamic nature of policy formulation.

From this chapter we have also witnessed how appreciations of the location of evidence in decision making are tied to deep core beliefs about policy. It is necessary to point out that while the focus of the current and previous chapters has primarily been to highlight the differences between the various perspectives' appreciations on the nature of evidence and evidence-based policy making, there has also been a non-trivial amount of consensus across the subsystem on what counts as evidence (the differences being whether its prevalence in the process constituted evidence-based policy making) and whether evidence should be restricted to the evaluation of policies and/or should be a key part of policy formulation. In other words, 'evidence', as a concept, has been shown to be primarily, but not wholly, contested. This further undermines the default zero-sum position that is resorted to in highly charged policy debates. If zero-sum explanations of the evidence and policy connection in politicised areas are not accurate, how is the relationship to be explained? The following chapter attempts to answer this question.

EIGHT

Conceptualising and modelling evidence use in politicised policy areas

> Despite considerable effort at bridging the gap between evidence and policy, rare is the study that leads to direct change in direction. (Weiss et al, 2008, p 34)

Previous chapters have raised a number of quandaries for the analyst trying to explain the nature of the evidence and policy relationship with particular reference to heavily politicised areas. It has been suggested that particularly in these contexts zero-sum accounts of the evidence and policy relationship are the most frequent default position resorted to by supporters and detractors alike. It was suggested at the end of Chapter Seven that zero-sum views cannot readily account for the subtleties in the evidence and policy connection in politicised areas and, consequently, an alternative view is put forward here. Previous chapters have shown the inherently fluid nature of politicised policy areas and the connection therein between evidence and policy, which is likewise unpredictable and non-linear.

To offer a comprehensive overview of evidence utilisation in politicised policy areas, a number of factors must be accounted for. These can be summarised as follows: (a) the recognition that evidence of some kind is embedded within the policy process, but that (b) the concept of evidence contains vestiges of contestation and certitude. In turn, it requires (c) a model of the policy process that demonstrates how policy (particularly in politicised areas) is inherently dynamic or unstable, which raises the possibility that (d) the connection between evidence and policy is rarely linear where evidence shapes policy outcomes or is used solely in policy analysis, in the form of evaluation for instance.

The quest of this chapter is to synthesise the lessons of the previous chapters. In doing so, it seeks clarification on the nature and role of evidence in the policy process. Initially this involves some brief recourse to philosophical and social scientific discussions of concept formation, looking at the notion of conceptual contestation, certitude and flux. This is because to develop a model of evidence-based policy making one needs to be clear not only about the view of the policy process, but also about the nature of evidence itself. Existing models of research utilisation have been developed over a number of years (see, for example, Weiss, 1986); these have tended to focus on the former, but have neglected the latter. From the discussion of concept formation, and drawing on the findings of previous chapters, it is suggested that the best platform to explain the concept of evidence is to view it in terms of its fluctuating nature. Armed with this understanding of evidence, the debate turns towards established models of research utilisation. These are considered as a means of explaining the complex selection or exploitation of research in politicised areas. They are also considered because any new model will inevitably be influenced by the existing literature. For a variety of reasons, it is proposed that these existing models are not up to the task of explaining the minutiae of evidence utilisation in politicised areas. Consequently, more recent additions to the literature are then discussed, which are more fit-for-purpose. The chapter concludes with a summary.

Contestability, certitude and flux in concept formation

The view of evidence emerging from discussions of drug classification is of a concept that is contested, but simultaneously has vestiges of consistency. Applying this to a model of evidence utilisation is the task ahead. The contested and certain nature of concepts poses a challenge for various thinkers, who prefer to see them in one way or another. An outline of these debates is briefly documented here (readers who wish to know more should refer to Pawson, 1989 and Bryant, 1995). Parsonian social theory represents a good example of where concepts are viewed as reflecting the real world and have a consistent meaning (Parsons, 1937). These are referred to as 'operationalist' concepts. Here scientific discourse is consistent and understood in the same way by everyone, as are the concepts that are used in explanation. For others (Gallie, 1956; MacIntyre, 1973; Connolly, 1974), this is impractical as different interpretations of concepts are always possible and researchers have little control over how this occurs. In this way, for Gallie (1956), concepts are always 'essentially contested'. Essentially contested concepts are the epitome of the 'contestabilist' tradition of concept formation. Essential contestation equates to more than mere disagreement over the meaning of concepts, but refers also to fundamental disagreement as to their application in science. This is because concepts can never be free of values that seep into science at every available opportunity. The operationalist and contestabilist traditions represent the extreme poles of concept formation in terms of consistency and contestability.

In his discussion of conceptual analysis, Bryant (1995, p 53) concludes that neither stance accurately describes the nature of concepts in research and it is necessary to 'move beyond' such accounts. He claims that an acceptance that concepts are both is the path to follow and the task of researchers or scientists is to come to an agreed upon and useable definition. This mirrors the view of evidence advanced here. Bryant's analysis is, however, rooted in a particular kind of logic. Kilminster (1998) suggests that such reasoning is typical of the philosophy of science. Here, one is forced to choose how one sees particular situations based around long-standing dichotomies, for example whether social phenomena are best explained from the starting point of structure or agency, or whether the social world is an open or closed system. If a choice is not or cannot be made, then it becomes necessary to reconcile these opposing views in some way. Bryant's strategy for such a reconciliation is that there should be dialogue between rival traditions, which can result in a jointly agreed meaning of concepts emerging. This view is consistent with what is often referred to as the 'reconstructionist' tradition of concept formation (Oppenheim, 1981; Sartori, 1984), although Bryant is critical of some of the manifestations of this tradition, referring to its adherents as the 'conceptual thought police' (Bryant, 1995, p 43).

It is the solution of 'dialogue' that is, for current purposes, problematic. As has been illustrated throughout this book, in debates where deeply held views are apparent, there is limited opportunity for the deep core of that view to alter through the process of dialogue and this is, furthermore, likely to be a futile pursuit in terms of fostering change. If agreement on the nature of concepts stemming from productive dialogue between diverging groups is unlikely, then an alternative form of synthesis is required. Salvation comes in the form of 'formalist' thinking and with recourse to the sociology of knowledge, particularly that of Elias (1978, 1991, 2000):

> Few controversies are as unattractive as that in which two groups of antagonists run around in circles, each defending its own speculative and untestable thesis by attacking another that is equally speculative and untestable on the grounds that no third alternative is possible. (Elias, 1978, p 73)

Elias's sociological project can, on one level, be seen as a concerted attempt to move beyond the circular debates described above (Kilminster, 2007). Meanwhile, formalism provides something of a halfway house for the conceptual contestability and certitude debate. Pawson (1989) demonstrates the principle of formalism via an analysis of the concept of social class, which has been operationalised in various different ways with a range of propositions, yet this concept is still widely understood, at the very least, by most social scientists. This is not because some common ground has been established between rival perspectives, but as a result of how it relates to other concepts – income, status, stratification and so on – within a wider system. Pawson (1989, p 237) further suggests that this entails the 'genuine appraisal of the conceptual structure of sociological theory'. In effect, social theories should not strive to be all-encompassing, but should operate at a middle level of abstraction (Merton, 1957), and take their meanings from other theories operating in other spheres, as should the concepts that are central to them.

Taking the concept of evidence, then, any argument made with recourse to this, on some level, shows signs that it has been thought about in relation to other phenomena. A formalist-led view of evidence would therefore view the concept as internally diverse, but as having a simultaneously consistent level of application in wider discourse. The previous chapters have identified the miscellany of evidence, linking this to wider beliefs about preferable directions for policy. Writing in the context of health policy, Culyer and Lomas (2006, p 360) highlight its internal diversity of evidence, suggesting that:

> Clinical or programme effectiveness data compare with assertion (sometimes claimed to be expert assertion), cost–utility algorithms sit alongside political acceptability and public or patient attitude data are combined with vivid recollections of personal encounters. What Ministers call evidence is what they get from their constituents at Saturday surgery. (Culyer and Lomas, 2006, p 360)

They also suggest, however, that on a higher level of abstraction, 'evidence is anything that claims to be an empirical fact' (Culyer and Lomas, 2006, p 360). Locating a meaning of the term in jurisprudence, they claim that 'evidence is to do with the facts of a case', before continuing that 'the kind of evidence that is relevant in any situation consists of material facts that help establish the truth of someone's assertions or the cause of a consequence' (Culyer and Lomas, 2006, p 360). On this level, it is broadly understood by those who comment on, or attempt to formulate, evidence-based policy. Culyer and Lomas are at pains to point out, however, that because of its retrospective nature, the jurisprudential meaning of evidence is unsuitable in the context of evidence-based policy, whereas health evidence is concerned with 'forecasting, prediction and prognosis' (Culyer and Lomas, 2006, p 360). A case can be made, however, that evidence in policy is linked to that in the legal process. Jurisprudential evidence need not always be retrospective. There is always the possibility for 'new' evidence to come to light in criminal trials, for example, which can lead to the re-opening of criminal investigations.

This leads on to another key point about the nature of evidence. Transposed into the current debate, we can say that the concept of evidence in evidence-based policy making (particularly in politicised areas), like that in jurisprudence, should not be viewed as a motionless entity. This is primarily because the contexts in which it is applied are dynamic. The influence of politics on policy can be drawn on to explain this. Indeed, the dynamic nature of policy subsystems can be illustrated by the fluctuating nature of cannabis legislation in the UK that has been subservient to the political winds of change, to-ing and fro-ing between classes B and C. As regards the fluctuating nature of evidence, the association between cannabis use and mental illness, along with the debates over cannabis potency, reveal how this is an inherently dynamic area. The media and public interest in the topic also mean that there is a market for research to be continuously conducted. It is worth pointing out that for this very reason the ACMD (2008) recommended that the evidence base for cannabis classification be placed under permanent review.

In effect, the concept of evidence and the context to which it is applied must be seen to be in flux. It is suggested here that it is possible for concepts to show signs of both contest and certitude, precisely because of this. Again, this line of thinking has similarities with that of Elias. One of Elias's main concerns was that at his time of writing, the means of speaking and thinking available to sociologists, for the most part, were unequal to the task asked of them. A by-product of the lexicon of the social sciences, for Elias, was that numerous technical terms seemingly relate to independent static artefacts. On closer scrutiny, however, the phenomena under consideration were dynamic. Drawing on Whorf's (1956) philosophy of language, he develops this point by referring to the nature of wind:

> We say, "The wind is blowing", as if the wind were actually a thing at rest which, at a given point in time, begins to move and blow. We speak as if the wind were separate from its blowing, as if a wind could exist which did not blow. (Elias, 1978, p 112)

Elias then pointed out how the same was true for the concept of 'society' and other related sociological concepts:

> The very concept of society has this character of an isolated object, in a state of rest, and so has that of nature. The same goes for the concept of individual. Consequently, we always feel compelled to make quite senseless conceptual distinctions, like 'the individual *and* society', which makes it seem that 'the individual' and 'society' were two separate things, like tables and chairs, or pots and pans. One can find oneself caught up in long discussions of the nature of the relationship between these two apparently separate objects. Yet on another level of awareness one may know perfectly well that societies are composed of individuals, and that individuals can only possess specifically human characteristics such as their abilities to speak, think, and love, in and through their relationships with other people – 'in society'. (Elias, 1978, p 113)

This is a useful premise on how evidence should be viewed for policy. It is difficult to think of evidence without it being linked to the nature of the policy area to which it relates. Formalist reasoning accounts for this nuance. A modified formalist account of conceptual explanation is, therefore, advocated here. There are, then, traces of both certitude and contestability in the concept of evidence. Taking this as the starting point and recognising that contestability and certitude are apparent can be a good platform for developing a model to explain the role of evidence in politicised areas.

Modelling the evidence and policy connection

Drawing on the work of Weiss (1998), Nutley et al (2003) demarcate four main 'types' of research utilisation from 'models' of research utilisation. These are:

- *instrumental use*, where research feeds directly into decision making for policy and practice;
- *conceptual use*, where even if practitioners are blocked from using findings, research can change their understanding of a situation, provide new ways of

thinking and offer new evaluative insights into particular courses of action. In this way conceptual use can become instrumental;

- *mobilisation of support*, where research becomes an instrument of persuasion or the act of research is a tool to legitimate particular courses of action or inaction;
- *wider influence*, where research can have an influence beyond the institutions studied.

There is significant overlap between the 'types' and 'models' of research utilisation, as will become apparent. The latter are favoured here on account of their prevalence in the wider literature.

According to Harré and Secord (1972, p 72), 'the key to understanding of the epistemological and logic of creative science is to be found in the logic of the model'. Stevens (2007a), by drawing on the work of Weiss (1986), among others, has produced a four-tier typology of models of the evidence-based policy-making process. He suggests that the evidence and policy relationship can be divided into the following: the 'linear model', the 'enlightenment model', the 'political/tactical model' and finally, the 'evolutionary model', for which he claims superiority. Although not mentioned by Stevens (2007a), Weiss (1986) also refers to an 'interactive model' and the model of 'research as part of the intellectual enterprise of society' as plausible accounts of the research and policy connection. All are expounded below, with the exception of the evolutionary model, which is reserved for a subsequent discussion. Bryant (1995), in his review of this area of the literature, covers much the same ground, but uses a slightly different lexicon. Of prime significance, for current purposes, is his reference to a 'dialogical model'. It is worth pointing out that although the models are discrete, the many features that make them up overlap with other models.

With the exception of Stevens' (2007a) evolutionary model, these constitute the established models of research utilisation. It must be stressed that although there are differences between 'research' and 'evidence', in what follows the terms are used interchangeably. In the context of highly politicised policy areas, all the established models have their relative strengths and weaknesses. The models are judged as to their effectiveness based on a range of criteria discussed over the course of previous chapters. It is maintained that in order to develop a useful model of evidence utilisation in politicised policy areas, an understanding of evidence-based policy making that accounts for the use of evidence in both the analysis of policy (outcomes) and the development of policy (process) is necessary. In addition, a view of the concept of evidence is required that can account for both certitude and contestability. This is because evidence is always in a state of flux. A dynamic view of the link between evidence and policy is another pre-requisite. This allows for the fact that the link between the two is rarely linear or short term, but is much more ad hoc and usually takes place over a prolonged time frame. The next criterion is that a view of the decision-making process is required where evidence is only one spoke in the wheel of decision making, fighting for influence alongside things such as polling and punditry, for instance.

Finally, any model must incorporate a sophisticated account of the mechanisms by which evidence comes to play a role in decision making.

In recent times, multi-criteria decision making or a variant thereof has been employed to adjudge between various evidence bases in various policy domains including, for instance, in the disposal of nuclear waste (see, for example, Morton et al, 2009). Multi-criteria decision making attempts to allow policy makers to adjudicate between rival interpretations of data on the same problem by establishing a set of criteria which must be met. The focus of evidence selection here, is similar; however, the focus is more on what Bulmer (1986, p 10) terms the 'content of the negotiations' of research use – these are the means by which research is selected for use in policy or practice. In effect, it is the interplay between structure and agency in the decision-making process and how evidence flourishes or flounders under the conditions of heavy politicisation that is of prime concern. For the sake of clarity, the key criteria for a useable model of evidence are produced in table form alongside a brief description of the key tenets of each, as Table 8.1 illustrates. The top five rows relate to various issues of the research and policy relationship discussed in previous chapters, and in the pending discussion of the models. The final row emerges out of the pending discussion of the existing models of research utilisation.

Table 8.1: Key issues for models of research utilisation in heavily politicised policy areas

Issue	Description
Outcome	A view of evidence that is equated to policy outcomes (analysis of policy), primarily in the form of policy evaluation
Process	A view of evidence that sees its role in the process of policy decision making (analysis for policy) in policy formulation
Nuanced account of the nature of evidence	A view of evidence that is diverse and encompasses a range of possible manifestations of what it is and/or should be, but also accepts that despite its contestation it has vestiges of certitude
Dynamic view of policy making	A view of the policy process that assumes an indirect or arbitrary link between evidence and policy. This is often accompanied by a long-term view of the relationship between evidence and policy, where policy making is ad hoc and complex
Evidence central to policy	A view of the relationship between evidence and policy that sees a deterministic relationship between evidence and policy where evidence is the key driver of policy. This factors out or downplays other key influences such as the role of politics and the media
Explanation of evidence selection	A view of the relationship between evidence and policy that gives a detailed account of how evidence is utilised in policy making including how it is selected

Linear model

Also referred to as the 'rational model' or 'purist model', as the name suggests, the linear model portrays a direct link between evidence production and policy decision making. It can be read as an amalgamation of what Weiss (1986) terms the 'knowledge-driven model' and the 'problem-solving model' of research utilisation. For Weiss, the knowledge-driven model is derived from the natural and/or physical sciences and assumes a linear application of research findings to policy making. This occurs along the lines of the following sequence (see Weiss, 1986, pp 31-2):

> basic research → applied research → development → application

In this formulation, basic research highlights an opportunity, applied research is then conducted to define and test these findings, appropriate technologies are then developed, and finally, application occurs. This model is premised on the assumption that because knowledge exists, it will subsequently come to be used in policy making.

Also premised on a linear sequence of the research–policy relationship, the problem-solving model suggests that research is used to fill gaps in knowledge where problems have arisen. This research can be of any variety. This process takes the following sequence (see Weiss, 1986, p 32):

> definition of pending decision › identification of missing knowledge → acquisition of social science research → interpretation of the research for the decision context → policy choice

In this model there are two main ways in which research enters the domain of the policy maker: first, the research antedates the policy problem and can then be drawn on if required, a notion not dissimilar from Kingdon's (1984) 'primeval soup'. In this respect, policy makers or their associates may go and search for, happen upon or be familiar with, prior existing research from a variety of different sources that can be tapped into. Second, there is also the notion that research may be specially commissioned to fill the knowledge gap. This is based on the assumption that 'decision makers have a clear idea of their goals and a map of acceptable alternatives and that they have identified some specific informational needs to clarify their choice' (Weiss, 1986, p 32). In this scenario, social scientists are purposively contacted to fill the knowledge gap and it is perceived that research directly influences policy choices and decisions by providing evidence, information and knowledge that help to solve and illuminate a particular policy problem.

The most common manifestation of this model lies in evidence-based medicine. The Cochrane Collaboration is premised on this, as is the social science equivalent, the Campbell Collaboration, with its experimental approach to social inquiry. For Stevens (2007a), underpinning this model is an 'instrumentally rational' approach for choosing the means to arrive at pre-determined ends, a point also recognised by Richardson and Jordan (1979, p 19), who suggest that its potential influence stems from the way it points to a clear direction in which research can shape policy. As a result, the linear model has enjoyed significant longevity. According to Lindblom, the linear model represents the 'typical' understanding of the relationship between research and policy. This stems from the fact that there is a general view that to make policies more effective, it is necessary to bring 'more information, thought and analysis into the policy-making process' (Lindblom, 1980, p 11).

This is, however, a static view of the evidence and policy relationship. It is questionable as to the extent that the policy-making process is characterised by rational decisions made on the basis of the best information (Young et al, 2002, p 18), or whether this is possible or desirable. A related point is that this model factors out issues concerning the 'fuzzy' production of data in scientific research. As illustrated in previous chapters, there are prominent schools of thought that show that social research is inevitably contested (Gallie, 1956; MacIntyre, 1973; Connolly, 1974), or part-contested (Pawson, 1989; Bryant, 1995), and there are inevitable discrepancies between the evidence producers and the requirements of the policy makers (Caplan, 1979). In effect, the knowledge produced by science 'does not readily lend itself to conversion into replicable technologies, either material or social' (Weiss, 1986, p 32). It is also important to remember that evidence often stems from the diverse interests of those responsible for its creation and carries with it ideological baggage.

This notion of diverse interests, then, is in direct contrast to the one-size-fits-all approach of the linear model's assumptions on the nature of evidence. There is, in politicised areas, conflict between groups with competing interests, which impacts on the nature of evidence production. For evidence to be utilised in decision making, it must be perceived to be useable by those in positions of power. In this sense, it helps if it is consistent with their view of the policy in question (Monaghan, 2010). There is no account in this model of these issues or other factors explaining policy formulation such as political or media imperatives. Within this model an assumption is also made that both researchers and policy makers will share a common outlook on the relationship between research and policy, and that if they do, they will agree on the research findings, which is not always the case. As a result, the insights gained from this research suggest that evidence utilisation involves issues of power, a point that is neglected in the linear account. For these reasons and notwithstanding debates concerning the inadequacies in the links between the research and policy communities (see also Chapter Three), there are various barriers to a linear version of evidence utilisation. In effect, the connection between evidence and policy is not deterministic and there is a significant element of luck involved in having relevant social research on hand for use in policy making; it cannot be viewed as a consistently linear process and other means of explaining the connection are required.

Enlightenment model

For its supporters (Janowitz, 1972; Sabatier and Jenkins-Smith, 1993b; Young et al, 2002; Pawson, 2006a), the enlightenment model represents a more urbane explanation of the evidence and policy relationship. Given one of its first expressions in the work of Weiss (1977), it refers to the arbitrary way research can enter the policy arena. Weiss and Bucuvalas (1980) suggest that this is the model that most closely typifies the relationship between research and policy formulation. Duke (2003, p 17) claims that the relationship between research and policy, in this model, is characterised by the process of 'indirect diffusion'. Thus, it offers a more dynamic perspective of the research and policy relationship. In this scenario, social science research 'percolates' into the 'informed public's consciousness' and comes to shape the way the public sees the world.

In effect, in the enlightenment model research supplies the conceptual tools to policy makers to aid their decision making. It is important to stress that within this model, single pieces, or even an entire body of research or evidence, rarely, if ever, have a direct impact on policy. Instead, the process of cumulating research and information over time serves to sensitise policy makers to new issues. In this way research influences the way policies are defined and framed and can thus help to reshape the policy agenda. It also highlights how research can be conceived as part of the process of policy making, as opposed to just helping shape the outcomes, as in the linear approach. For Weiss, enlightenment is a two-way process. On the one hand, it raises the awareness of decision makers to issues. This can help set the agenda and construct certain problems as requiring solutions. In this regard, as Banting (1986, p 42) has pointed out, the vast outputs of Richard Titmuss, among others, while documenting the failures of the welfare state, also helped to establish poverty and inequality as key policy issues in the 1960s. On the other hand, research can turn what were once potentially pressing problems into lesser policy issues and can change the boundaries over where solutions are sought.

Although the enlightenment model offers a most promising opportunity for research evidence to influence the policy agenda, critics highlight various problems, which ultimately mean that the enlightenment model is characterised by its explanatory under-ambition. First, the notion of the 'indirect diffusion' of evidence that typifies the enlightenment model can lead to 'distortion' and 'over-simplification'. The end result can be that policies become 'endarkened' (Weiss, 1986, p 39), as research clouds the issue as opposed to providing guidance on it. Second, it can take a long time for research to reach its intended audience in the policy domain, which can serve to detract from its utility and relevance. In this sense, research can easily be neglected and this can be a wasteful process. Third, and related to the point of endarkenment, as issues become more widely researched, there is an increasing chance that policy solutions become more contested and the process of research utilisation becomes more intricate. This is magnified with more social research, but is applicable to all of the sciences. Research findings do not always converge on a point that could be used as a barometer to guide policy; debates over the potency of contemporary cannabis and its links with mental illness documented in Chapter Six are indicative of this. Fourth, there is also little consideration of the fact that evidence is often not the only factor in policy decision making. For Stevens (2007a), a related and final shortcoming of this model revolves around the notion that there is no filtration process by which inadequate or invalid research is siphoned out of the process. Consequently, there is an assumption that all kinds of research, regardless of theoretical standpoint and methodological preference, have an equal chance of influencing the policy agenda. The ability to shape or affect the agenda, as we have seen, is not an equal playing field (Stevens, 2007a; Monaghan, 2010).

Political/tactical model

The political/tactical model is characterised by the selective use of evidence to satisfy the 'short-term' interests of policy makers. For Weiss (1986), the political model can be distinguished from the tactical version. In the 'political model' various interests and ideologies coalesce to pre-determine the position of policy makers on particular issues or problems. It is claimed that new research is unlikely to have a bearing on these positions and, instead, has a legitimising or justificatory function for a particular policy decision. Duke (2003, p 17) illustrates how often research that confirms existing arguments is used by advocates as 'ammunition', to attempt to neutralise opponents and persuade those who doubt the wisdom behind certain decisions. This is achieved even if the research is taken out of context.

In the 'tactical model' the findings of research are less significant than the actual process of undertaking research. Policy makers are able to procrastinate on policy formulation by stating that they are awaiting the results of ongoing research activity. Oral evidence from the Science and Technology Select Committee (2006b), between the chair, Phil Willis MP, and Vernon Coaker MP, the drugs minister at the time, illustrates this:

> **Q1205 Chairman:** In January [2006] the then Home Secretary Charles Clarke announced that a consultation paper on the ABC classification system would be published within a few weeks. There was obviously a concern about it at that time. Why has it not happened?

> **Mr Coaker:** Two things. First of all, the Home Secretary [John Reid] – in post for four weeks – has not yet taken a decision on how to proceed with the review of the classification system. With respect to the consultation document which is in draft form in the department, the view is that we will need to wait until such time as we decide how to proceed with respect to the review of the classification system and also, similarly, wait for the report of this Committee, which we want to take into account in determining the best way forward. (Science and Technology Select Committee, 2006b, Evidence 43)

In the tactical model, research findings are also used strategically. Weiss (1986, p 37) has suggested that social researchers and the research they produce can 'deflect criticism' away from the government in relation to policies that have proved unsuccessful and unpopular. Tizard (1990) likewise claims that, as a result, many research reports remain unread and are left collecting dust on the shelves of government departments.

The political/tactical model, in contrast to the linear and enlightenment versions, does start to descend the ladder of abstraction to consider the ways in which evidence is (or is not) selected in policy decision making. There is also some recognition that political imperatives, along with evidence, are central to the policy-making process and that evidence is not the only driver of policy formulation. The logic underpinning this position is, however, ultimately linear (especially in the political version). It also offers a static, short-term view of the policy-making process, factoring out the potentially unintentional or serendipitous ways evidence can come to be used in policy making. It also suggests that if evidence survives political manipulation, it will be used in decision making, but as we have seen with the sacking of David Nutt, this is not always so. In short, it offers a restrictively narrow vista of the research and policy connection, as if it was somehow deterministic and thus neglecting the unstable nature of policy development. There is, then, little consideration of issues pertaining to the often contested nature of evidence and how evidence may still not be used despite having powerful sponsors in policy debates. Of all the established models, Stevens (2007a) is most supportive of the political/tactical variety and sees an affinity between this and his evolutionary version, as we shall see.

Interactive model

On one level, the interactive model is consistent with pluralist models of policy analysis. Here, information is sought not only from (social) scientists, but also from a range of actors in the policy process. As a result, research is not the only factor influencing the decision-making process. There is also a non-linear relationship from research to policy decision. Instead, the process, according to Weiss (1986, p 35), consists of a 'disorderly set of inter-connections and back-and-forthness that defies neat diagrams'. Social scientists are just one group of a multitude of actors who can have an impact on policy. This is highly unlikely to happen as a result of some of their research impacting directly; it is more the case that researchers and policy makers engage in 'mutual consultations' that eventually move towards a policy response to a potential problem.

The interactive model offers, then, a dynamic and long-term understanding of the evidence and policy relationship. Weiss (1986, pp 35-6) draws on Donnison's (1972, p 527) experience of the legislation formulation process, to illustrate how policy makers cannot always rely on the findings of research when considering certain policy responses:

Research workers could not present authoritative findings for others to apply; neither could others commission them to find the 'correct' solution to policy problems: they were not that kind of problem. Those in the four fields from which experience had to be brought to bear [politics, technology, practice and research] contributed on equal terms. Each was an expert in a few things, ignorant about most things, offered what he [sic] could, and generally learnt more than he [sic] could teach.

To reiterate, in this account research or evidence is just one element of a more complex process. Researchers can play an important role in promoting and acting as partisans for their research. In this sense, their role is similar to that of knowledge brokers, but there are, however, clear barriers to research directly entering policy, ignorance being one of them, according to Donnison. There are omissions from the interactive model, however. For instance, no information is forthcoming about the propensity of decision makers to favour certain kinds of information over others in terms of reliability or expediency. Also, little is said about the nature of evidence and how this may contribute to its lack of efficacy. Nor is any information forthcoming about the kinds of research evidence that could be used and how they are selected.

Research as part of the intellectual enterprise of society

In a similar vein to the interactive model, the notion of research as part of the intellectual enterprise of society suggests that it is one of many 'intellectual pursuits' in society. Unlike in the other models, here the relationship between research and policy is not considered in causal terms. Unlike all the other models, in this scenario research is another 'dependent variable running side by side with policy and philosophy, journalism, history, law and criticism etc' (Weiss, 1986, p 39). Weiss (1986, p 39) suggests that in such cases 'social science and policy interact, influencing each other and being influenced by the larger fashions in social thought'. In both the interactionist model and here, there is little concern with the vagaries of evidence in terms of contestability or certitude. The view of the policy process is one of long-term trends and is, therefore, dynamic. There are, however, no appreciations of the mechanisms of selection concerning what research plays a part in policy discussions.

Dialogical model

In addition to the models identified by Weiss (1986), Bryant (1995) highlights a dialogical model of the research and policy relationship. For Bryant (1995, p 142), this is a departure from all the previous ones, which, he suggests, are 'unambiguously empiricist'. The general premise for this assertion is that little attention is given to the fact that research can be contested and, therefore, is not always useable for policy makers. In addition, instead of offering a description of the relationship between research or evidence and policy, it is very much a rallying cry for how the connection can be consolidated.

Drawing on the various works of Giddens (1982, 1984, 1987), the dialogical model, then, offers a 'post-empiricist' view of social science and research. It is keen to stress the limitations of scientifically produced knowledge from research via recourse to the 'double hermeneutic'. In effect, for Bryant, concepts and therefore knowledge are inherently contested and meaning emerges from negotiation and dialogue between relevant constituents. Key to the dialogical model, then, is Giddens' (1987, p 47) view that research will most effectively inform policy through 'an extended process of communication between researcher, policy makers and those affected by whatever issues are under consideration'. There is also a re-framing of the temporal framework of research and policy as research helps to highlight 'where the most urgent practical questions cluster' and offers 'frameworks for seeking to cope with them' (Giddens, 1987, p 47). In terms of its view of the policy-making process, this is not dissimilar to the notion of research as part of the intellectual enterprise of society, the interactive model and the enlightenment model. This premise sets the dialogical model apart from what Bryant refers to as the 'control' model of applied sociology, for which we can read linear model.

For Bryant (1995, p 147), there are three central assumptions of the dialogical model. First, social research cannot just be 'applied' to an independently given subject matter. Instead, it has to be aimed at persuading actors to expand or modify the forms of knowledge or belief that they draw on in organising their action. This should include 'direct consultation of a prolonged kind where feasible' (Bryant, 1995, p 147). Second, there is the 'mediation of cultural settings'. This involves the 'communication, via social research, of what it is like in one cultural setting to those in another' (Bryant, 1995, p 147). This requires conceptual innovation or 'reconstruction' because the desire to make positive changes involves positing 'possible worlds' of what might become, via programmes of social reforms. For Giddens (1987, p 48), novel conceptual frameworks open up possible fields of action previously unperceived either by policy makers or by the agents involved. Third, there are the practical issues of the double hermeneutic. Again reminiscent of the enlightenment model, these mean that social research produces:

> ... not sets of generalisations which facilitate instrumental control over the social world but, rather, the constant absorption of concepts and theories into that 'subject matter' they seek to analyse, constituting and reconstituting what the subject matter is. (Giddens, 1987, p 48)

Ultimately, this model casts doubt on evidence being able to inform policy unless there is a commitment to dialogue between policy makers, researchers and the wider community. The dialogical model therefore offers a dynamic view of the policy process, showing how the connection between evidence and policy is complex, but properly reconstructed evidence plays a role in the process of policy formulation. Little is mentioned about the use of evidence in the evaluation of policy. The dialogical model is more concerned with evidence in the process of decision making. A key strength, however, is the way it descends the ladder of abstraction to show how agency is a key aspect of policy deliberations. This is not immediately obvious in many of the previous models, most obviously the linear version. Little account is given, however, of the likely outcomes of consultations between the evidence producers and key policy stakeholders, only that they are necessary. A repeated theme throughout this book has been that in heavily politicised areas, dialogue between rival perspectives is rarely a guarantee of influencing agendas. It is difficult to have fruitful dialogue over issues such as required policy directions in heavily controversial areas, because deeply held views are rigid. Often, the best that can be hoped for is consensus over the less stringently held views, changes to which do not significantly alter the overall direction of policy (Sabatier and Jenkins-Smith, 1993b). Although to date this was the least abstract of models of research utilisation, caution is urged about how successful this strategy will be in overcoming the various challenges of influencing the policy process and how accurate it can be as an explanation of the connection between evidence and policy.

An overview of the established models of research utilisation

Based on the findings of this and previous chapters, and as Table 8.1 surmised, in explaining the role and nature of evidence in a heavily politicised policy area a sophisticated model is required that moves beyond simple zero–sum appreciations of the evidence and policy connection. Table 8.2 offers an overview of each model in relation to the criteria established at the outset of the chapter. It serves as a summary of the relative merits and weaknesses of all the established models of research utilisation.

Table 8.2: An overview of the applicability of existing models of research utilisation in politicised policy areas

Model/criteria	Outcome	Process	Nuanced account of the nature of evidence	Dynamic view of policy making	Evidence central to policy	Explanation of evidence selection
Linear	✓	X	X	X	✓	X
Enlightenment	X	✓	X	✓	✓	X
Political/tactical	✓	X	X	X	X	✓
Interactive	X	✓	X	✓	X	X
Intellectual enterprise	X	✓	X	✓	X	X
Dialogical	X	✓	✓	✓	X	✓

Of all the established models, none possesses all the required criteria for explaining the complexity and nuance of evidence utilisation in politicised policy areas. First and foremost, this is because none recognises that evidence utilisation can occur in both the development and in the analysis of policy. Only the dialogical variety and the political/tactical model begin to descend the ladder of abstraction to explain how evidence is selected rather than what the connection is. Although it would be fair to say that the dialogical model pays more attention to the problems associated with the nature of research (which can be transferred to the nature of evidence), the discussion is skewed by its insistence on focusing on its inherently contested nature. In a bid to develop a more comprehensive model, the discussion now turns to two newer additions to the literature that have recently been developed; the evolutionary model and the processual model. These offer alternative explanations of the evidence and policy relationship. The first is a recent addition to the existing literature and the second is an original contribution based on the shortcomings of other models.

Evolutionary model

Unlike the previous models, the evolutionary model was conceived specifically as a model of evidence-based policy rather than as a model of research utilisation. The focus of this model is to uncover the bias that occurs in evidence use in policy. The analysis commences with evidence being equated to ideas. These may be 'facts, findings or recommendations that have been produced by academics, journalists, think tanks, pressure groups or others' (Stevens, 2007a, p 28). By focusing the analysis at the level of ideas, a broader appreciation of evidence can be ascertained. This does not extend to an in–depth synopsis of the concept in terms of concern over the often contested nature of evidence, but it does illustrate how evidence can be more than the product of research. It can also be suggested that the model is premised on a pluralist view of the policy process that considers how various constituencies are embroiled in the process. Furthermore, it accepts that evidence of some kind is embedded therein. In addition, this model does not rely on a deterministic explanation that equates the phenomenon with the deliberate manipulation of evidence by policy makers.

Whereas most of the established models remain unconcerned with the 'content of the negotiations' of research use, this is precisely the concern of the evolutionary model. In short, influenced by the ideas of John (1999), according to Stevens (2007a), it is able to explain the pattern of selection of evidence used in policy making by descending the ladder of abstraction to look at how evidence selection is premised on Darwinian, 'classic' evolutionary social theory and the notion of 'survival of the fittest' (Spencer, 1891):

> Some of these ideas fit the interests of powerful groups and some do not. Ideas that do fit will find powerful supporters. Others will not. Those ideas that fit will therefore have groups and individuals that

can carry them into policy, as would a gene be reproduced if it finds a place in organisms that survive. The ideas that do not fit will tend not to be picked up by people who have the power to translate them into policy. This evolutionary advantage leads to the survival of the ideas that fit. (Stevens, 2007a, p 28)

The evolutionary model is also premised on Giddens' (1984) theory of structuration. There is a reciprocal relationship between the idea and the carrier (the powerful supporter). The idea exists within certain structural conditions that are partly created by the agents. The conditions under which an idea either flourishes or flounders are shaped in terms of what Stevens (2007a) calls the 'mechanisms of selection'. These are similar to ideas expressed in the political/tactical model of research utilisation but are ultimately more advanced and detailed. Stevens (2007a) identifies four main ones which can be illustrated with recourse to recent debates in UK drug policy.

The first mechanism focuses on how policy makers or other powerful groups may 'fish' or 'trawl' for evidence. Here, they haul in the bits they require and throw back those not needed. A common tactic employed in this regard is the use of 'repetition'. Powerful actors are able to focus the attention of potential critics towards evidence that supports a said policy, even if the evidence has been taken out of context (Weiss, 1986). In doing so, this evidence becomes a key part of the knowledge base, justifying the 'validity' of the policy to which it equates. This can be seen in the frequent proclamations that in drug policy 'treatment works', even though the evidence for this is often conflicting (Bean and Nemitz, 2004), and there is little uniformity surrounding the concept of treatment.

In a somewhat similar vein, the second mechanism suggests that powerful groups can 'farm' for or cherry-pick evidence. Here, research is specifically commissioned to provide evidence for the proposed policy, although only that which actually supports the policy is published. The drug debate is awash with examples of where this has happened. In 2003, the Prime Minister's Strategy Unit produced a report detailing the (lack of) progress of the current drug strategy. Chaired by Sir John Birt, the report amounted to a damning failure of the current approach, and was consequently not published. The detail of the report became public knowledge when it was leaked to *The Guardian*. Farming and trawling are not far removed from the linear model's description of evidence selection.

The tactic of creating 'flak' is the third mechanism. Here, a significant amount of disquiet is created over evidence that enters the public arena that is detrimental to the chosen or established policy direction. The media play a powerful role in this regard. Specific kinds of 'journalistic philosophy' have a regulatory effect when it comes to policy through the reportage of selected information about certain policies (Prideaux, 2004, p 18; see also Chibnall, 2004). Thus, if a policy suggestion departs from or conflicts with the stance advocated by the editorial board of a newspaper, then the media have the power to undermine the stance, perhaps via ridicule. The reception of evidence relating to the abandonment of the prohibition of legal drugs and that advocating more rigorous drug law enforcement have, typically, been the victim of flak. This is on the grounds that they are perceived as being contrary to the principles of evidence-based policy making, as these stances have never been fully trialled in the UK. Consequently, a degree of speculation surrounds whether they would be successful in dealing with the drug problem in the UK in terms of reducing the harm associated with drugs (Monaghan, 2010).

Imposing 'strain' on organisations or individuals who produce and advocate 'unhelpful' evidence to those in power is the final mechanism. This can be illustrated by the way that funding is allocated for the drug policy sector. This is worthy of elaboration. As Chapters Five to Seven have illustrated, groups and agents making up the rational perspective were more likely to be the recipients of central funding, being in a structurally and favourable position in the debate, and sharing a similar outlook on the nature of the problem to that of the government. To rephrase, the rational perspective's appreciation of evidence is consistent with the government's picture, hence its barriers to central funding are greatly reduced, evidenced by the way that DrugScope, a leading group in the rational perspective, receives some of its funding from central government (DrugScope, no date).

Ultimately, these mechanisms relate to the way that power is a central feature of evidence-based policy making. As Stevens (2007a, p 29) comments, the 'groups with the most power in society will be most able to implement these mechanisms'. Power is not a zero-sum game, however, and 'weaker social groups' can also attempt to 'make the mechanisms work for them' (Stevens, 2007a, p 29). This task is difficult due to restricted access to the resources required to make this happen. As a result, ideas that make it into the policy arenas are those that are fit enough to survive the filtration process, mainly from gaining powerful sponsors. Evidence that is not used is that which cannot get a powerful sponsor. In this respect, there is, again, recognition of the limitations of evidence alone in influencing decision making and that politics and the media may play a key role in deciding what is permissible in decision making. The manipulation of evidence is not merely a product of policy makers tampering with 'pure' evidence, although undoubtedly, this does happen.

An appraisal of the evolutionary model and the potential of a processual model

In understanding the role of evidence in politicised policy areas such as UK drug legislative change, the evolutionary model has much to its credit. It starts from the premise that evidence is embedded in policy debates and, unlike most of the established models, highlights how it plays a role, via the mechanisms of selection. The evolutionary understanding of evidence utilisation can be interpreted in such a way that evidence can be utilised in both the process and in the evaluations or outcomes of policy. Indeed, the mechanisms relate to the way that unhelpful evidence will be sidestepped in policy formulation, but also unhelpful evaluations of policy can be 'buried' by decision makers. For evidence to play a role in policy, it needs to be consistent with the view of what evidence ought to be from powerful groups, in this case, central government and policy makers. Although it has much to its credit, there are significant issues with the model that need to be addressed and ultimately make it problematic as an explanation for the role and nature of evidence in politicised areas. One key omission is any nuanced discussion of the nature of evidence, save for that which suggests that it can be produced by various agents and agencies and is broader than research.

To fully appraise the utility of the evolutionary model, it is worth considering it alongside the more established models. As Table 8.3 shows, the evolutionary model shares many similarities with, but also departs from, the established models of research utilisation. In a similar vein to the enlightenment and dialogical models, the evolutionary model views utilisation in the process of decision making and not just in an evaluation of outcomes. In contrast to the enlightenment view, it offers an analysis of power relationships via a discussion of the mechanisms of evidence selection. In doing so, it highlights the filtration process by which certain kinds of evidence play a role in policy making, whereas others do not. This detailed discussion of evidence selection is its most striking and original contribution to the literature on utilisation.

Table 8.3: An overview of the applicability of existing models of research utilisation and the evolutionary model in politicised policy areas

Model/criteria	Outcome	Process	Nuanced account of the nature of evidence	Dynamic view of policy making	Evidence central to policy	Explanation of evidence selection
Linear	✓	X	X	X	✓	X
Enlightenment	X	✓	X	✓	✓	X
Political/tactical	✓	X	X	X	X	✓
Interactive	X	✓	X	✓	X	X
Intellectual enterprise	X	✓	X	✓	X	X
Dialogical	X	✓	✓	✓	X	✓
Evolutionary	✓	✓	X	X	X	✓

Somewhat paradoxically, it is also this contribution that leaves the evolutionary model open to criticism. Three main and interrelated criticisms can be garnered from the above discussion. First, like the political/tactical model, the evolutionary model does not manage to move beyond a static view of the policy-making process, often assuming that there will be a direct link between evidence and policy if evidence survives the filtration process. This line of argument, it is suggested, is too close to that of the linear model. It is premised on a linear causal connection between evidence production and policy making.

The second point follows on from this. The assumption that ideas that survive the filtration process will somehow be used in policy formulation is far from a foregone conclusion or clear-cut. It is worth reminding ourselves that the Nutt et al matrix was initially adopted by the New Labour government. This was demonstrated by Vernon Coaker's statement in 2007 (referenced in Chapter Seven) that illustrated how the government was committed to using the findings of the Nutt et al matrix. The sacking of David Nutt has cast a huge question mark over this. This is not to suggest that the Nutt et al matrix has never played a part in policy deliberations, only that the connection is not straightforward, but one would be hard pressed to demonstrate that it has influenced any policy outcomes as the evolutionary model suggests it should. As a result, even evidence that survives filtration may not be used if the political conditions are not favourable. The third point is that the evolutionary model does not fully escape the spectre of teleology. At its most simple level, it has a deterministic view of the evidence and policy connection. This means that it views policies as moving towards some fixed point where they become 'evidence-based' or not. As has been stressed throughout this book, the relationship between evidence and policy is much more nuanced. Again, the recent fortunes of Professor Nutt are indicative of this.

In sum, when explaining evidence use in the context of politicised policy areas, despite being an improvement on the established models, the evolutionary model is still found wanting. Its strength lies in its specific analysis of the content of the negotiations that take place in evidence debates. This manifests itself in a consideration of the mechanisms of selection, which show the relationship between evidence and policy to be complex because of other factors impacting on the policy process. Ultimately, however, the evolutionary model is not a radical enough departure from the more established versions, particularly the problematic linear version. Consequently, a modified version of the evolutionary model has been advocated – the 'processual model' (Monaghan, 2010).

The processual model can be seen as a synthesis of various aspects of other established models. First and foremost, in this model evidence-based policy can refer to evidence use in both the process of policy formulation and its analysis. It is also preoccupied with the concept of evidence itself, which must be seen as both contested but with vestiges of consistency. It therefore advocates a view of evidence that is consistent with the modified version of formalism and thus takes its departure from the dialogical model. It shares the evolutionary model's views of the mechanisms of evidence selection. It does not, however, draw the same conclusions about utilisation. In effect, the processual model is not deterministic about the connection between evidence and policy. In common with the enlightenment model, it shares a dynamic view of the policy-making process, where there is no assumption that evidence will have a direct link with policy formulation, particularly in terms of policy outcomes. It sees the evidence and policy connection, particularly in politicised areas, as being dynamic, and in constant flux. The key aspects of the processual model are succinctly illustrated in Table 8.4, alongside those of the evolutionary model, for the purposes of comparison.

Table 8.4: The key aspects of the evolutionary and processual models

Model/criteria	Outcome	Process	Nuanced account of the nature of evidence	Dynamic view of policy making	Evidence central to policy	Explanation of evidence selection
Evolutionary	✓	✓	X	X	X	✓
Processual	✓	✓	✓	✓	X	✓

The view of the policy process advocated in the processual model is one of 'bounded pluralism' where a range of groups compete in shaping the policy agenda. This competition is open, but it is also unequal and unpredictable (Hall et al, 1975, pp 150-1). The processual model accepts that evidence is embedded in the policy process and could percolate into decision making, but this is by no means a foregone conclusion, nor is the connection straightforward. It is here that it also departs from its evolutionary kin. The analogy of evolution assumes a logical and sequential form of policy making, and that reasonable predictions can be made about likely outcomes when in receipt of sufficient knowledge. But politicised policy areas are unpredictable and unstable. A model is therefore required that can account for the to-ing and fro-ing of policy decision making. The blueprint for this can be found in Eliasian social theory, particularly in *The symbol theory* (Elias, 1991) and in *The civilizing process* (Elias, 2000), among other works.

It is not possible at this stage to offer a detailed overview of Elias's understanding of evolution (see Kilminster, 2007, for an introduction and Elias, 1991, for a comprehensive account), but for current purposes we can state that Elias deemed evolutionary accounts of social phenomenon, particularly those associated with Darwin (and Spencer), as being incomplete. Instead, for Elias, evolution or progress occurs in different layers and is the product of the needs of key groups at particular times. This is the epitome of his 'figurational' approach to social analysis. For current purposes, it is Elias's recognition that state formation and the concomitant 'reduction in contrasts' between members of society – a key aspect of the civilising process – that is of concern, in particular, the way that these developments of human society do not correspond to the teleological accounts offered by Marx or, indeed, other evolutionary analyses. According to Elias (2000, p 383):

> … [t]he movement of society and civilization certainly does not follow a straight line. Within the overall movement there are repeatedly greater

or lesser counter-movements in which the contrasts in society and the fluctuations in the behaviour of individuals, their effective outbreaks, increase again.

This civilising process challenges the uni-directional assumptions of the progress of knowledge and human society. Kilminster (2007, p 135) effectively makes this point, claiming that when formulating the theory of the civilising process, Elias anticipated the accusation of evolutionary determinism by making a distinction between 'largely irreversible biological evolution and potentially reversible social development':

> The life cycle of stars and the development of societies are not of the same kind: unlike a star, it is possible for social development to go into reverse and go back to an earlier stage, say, to feudal social relations or to a stage where mutual identification is less. With this point in mind, Elias thought of civilizing and decivilizing processes, for example, as going hand in hand. (Kilminster, 2007, p 135)

Although Kilminster is referring to Elias's discussion of large-scale, macro-social processes, this provides a useful model or analogy for policy development and the evidence and policy relationship. The key phrase is 'potentially reversible social development'. As this is the case, there is always the potential for policies to wax and wane, reverse or move forward. This may be a product of new evidence, but it could also be because of political imperatives, and relates primarily to the fact that policies are made by specific configurations of agents who act of their own volition, making choices within the confines of what is possible. These choices are not always predictable, however. Indeed, one of the only predictable aspects of politicised policies is that they are inherently unpredictable. It is this nuance that is ultimately absent from the evolutionary model.

The processual model is put forward here as a realistic account of the evidence and policy connection. The key contribution made by the model, however, is its focus on the minutiae of evidence and how this can be operationalised as being both contested but having vestiges of certitude. To reiterate, this is because evidence and policy are always in a constant state of flux. The dynamic nature of drugs policy as a politicised area is illustrated neatly by reminding ourselves of the purpose of the ACMD, whose remit is to keep 'under review' the UK drug situation with respect to the drugs which 'are being or appear to them likely to be misused' (Science and Technology Select Committee, 2006b, p 13). In effect, they have a monitoring brief and this is precisely because the drug situation is constantly changing. The emergence on the media and political agenda of so-called 'legal highs' such as Gamma-Butyrolactone (GBL), Benzylpiperazine (BZP) and Mephedrone over recent years is indicative of this, as obviously is the to-ing and fro-ing over cannabis.

The processual model also offers a view on the tumultuous relationship between evidence and policy. The bridging of the gap between the two communities of evidence and policy is an ongoing problem, particularly in politicised areas. Whereas knowledge brokering, knowledge transfer or action research offer the potential to increase communication between the two communities, thus maximising the scope of evidence in influencing policy, they are likely to flounder in politicised areas because of the deeply held views that the protagonists hold which are fundamentally resistant to change. As a result, if research or evidence is utilised in policy then this is likely to percolate over time rather than inform directly. Consequently, the evidence into the policy process is characterised by one certainty; this is that the connection is always uncertain. With this in mind, the design, realisation and rallying cry of the processual model is perhaps best expressed by Rein's intuitive assertion that 'social science does contribute to policy and practice, but the link is neither consensual, graceful nor self-evident' (Rein, 1976, p 12).

Summary

It has been argued in this chapter that for various reasons the established models of research utilisation do not translate successfully into models of evidence-based policy making in politicised areas. First and foremost, they say little about the tumultuous nature of evidence (or research) itself. In effect, the term evidence-based policy making is treated as if it was understood in the same way by all those who appropriate it, leaving behind a scent of universalism and essentialism. A closer appreciation of the role and nature of evidence in UK drug classification policy has revealed that, in reality, 'evidence' is highly contested, albeit with vestiges of consistency. Much of this contestation, but not all, comes from the fact that politicised policy areas are hotly debated by stakeholders who have particular normative views on what should (and does) count as evidence in these domains. In addition, an often overlooked feature of policy making is its dynamism. This is accelerated in politicised areas with the knock-on effect that evidence production is, likewise an iterative process.

The established models of research utilisation also operate at too high a level of abstraction and pay scant attention to how evidence comes to play a role in the policy-making process. In this regard, the newer additions to the literature offer significant potential. These illustrate not only what the link is between evidence and policy making, but also precisely how this relationship is consolidated. The evolutionary model pioneered the journey down the ladder of abstraction to explain how evidence comes to be used in policy, but it is ultimately premised on problematic logic and has a short-term outlook on the relationship. By contrast, the processual model stops short of making deterministic assumptions. In doing so, it advocates a view of the policy process that is characterised by ad hoc, back-and-forth decision making, typical of highly politicised areas.

NINE

Conclusion

> Almost everyone can appreciate, intuitively, the advantages of evidence-based policy; it is another matter entirely to make this concept clear, operational and valid. And it is another matter still to know if and how the field should respond. (Feuer et al, 2002, p 4)

In contemporary society, evidence-based policies have become the benchmark by which most policies are judged. As suggested in Chapter Two, in recent times throughout the UK, the US, Europe and further afield, a range of agencies has been installed with the mission to gather, review, synthesise, interpret and broker evidence in order to better inform public policy. This has ushered in the 'evidence age'. Mulgan (2005, p 216) suggests that the 'Western' world is currently in an era where the demand for knowledge is paramount and where today's citizens are 'far more educated, knowledgeable and confident than their predecessors'. This manifests itself in the fact that they use scientific knowledge to inform a range of choices, for example, from business decisions to dietary preferences. This scientific knowledge is tied in with the notion of 'best practice' that has become paramount in various policy spheres. For Mulgan (2005, p 216), governments are often cajoled into searching for this by the increasing influence of various transnational bodies such as the UN, the World Bank, the IMF, the OECD and the EU. This search for best practice and spirit of coordination is leading to the creation of an evidence-based policy infrastructure across these domains.

Most European and other 'Western Hemisphere' governments have committed themselves, then, to a programme of evidence-based policy under the aegis of knowledge-based societies. Here, the development of public policy increasingly calls on independent, expert inquiry. Evidence-based policy is the latest incarnation of this trend. Although in the UK evidence-based policy making became an established part of the New Labour project, the relationship between research and policy is long and uncertain. The continuing friction between the two communities can be traced via the colourful titles of, and key phrases from, landmark papers and monographs in the debate, for example: *Knowledge for what?* (Lynd, 1940), *Can science save us?* (Lundberg, 1947), *Nothing as practical as a good theory* (Lewin, 1952), 'The (f)utility of knowledge' (Gusfield, 1975), *Why sociology does not apply* (Scott and Shore, 1979), 'No good applied research goes unpunished' (Rossi, 1987), *The impossible science* (Turner and Turner, 1990), 'The haphazard connection: social science and public policy' (Weiss, 1995) and 'Rationality can be dangerous to your reasoning' (Fine, 1998).

The path of the evidence movement has rarely run smoothly. Almost since its incarnation, recognisable criticisms of the endeavour emerged. These were documented in Chapter Three. They generally revolved around the mutual suspicion that exists between the evidence providers (the research community) and evidence consumers (politicians and policy makers). Attempts to mediate between the two communities exist, but these are also beset with problems, premised as they are on encouraging dialogue between groups with very different occupational functions. These issues are magnified in heavily politicised areas, primarily a result of problems in generating evidence in such domains and the fact that such policy areas are politically sensitive so that political imperatives are more of a driver of policy than evidence. Indeed, it was these issues that, for instance, led Scott and Shore (1979) to their gloomy conclusion about the applicability of the social sciences in policy.

The maxim that 'evidence never speaks for itself' is nowhere more apposite than in adversarial policy domains. These are arenas where the political stakes are high, where there is intense media scrutiny of policy, where policy options are considerable and multi-layered, where there is a lack of consensus on its direction and where there is prolonged conflict between competing interest groups. Often, these are policy areas lying at the intersection of autonomous department boundaries. In such instances debates over the evidence base for policies are heavily contested, with different interest groups declaiming the significance of quite different bodies of research.

A central theme running through this book is that in contemporary society, the spectre of this history remains, but the lure of the evidence movement is strong. These pull analysts and advocates in differing directions in their accounts of evidence use in policy. Debates in UK drug classification are indicative of this and have been the case study through which the turbulent nature of evidence has been explored in this book. In the aftermath of the publication of the Science and Technology Select Committee report (2006b) into the evidence base for the UK drug classification system, derivatives of these two positions emerged. Independent research commissioned for the inquiry suggested that 'recent evidence is feeding into new policy' (Levitt et al, 2006, p xvi). By contrast, based on its findings, MacDonald and Das (2006) claimed with some assertiveness that the UK drug classification system is an 'un-evidence-based mess'. In this scenario, policies are seen, in effect, to be either wholly evidence-based or wholly evidence-free. The former position represents a positive, zero-sum stance and the latter a negative, zero-sum stance.

An integral argument of this book has been that understandings of the evidence and policy relationship in highly politicised areas are frequently underpinned by these linear, zero-sum conceptualisations of the relationship. But if evidence-based policy is to continue to have currency then more sophisticated analysis is required. Politicised policy areas can gain from more nuanced accounts of the evidence and policy connection, but as it stands these are areas where zero-sum accounts flourish. Typically, evidence is most frequently considered to be missing from the process.

Scepticism of the impact of social research is stronger than claims for its success in influencing policy. No matter how vociferously they are made, and no matter how understandable, zero-sum views do not accurately describe the relationship between evidence and policy. Chapters Six and Seven reported on some primary research carried out by the author into appreciations over the evidence base for UK drug classification decision making. It was suggested that the negative zero-sum account is paradoxical because it assumes policies to be evidence-free, while in some cases accepting that evidence was present in the decision–making process. The positive zero-sum account is also problematic because it assumes that favourable evidence will be used in the process, but there is always evidence that is missing. These chapters also revealed that much confusion abounds on the nature of evidence itself and its role in policy, which goes some way to explaining often opposing accounts of whether the same policy is evidence-based or not. In addition, there is the possibility – particularly in heavily politicised areas – that decisions made will be reversed or renegotiated in some way, due to the dynamic nature of policy formulation, and any attempt to explain the connection between evidence and policy should account for this.

The true picture is, then, characterised by complexity and opacity. Indeed, Saunders (2005, p 385) has noted that political strategies and functions are hugely significant factors in decision making and with this in mind the role of scholarly research 'may be subtle and hard to trace'. This is undoubtedly true, but 'hard to trace' does not equate to 'non-existent' or not evidence-based. Instead, it has been argued here that evidence of some kind is embedded in the decision-making process and the challenge for analysts is to unpick the mechanisms by which it comes to play a role in policy. In other words, the focus on uncovering the mechanisms of evidence use in the context of heavy politicisation starts with the premise that it is mistaken to label heavily politicised policy areas as being un-evidenced or evidence-free. As it is widely understood, even by enthusiastic adherents, that the influence of evidence on policy is fragile and often trumped by political considerations, models of research utilisation thus require a sophisticated understanding of the political mechanisms through which evidence is selected and filtered. So while 'evidence' has become a vital part of the argot of modern policy, its usage is always mediated, as when policy makers trawl or cherry-pick for evidence favouring their plans, or when they squeeze funding, load advisory committees and procrastinate over publication. In practice, the use of expertise turns out to be an admixture of evidence-based policy and policy-based evidence. It is not advocated that policies are, or can be, free of political interference (Leicester, 1999); but on the other hand, this does not preclude the utilisation of evidence in decision making.

The mistaken perception of zero-sum conceptualisations is their reliance on a linear view of the evidence and policy connection. Black (2001) suggests that these can factor out of the equation a commonly held view detailing the interactive relationship of evidence and policy. The various different ways of considering the relationship between evidence and policy have been widely documented and were covered in Chapter Eight. The linear model represents one such account, albeit one that is widely discredited. For current purposes, the established models cannot explain the subtleties of evidence utilisation. A key reason for this concerns the fact that evidence as a concept differs to a significant extent from that of research. In recent times there has been revived interest in this area and more recent additions to the literature can also be identified in the form of an evolutionary model (Stevens, 2007a) and a processual model (Monaghan, 2010). These are specifically models of evidence utilisation. The main contribution of the former was to address the pertinent issue of the way that evidence is selected in decision making. The main contribution of the latter was to factor into the account the complexity surrounding the concept of evidence and how this can (and should) be operationalised. A key feature of the processual model of evidence utilisation is that evidence is a complex concept. It has many internal variants, stemming from conflict within the policy subsystem over how it is perceived.

As this is the case, this book makes the case that of all the available theories and methods, the processual model offers the most potential for exploring and explaining the evidence and policy connection in heavily politicised areas. It is underpinned by a formalist understanding of concept formation, which recognises the complexity of the concept of evidence. It also underscores a view of decision making that does not restrict the role of evidence to one of policy outcomes, in other words, 'analysis of policy'. But evidence also needs to be considered as part of the process of policy making, or as 'analysis for policy' (Gordon et al, 1993, p 5). In this sense, evidence is seen to be embedded in the decision-making process, but does not assume a determinist account of utilisation. The processual model can, therefore, account for the many perturbations that impact on the policy process, but importantly it avoids viewing policy as a static system. In this way, it differs from most established models of research utilisation. These have an explanatory end point, whether this is research informing policy, as in the linear approach and even in the evolutionary model, or whether this relates to the way research (metaphorically) gathers dust on shelves in government departments. The processual model has no such point as it is premised on a model of the policy process that stresses dynamism. As Fischer (2003, p 95) points out, policy making is 'an ongoing process with no clearly demarcated beginnings or terminations'. And so it is with evidence-based policy. The processual model outlines an ongoing process between evidence production and policy formulation. It does not accept the inevitability of favourable and powerful research being utilised, although it accepts that this often happens. Herein lays an affiliation with realism and the enlightenment tradition (Pawson, 2002; Sanderson, 2002).

A word of caution is needed at this stage, however. The efficacy of the processual model in explaining evidence utilisation is tentatively advocated. This tentativeness stems from the realisation that generalising from one case study to other areas of policy is problematic. This is typical of any small *n* analysis. Generalisation must, however, be the goal of research. Hammersley (1992, p 68) has pointed out how research should provide 'information that is both true and relevant to some legitimate public concern'. In this sense, it is intended that the processual model be put to empirical test in other, similar areas of policy. Other policy areas have been alluded to as examples illustrating how evidence utilisation is complex; these include alcohol policy, tobacco smoking prevention policies and debates in climate change science. All are highly politicised and this is not an exhaustive list. Although beyond the scope of the current inquiry, all would perfectly suit the remit of closer scrutiny of evidence utilisation. Readers may have other examples in mind. In effect, the full theoretical implications remain to be seen, but it is contended here that the processual model offers some potential for further use in the research utilisation and evidence-based policy literature, particularly in the context of politicised areas. With the model in place, it is worth pausing to ponder on the future of the movement.

Whereunto for evidence-based policy?

As indicated, most European and other 'Western hemisphere' governments have committed themselves to a programme of evidence-based policy. Here, the development of public policy increasingly calls on independent, expert inquiry. At exactly the same time, the study of the social or public policy-making process has become the study of the evidence-based policy process. In effect, an industry is springing up that no longer focuses on the analysis of the policy-making process but is concentrating on an analysis of the evidence-based policy-making process (see, for example, Dobrow et al, 2004, 2006; Culyer and Lomas, 2006; Jewell and Bero, 2007; Nutley et al, 2007; Stevens, 2007a; Jung and Nutley, 2008; Monaghan, 2008). This represents a delicate but significant shift in the paradigm.

One by-product of this movement has been to pay particular attention to the way that 'evidence' is conceived by those engaged in the evidence-based policy-making process on any level. Recent publications from the Research Unit for Research Utilisation at the University of Edinburgh have moved away from a focus on 'what works' to consider the way evidence is utilised in policy formulation (see, for example, Nutley et al, 2007). In the UK, the institutions and research clusters that were formed in the initial expansion of the evidence-based movement are becoming increasingly reflective and reflexive about the whole phenomenon. This can be seen in the way the Centre for Evidence-based Policy has now become the Centre for Evidence and Policy in light of changing appreciations over what the connection is between the two aspects of the phenomenon (Boaz et al, 2008). The current account can be added to this list.

The first step in the argument has been that the bolder claims of evidence-based policy need to be muted. This proposition is not new. Indeed, Nutley et al (2002, pp 76-7) suggest that when the expectations of evidence are toned down, that is, anticipation that evidence production will lead to more effective policies, there is more cause for optimism over the way research findings can be incorporated into policy making (see, for example, Weiss, 1999). In recognition of similar issues, other authors have adopted alternative maxims to explain the evidence and policy relationship. 'Evidence-informed' policy (see, for example, Chalmers, 2005), or 'evidence-inspired' policy (Duncan, 2005) are phrases that have been coined to highlight potential discrepancies between evidence production and policy making. This book proposes a new addition to this list. Drawing on its key thesis that we now live in an evidence age where evidence is embedded in the policy process, the message is that 'evidence within policy' best describes the relationship.

This is a message of cautious optimism. Supporters of consistently inconsistent sports teams will know only too well that it is hope that kills you in the end, but adopting this realistic standpoint can be healthy. We have witnessed how initial enthusiasm for evidence-based policy has been replaced with doubt and, at times, despair, yet the evidence-based policy message is spreading. As was demonstrated in Chapter Two, the knowledge utilisation agenda is central to EU governance and its member states. It has also filtered into the consciousness of politicians and policy makers in the US (Clear, 2010). It is hoped that this cautionary tale can contribute to realistic expectations in jurisdictions where the evidence organism is even more embryonic. At the same time, the future of evidence-based policy in this guise remains uncertain. What is beyond doubt is that the relationship between the ivory tower and the corridors of power will continue to be of interest for some, and a concern for others. In the UK it is now commonplace for research councils to ask applicants searching for funding to demonstrate the 'impact' of their research, which, although not exclusively, equates to policy relevance. This has coincided with or can be tied to the increasing interest in knowledge exchange or knowledge translation. The lessons from evidence-based policy making can, and should, speak to these debates, particularly advocating that the relationship is not always self-evident and is more often than not characterised by percolation of evidence into policy over time; it would be unwise to suggest otherwise.

It would be a missed opportunity if this message for moderation was not delivered to commentators, policy makers and evidence suppliers in the drugs and criminal justice fields. At the time of writing, a new body has been established by Professor David Nutt – the Independent Scientific Committee on Drugs (previously the Independent Council on Drug Harms) – which vows to pursue an agenda close to the one which led to Professor Nutt being removed from his post as chair of the ACMD. This will entail assessing the science that is likely to challenge 'some of the aberrations' in the current MDA 1971 (Boseley, 2010). This is expected to keep the evidence and drug policy debate alive for some time.

Meanwhile, Professor Les Iversen – a retired University of Oxford Professor of Pharmacology – has taken interim charge of a streamlined ACMD. Although Iversen is the author of more than 350 scientific papers and has a long-standing advisory relationship with the government, it was his views on cannabis regulation that prompted interest in his background in certain sections of the media, in particular, his claim in 2003 that cannabis is one of the 'safer' recreational drugs and that it was misclassified over 50 years ago (BBC, 2010). Yet this is not the central message of his book or, indeed, its second edition published in 2008. This sweep of the science of cannabis entails interesting sections on culture, history and policy and leaves the reader with a final message, summarised from a *Lancet* editorial in 2004. This resonates with the message put forward here:

> Cannabis can cause anxiety, agitation and anger amongst politicians. The consequences of this cannabis-induced psychological stress syndrome (CIPDS) include over-reaction with respect to legislation and politics…. (cited in Iversen, 2008, p 241)

Politicians are not alone in this. When debates turn to the evidence base for drug policy formulation, agitation and anxiety are symptoms displayed by many policy actors, and misleading explanations of evidence-based policy making abound as a result.

The processual model is put forward as a stepping-stone in curbing this impulse. It recognises that many other factors are involved in the decision-making process. These include the impact of politics and the media. To reiterate, the processual model warns against drawing the conclusion that these are somehow obstacles to the utilisation of evidence in policy. In effect, it challenges the widespread assumption that heavily politicised policies are evidence-free, but also challenges supporters of the said policies to refrain from claiming them to be wholly evidence-based. The quest is to show the role and nature of evidence in the decision-making process and to contribute towards a toning down, and more realistic appreciation, of what evidence-based policy is and can be. It ultimately assumes that research is frequently 'exploited' in decision making. This may sound like a negative conclusion, but it is worth pausing to consider the *Collins English Dictionary* definition of 'exploit':

> **exploit** 1) notable deed or feat, especially one that is heroic; 2) to take advantage (of a person, situation etc) for one's own end; 3) to make best use of

It is for the reader to decide which aspect most accurately explains the evidence and policy connection. What is hopefully beyond debate is that evidence utilisation is more than simply a case of yes or no. It is also hoped that the current endeavour can contribute towards more reasoned debate over the use of evidence and what this entails. That will be a notable deed.

References

Academy of Medical Sciences, The (2008) *Brain science, addiction and drugs*, London: The Academy of Medical Sciences.

ACMD (Advisory Council on the Misuse of Drugs) (1988) *AIDS and drug misuse*, London: Home Office.

ACMD (2002) *The classification of cannabis under the Misuse of Drugs Act 1971*, London: Home Office.

ACMD (2005) *Further consideration of the classification of cannabis under the Misuse of Drugs Act 1971*, London: Home Office.

ACMD (2008) *Cannabis: Classification and public health*, London: Home Office.

ACMD (2009) *MDMA ('ecstasy'): A review of its harms and classification under the Misuse of Drugs Act 1971*, London: Home Office.

Adler, M.W. (1995) 'Human subject issues in drug abuse research – College on Problems of Drug Dependence', *Drug and Alcohol Dependence*, vol 37, no 2, pp 167-75.

Albaek, E. (1995) 'Between knowledge and power: utilization of social science in public policy making', *Policy Sciences*, vol 28, pp 79-100.

Aldridge, J., Parker, H. and Measham, F. (1999) *Drug trying and drug use across adolescence: A longitudinal study of young people's drug taking in two regions of Northern England*, DPAS Paper 1, London: Drugs Prevention Advisory Service.

Alkin, M.C. (2004) *Evaluation roots: Tracing theorists' views and influences*, Thousand Oaks, CA: Sage Publications.

Anderson, L. (2003) *Pursuing truth: Exercising power: Social science and public policy in the twenty-first century*, New York: Columbia University Press.

Apparduri, A. (1997) 'The research ethic and the spirit of internationalism', *Items*, Social Science Research Council (December), vol 51, no 4, pp 55-60.

Arseneault, L., Cannon, M., Witton, J. and Murray, R.M. (2004) 'Causal association between cannabis and psychosis: examination of the evidence', *British Journal of Psychiatry*, vol 184, no 2, pp 110-17.

Bache, I. and George, S. (2006) *Politics in the European Union* (2nd edn), Oxford: Oxford University Press.

Banting, K.G. (1986) 'The social policy process', in M. Bulmer, K.G. Banting, S.S. Blume, M. Carley and C.H. Weiss (eds) *Social science and social policy*, London: Allen Unwin, pp 41-59.

Barton, A. (2003) *Illicit drugs: Use and control*, London: Routledge.

Baumgartner, F. and Jones, B. (1993) *Agendas and instability in American politics*, Chicago, IL: Chicago University Press.

BBC (2009) 'Ecstasy "should be class B drug"' (http://news.bbc.co.uk/1/hi/uk/7882708.stm).

BBC (2010) 'Profile: Leslie Iversen, chief drugs adviser' (http://news.bbc.co.uk/1/hi/uk/8456726.stm).

Bean, P. (2002) *Drugs and crime*, Cullompton: Willan.

Bean, P. and Nemitz, T. (eds) (2004) *Drug treatment: What works?*, Abingdon: Routledge.

Beck, U. (1992) *Risk society: Towards a new modernity*, Cambridge: Polity Press.

Bennett, T. and Holloway, K. (2005) *Understanding drugs, alcohol and crime*, Buckingham: Open University Press.

Bergeron, H. and Griffiths, P. (2006) 'Drifting towards a more common approach to a more common problem: epidemiology and the evolution of a European drug policy' in R. Hughes, R. Lart and P. Higate (eds), *Drugs: Policy and politics*, Maidenhead: Open University Press.

Berridge, V. (1984) 'Drugs and social policy: the establishment of drug control in Britain 1900–1930', *British Journal of Addiction*, vol 79, pp 17-29.

Berridge, V. (2005) 'The "British system" and its history: myth and reality', in J. Strang and M. Gossop (eds) *Heroin addiction and the British system*, Abingdon: Routledge, pp 7-16.

Berridge, V. and Edwards, G. (1981) *Opium and the people*, New Haven, CT: Yale University Press.

Black, N. (2001) 'Evidence-based policy: proceed with care', *British Medical Journal*, vol 323, no 7307, pp 275-80.

Blackman, S. (2004) *Chilling out: The cultural politics of substance consumption, youth and drug policy*, Buckingham: Open University Press.

Blaikie, N. (2000) *Designing social research*, Cambridge: Polity Press.

Blumer, H. (1956) 'Sociological analysis and the "variable"', *American Sociological Review*, vol 19, pp 3-10.

Blunkett, D. (2000) 'Influence or irrelevance: can social science improve government?', *Research Intelligence*, vol 71, March.

Boaz, A. and Pawson, R. (2005) 'The perilous road from evidence to policy: five journeys compared', *Journal of Social Policy*, vol 34, pp 175-94.

Boaz, A., Grayson, L., Levitt, R. and Solesbury, W. (2008) 'Does evidence-based policy work? Learning from the UK experience', *Evidence & Policy*, vol 4, no 2, pp 233-53.

Bochel, H. and Duncan, S. (eds) (2007) *Making policy in theory and practice*, Bristol: The Policy Press.

Boekhout van Solinge, T. (1999) 'Dutch drug policy in a European context', *Journal of Drug Issues*, vol 29, no 3, pp 511-28.

Boister, N. (2001) 'Decriminalising the personal use of cannabis in the United Kingdom: does international law leave room for manoeuvre?', *Criminal Law Review*, pp 171-83.

Booth, T. (1988) *Developing policy research*, Aldershot: Gower.

Boseley, S. (2010) 'Sacked drugs adviser David Nutt launches rival committee', *The Guardian* (www.guardian.co.uk/society/2010/jan/15/david-nutt-drugs-independent-committee).

Boswell, C. (2008) 'The political functions of expert knowledge: knowledge and legitimation in European Union immigration policy', *Journal of European Public Policy*, vol 15, no 4, pp 471-88.

Braybrooke, D. and Lindblom, C.E. (1963) *A strategy of decision*, New York: Free Press.

Bridgman, P. and Davies, G. (2000) *The Australian policy handbook*, Sydney: Allen Unwin.

Brocklehurst, N. and Liabo, K. (2004) 'Evidence nuggets: promoting evidence-based practice', *Community Practitioner*, vol 77, no 10, pp 371-5.

Bryant, C.G.A. (1995) *Practical sociology: Post-empiricism and the reconstruction of theory and application*, Cambridge: Polity Press.

Buchanan, J. and Young, L. (2000) 'The war on drugs – a war on drug users?', *Drugs: Education, Prevention and Policy*, vol 7, no 4, pp 409-22.

Bullock, H., Mountford, J. and Stanley, R. (2001) *Better policy making*, London: Cabinet Office, Centre for Management and Policy Studies.

Bulmer, M. (1982) *The uses of social research: Social investigation in public policy making*, London: Allen Unwin.

Bulmer, M. (1986) 'The policy process and the place in it of social research', in M. Bulmer, K.G. Banting, S.S. Blume, M. Carley and C.H. Weiss (eds) *Social science and social policy*, London: Allen Unwin.

Bulmer, M., Banting, K.G., Blume, S.S., Carley, M. and Weiss, C. (eds) (1986) *Social science and social policy*, London: Allen Unwin.

Burawoy, M. (2005) 'For public sociology', *British Journal of Sociology*, vol 56, no 2, pp 259-94.

Cabinet Office (1998) *Tackling drugs to build a better Britain*, London: The Stationery Office.

Cabinet Office (1999a) *Modernising government*, London: The Stationery Office.

Cabinet Office (1999b) *Professional policy making for the twenty-first century*, London: Cabinet Office.

Caldwell, R. (2002) *Public policy resource guide*, Denver, CO: Institute for Public Policy Studies, University of Denver.

Callinicos, A. (1999) *Social theory: A historical introduction*, Cambridge: Polity Press.

Campbell, D.T. (1969) 'Reforms as experiments', *American Psychologist*, vol 24, pp 409-29.

Campbell, D.T. (1978) 'Reforms as experiments', in J. Bynner and K.M. Stribley (eds) *Social research: Principles and procedures*, Oxford: Oxford University Press, pp 79-112.

Campbell, H. (2002) 'Evidence-based policy: the continuing search for effective policy processes', *Planning Theory and Practice*, vol 3, no 1, pp 89-90.

Caplan, N. (1977) 'A minimal set of conditions necessary for the utilization of social science knowledge in policy formulation at the national level', in C.H. Weiss (ed) *Using research in public policy making*, Lexington, MA: Lexington-Heath, pp 183-97.

Caplan, N. (1979) 'The two communities: theory and knowledge utilization', *American Behavioural Scientist*, vol 22, no 3, pp 459-70.

Castells, M. (1996) *The rise of the network society*, Oxford: Blackwell.

Chalmers, I. (2005) 'If evidence-informed policy works in practice, does it matter if it doesn't work in theory?', *Evidence & Policy*, vol 1, no 2, pp 227-42.

Chancer, L. and McLaughlin, E. (2007) 'Public criminologies', *Theoretical Criminology*, vol 11, no 2, pp 155-73.

Chatwin, C. (2003) 'Drug policy developments within the European Union: the destabilizing effects of Dutch and Swedish drug policies', *British Journal of Criminology*, vol 43, no 3, pp 567-82.

Chibnall, S. (2004) *Law and order news: An analysis of crime reporting in the British press* (2nd edn), London: Routledge.

Cicourel, A.V. (1964) *Method and measurement in sociology*, New York: Free Press.

Cini, M. (1996) *The European Commission: Leadership, organisation and culture in the EU administration*, Manchester: Manchester University Press.

Cini, M. (2008) 'European Commission reform and the origins of the European Transparency Initiative', *Journal of European Public Policy*, vol 15, no 5, pp 743-60.

Clarence, E. (2002) 'Technocracy reinvented: the new evidence-based policy movement', *Public Policy and Administration*, vol 17, no 3, pp 1-11.

Clark, G. and Kelly, L. (2005) *New directions for knowledge transfer and knowledge brokerage in Scotland*, Edinburgh: Social Research and Knowledge Transfer Office (www.scotland.gov.uk/Resource/Doc/69582/0018002.pdf).

Clarke, J. (2004) 'Dissolving the public realm? The logics and limits of neo-liberalism', *Journal of Social Policy*, vol 33, no 1, pp 27-48.

Clarke, J., Gerwitz, S. and McLaughlin, E. (eds) (2000) *New managerialism, new welfare?*, London: Sage Publications.

Clear, T.R. (2010) 'Policy and evidence: the challenge of the American Society of Criminology: 2009 presidential address to the American Society of Criminology', *Criminology*, vol 48, no 1, pp 1-25.

Cochrane, A. (1972) *Effectiveness and efficiency: Random reflections on health services*, London: Nuffield Provincial Hospitals.

Cohen, S. (1972) *Folk devils and moral panics*, London: Palladin.

Colebatch, H.K. (2002) *Policy* (2nd edn), Buckingham: Open University Press.

Collin, M. (1997) *Altered state: The story of ecstasy culture and acid house*, London: Serpent's Tail.

Connolly, W.E. (1974) *Terms of political discourse*, Oxford: Martin Robertson.

Coomber, R., Morris, C. and Dunn, L. (2000) 'How the media do drugs: quality control and the reporting of drug issues in the UK print media', *International Journal of Drug Policy*, vol 11, no 3, pp 217-25.

Cope, S. (2001) 'Analysing criminal justice policy making: towards a policy networks approach?', in M. Ryan, S.P. Savage and D.S. Wall (eds) *Policy networks in criminal justice*, London: Palgrave, pp 1-23.

Crowther-Dowey, C. (2007) 'The police and drugs', in M. Simpson, T. Shildrick and R. MacDonald (eds) *Drugs in Britain: Supply, consumption and control*, Basingstoke: Macmillan, pp 108-24.

Culyer, A.J. and Lomas, J. (2006) 'Deliberative processes and evidence-informed decision-making in healthcare: do they work and how might we know?', *Evidence & Policy*, vol 2, no 3, pp 357-71.

Dahl, R.A. (1961) *Who governs? Democracy and power in an American city*, New Haven, CT: Yale University Press.

Dahl, R.A. and Lindblom, C.E. (1953) *Politics, economics and welfare*, New York: Harper and Brothers.

Daly, M. (2003) 'Governance and social policy', *Journal of Social Policy*, vol 32, no 1, pp 113-28.

Davies, H.T.O., Nutley, S.M. and Smith, P.C. (eds) (2000a) *What works? Evidence-based policy and practice in public services*, Bristol: The Policy Press.

Davies, H.T.O., Nutley, S.M. and Smith, P.C. (2000b) 'Introducing evidence-based policy and practice in public services', in H.T.O. Davies, S.M. Nutley and P.C. Smith (eds) *What works? Evidence-based policy and practice in public services*, Bristol: The Policy Press, pp 1-12.

DH (Department of Health) (1995) *Tackling drugs together*, London: DH.

Dobrow, M.J., Goel, V. and Upshur, R.E.G. (2004) 'Evidence-based health policy: context and utilisation', *Social Science and Medicine*, vol 58, no 2, pp 207-17.

Dobrow, M.J., Goel, V., Lemieux-Charles, L. and Black, N.A. (2006) 'The impact of context on evidence utilisation: a framework for expert groups developing health policy recommendations', *Social Science and Medicine*, vol 63, no 7, pp 1811-24.

Dobson, R. (2009) 'Insiderness, involvement and emotions: impacts for methods, knowledge and social research', *People, Place and Policy Online*, vol 3, no 3.

Donnison, D. (1972) 'Research for policy', *Minerva*, vol 10, no 4, pp 519-36.

Dorn, N. and Jamieson, A. (2001) *European drugs laws: Room for manoeuvre*, London: DrugScope.

Dorn, N. and South, N. (eds) (1987) *A land fit for heroin*, Aldershot: Gower.

Dostoevsky, F. (1866 [2000]) *Crime and punishment*, London: Wordsworth Classics.

Dowding, K. (1995) 'Model or metaphor? A critical review of the policy networks approach', *Political Studies*, vol 43, no 1, pp 136-58.

Dowding, K. (2001) 'There must be end to confusion: policy networks, intellectual fatigue, and the need for political science methods courses in British universities', *Political Studies*, vol 49, no 1, pp 89-105.

Downes, D. (1977) 'The drug addict as folk devil', in P. Rock (ed) *Drugs and politics*, New Brunswick, NJ: Transaction Books, pp 89-97.

DrugScope (no date) 'About us' (www.drugscope.org.uk/aboutus).

Duke, K. (2002) 'Getting beyond the "official" line: reflections on dilemmas of access, knowledge and power in researching policy networks', *Journal of Social Policy*, vol 31, no 1, pp 39-59.

Duke, K. (2003) *Drugs, prisons and policy making*, London: Palgrave.

Duncan, S. (2005) 'Towards evidence-inspired policy making', *Social Sciences*, vol 61, pp 10-11.

Dunlop, C.A. (2007) 'Up and down the pecking order, what matters and when in issue definition: the case of RbST in the EU', *Journal of European Public Policy*, vol 14, no 1, pp 39-58.

Durkheim, E. (1952) *Suicide: A study in sociology*, London: Routledge and Kegan Paul.

Easton, D. (1965) *Systems analysis of political life*, New York: John Wiley.

Elias, N. (1978) *What is sociology?*, New York: Columbia University Press.

Elias, N. (ed) (1991) *The symbol theory*, London: Sage Publications.

Elias, N. (2000) *The civilizing process* (revised edn), Oxford: Blackwell.

EMCDDA (European Monitoring Centre for Drugs and Drug Addiction) (2004) *An overview of cannabis potency in Europe*, Lisbon: EMCDDA.

EMCDDA (2009) *The state of the drugs problem in Europe: Annual report, 2009*, Lisbon: EMCDDA.

Erikksen, T. (2006) *Engaging anthropology*, Oxford: Berg.

European Commission (2001) *European governance: A White Paper*, Brussels: Commission of the European Communities.

European Commission (2002) *On the collection and use of expertise by the Commission: Principles and guidelines – Improving the knowledge base for better policies*, Brussels: Commission of the European Communities.

Fergusson, D.M., Horwood, L.J. and Ridder, E.M. (2005) 'Tests of causal linkages between cannabis use and psychotic symptoms', *Addiction*, vol 100, no 3, pp 354-66.

Feuer, M.J., Towne, L. and Shavelson, R.J. (2002) 'Scientific culture and educational research', *Educational Researcher*, vol 31, no 8, pp 4-14.

Finch, J. (1986) *Research and policy: The use of qualitative methods in social and educational research*, London: Falmer Press.

Fine, B. (1998) 'The triumph of economics: or rationality can be dangerous to your reasoning', in J.G. Carrier and D. Miller (eds) *Virtualism: A new political economy*, Oxford: Berg, pp 49-73.

Fischer, F. (1990) *Technocracy and the politics of expertise*, London: Sage.

Fischer, F. (2003) *Reframing public policy: Discursive politics and deliberative practices*, Oxford: Oxford University Press.

Forsyth, A.J.M. (2001) 'Distorted? A quantitative exploration of the reporting drug fatalities in the popular press', *International Journal of Drug Policy*, vol 12, nos 5/6, pp 435-53.

Fortson, R. (2005) *Misuse of drugs: Offences, confiscation and money laundering* (5th edn), London: Sweet and Maxwell.

Friedrich, C.J. (1963) *Man and his government*, New York: McGraw-Hill.

Frischer, M., Hickman, M., Kraus, L., Mariani, F. and Weissing, L. (2001) 'A comparison of different methods for estimating the prevalence of problematic drug use in Great Britain', *Addiction*, vol 96, pp 1465-76.

Gallie, W.B. (1956) 'Essentially contested concepts', *Proceedings of the Aristotlean Society*, vol 56, pp 167-98.

Garland, D. (2001) *The culture of control: Crime and social order in contemporary society*, Oxford: Oxford University Press.

Giddens, A. (1982) *Profiles and critiques in social theory*, London: Macmillan.

Giddens, A. (1984) *The constitution of society: Outline of the theory of structuration*, Cambridge: Polity Press.

Giddens, A. (1987) *Social theory and modern sociology*, Cambridge: Polity Press.

Ginsburg, M.B. and Gorostiaga, J.M. (2001) 'Relationships between theorists/researchers and policy-makers/practitioners: rethinking the two-cultures thesis and the possibility of dialogue', *Comparative Education Review*, vol 45, no 2, pp 173-96.

Glendinning, C., Powell, M. and Rummery, K. (2002) *Partnerships, New Labour and the governance of welfare*, Bristol: The Policy Press.

Goddard, J. (1997) 'Methodological issues in researching criminal justice policy: belief systems and the "causes of crime"', *International Journal of the Sociology of Law*, vol 25, pp 411-30.

Godfrey, C. (2006) 'Evidence-based illicit drug policy: the potential contribution of economic evaluation techniques', *De Economist*, vol 154, no 4, pp 563-80.

Goffman, E. (1963) *Stigma: Notes on the management of spoiled identity*, New York: Prentice Hall.

Goldstein, H. (2008) 'Evidence and education policy: some reflections and allegations', *Cambridge Journal of Education*, vol 38, no 3, pp 393-400.

Gordon, I., Lewis, J. and Young, K. (1993) 'Perspectives on policy analysis', in M. Hill (ed) *The policy process: A reader*, London: Harvester Wheatsheaf, pp 5-9.

Guba, Y. and Lincoln, E. (1989) *Fourth generation evaluation*, London: Sage Publications.

Gusfield, J. (1975) 'The (f)utility of knowledge? The relation of social science to public policy toward drugs', *The Annals of the American Academy of Political and Social Science*, vol 417, pp 1-15.

Haas, P.M. (1992) 'Introduction: epistemic communities and international policy coordination', *International Organization*, vol 46, no 1, pp 1-35.

Hajer, M. (1995) *The politics of environmental discourse*, Oxford: Oxford University Press.

Hall, P., Land, H., Parker, R. and Webb, R. (1975) *Change, choice and conflict in social policy*, London: Heinemann.

Hammersley, M. (1992) *What's wrong with ethnography?*, London: Routledge.

Hammersley, M. (2001) 'On "systematic" reviews of research literatures: a "narrative" response to Evans and Benefield', *British Educational Research Journal*, vol 27, no 5, pp 543-54.

Hammersley, R., Khan, F. and Ditton, J. (2002) *Ecstasy and the rise of the chemical generation*, London: Routledge.

Hansard (2007) 'Westminster Hall debates – drug classification: John Bercow in the Chair', 14 June (www.theyworkforyou.com/whall/?id=2007-06-14a.335.0).

Harden, A., Garcia, J., Oliver, S., Rees, R., Shepherd, J., Brunton, G. and Oakley, A. (2004) 'Applying systematic review methods to studies of people's views: an example from public health research', *Journal of Epidemiology and Community Health*, vol 58, no 9, pp 794-800.

Harré, R. and Secord, P.F. (1972) *The explanation of social behaviour*, Oxford: Blackwell.

Heclo, H. (1978) 'Issue networks and the executive establishment', in A. King (ed) *The new American political system*, Washington, DC: American Enterprise Institute, pp 87-124.

Heinemann, R.A., Buhm, W.T., Peterson, S.A. and Kearney, E.N. (1990) *The world of the policy analyst: Rationality, values and politics*, Chatham, NJ: Chatham House.

Henderson, M. (2008) 'Conservative MPs will be forced to keep up with science', *The Times* (www.timesonline.co.uk/tol/news/science/article5168006.ece).

Henquet, C., Krabbendam, L., Spauwen, J., Kaplan, C., Lieb, R., Wittchen, H.-U. and van Os, J. (2004) 'Prospective cohort study of cannabis use, predisposition for psychosis, and psychotic symptoms in young people', *British Medical Journal*, vol 330, no 11.

Herman, E.S. and Chomsky, N. (1988) *Manufacturing consent: The political economy of the mass-media*, New York: Pantheon Books.

Hill, M. (1997) *The policy process in the modern state* (3rd edn), London: Prentice Hall.

Hill, M. and Bramley, G. (1986) *Analysing social policy*, Oxford: Blackwell.

HMSO (Her Majesty's Stationery Office) (1946) *Report of the Committee on the Provision of Social and Economic Research*, Cmnd 6868 (Clapham Report), London: HMSO.

HMSO (1965) *Report of the Committee on Social Studies*, Cmnd 2660 (Heyworth Report), London: HMSO.

HMSO (1982) *An Enquiry into the Social Science Research Council*, Cmnd 8554 (Rothschild Report), London: HMSO.

HM Treasury (no date) 'Pre-budget report' (www.hm-treasury.gov.uk/pbr_csr07_psaindex.htm).

Hobbes, T. (1651/2004) *Leviathan*, Whitefish, MT: Kessinger.

Hodgkinson, P. (2000) 'Who wants to be a social engineer? A commentary on David Blunkett's speech to the ESRC', *Sociological Research Online*, vol 5, no 1.

Home Affairs Select Committee (2002) *The government's drugs policy: Is it working?*, London: Home Office.

Home Office (2002) *Updated Drug Strategy 2002*, London: Home Office.

Hood, C. (1995) 'The "new public management" in the 1980s: variations on a theme', *Accounting Organizations and Society*, vol 20, no 3, pp 93-109.

Hope, T. (2004) 'Pretend it works: evidence and governance in the evaluation of the reducing burglary initiative', *Criminal Justice*, vol 4, no 3, pp 287-308.

Howard, R. (1997) 'The service provider's perspective', in J. Braggins (ed) *Tackling drugs together: One year on*, London: Institute for the Study and Treatment of Delinquency.

Howard, R., Beadle, P. and Maitland, J. (1993) *Across the divide: Building community partnerships to tackle drug misuse*, London: Department of Health.

Hudson, J. and Lowe, S. (2004) *Understanding the policy process: Analysing welfare policy and practice*, Bristol: The Policy Press.

Iversen, L.A. (2008) *The science of marijuana* (2nd edn), Oxford: Oxford University Press.

Jann, W. (1991) 'From policy analysis to political management: an outside look at public-policy training in the United States', in P. Wagner, C. Weiss, B. Wittrock and H. Wollman (eds) *Social sciences and modern states: National experiences and theoretical crossroads*, Cambridge: Cambridge University Press, pp 110-30.

Janowitz, M. (1972) *Sociological models and social policy*, Morristown, NJ: General Learning Systems.

Jenkins, W.I. (1978) *Policy analysis: A political and organisational perspective*, Oxford: Martin Robertson.

Jenkins-Smith, H.C. and St Clair, G.K. (1993) 'The politics of offshore energy: empirically testing the advocacy coalition framework', in P.A. Sabatier and H.C. Jenkins-Smith (eds) *Policy change and learning: An advocacy coalition approach*, San Francisco, CA: Westview Press, pp 149-76.

Jewell, C. and Bero, L. (2007) 'Public participation and claimsmaking: evidence utilization and divergent policy frames in California's ergonomics rule making', *Journal of Public Policy and Administration*, vol 17, no 4, pp 625-50.

John, P. (1999) 'Ideas and interests: agendas and implementation: an evolutionary explanation of policy change in British local government and finance', *British Journal of Politics and International Relations*, vol 1, no 1, pp 39-62.

Jones, T. and Newburn, T. (2005) 'Comparative criminal justice policy making in the United States and the United Kingdom: the case of private prisons', *British Journal of Criminology*, vol 45, no 1, pp 58-80.

Jung, T. and Nutley, S.M. (2008) 'Evidence and policy networks: the UK debate about sex offender community notification', *Evidence & Policy*, vol 4, no 2, pp 187-207.

Kilminster, R. (1998) *The sociological revolution: From the Enlightenment to the Global Age*, London: Routledge.

Kilminster, R. (2007) *Norbert Elias: Post-philosophical sociology*, Oxford: Routledge.

Kingdon, J. (1984) *Agendas, alternatives, and public policies*, Boston, MA: Little Brown.

Knoke, D. (1990) *Political networks: The structural perspective*, Cambridge: Cambridge University Press.

Kübler, D. (2001) 'Understanding policy change with the advocacy coalition framework: an application to Swiss drug policy', *Journal of European Public Policy*, vol 8, no 4, pp 623-41.

Kuhn, T. (1970) *The structure of scientific revolutions* (2nd edn), Chicago, IL: University of Chicago Press.

Lakatos, I. (1970) 'The methodology of scientific research programmes', in I. Lakatos and A. Musgrave (eds) *Criticism and the growth of knowledge*, Cambridge: Cambridge University Press, pp 91-196.

Lart, R. (1998) 'Medical power/knowledge: the treatment and control of drugs and drug users' in R. Coomber (ed) *The control of drugs and drug users: Reason or reaction,* Amsterdam: Harwood Academic Publishers, pp 49-68.

Lasswell, H. (1951) 'The policy orientation', in D. Lerner and H. Lasswell (eds) *The policy sciences,* Stanford, CA: Stanford University Press, pp 3-15.

Lasswell, H. and Kaplan, A. (1950) *Power and society,* New Haven, CT: Yale University Press.

Layder, D.R. (1998) *Sociological practice: Linking theory and social research,* London: Sage Publications.

Lee, R.M. (1993) *Doing research on sensitive topics,* London: Sage Publications.

Leicester, G. (1999) 'The seven enemies of evidence-based policy', *Public Money and Management,* vol 19, no 1, pp 5-7.

Lenke, L. and Olson, B. (2002) 'Swedish drug policy in the twenty-first century: a policy model going astray, *Annals of the American Academy of Political and Social Science,* vol 417, pp 1-15.

Levitt, R., Nason, E. and Hallsworth, M. (2006) *The evidence base for the classification of drugs,* Cambridge: RAND Corporation.

Lewin, K. (1952) *Field theory in social science: Selected theoretical papers,* London: Tavistock.

Lincoln, Y.S. and Guba, E. (1985) *Naturalistic enquiry,* Beverly Hills, CA: Sage Publications.

Lindblom, C.E. (1959) 'The science of muddling through', *Public Administration Review,* vol 19, pp 79-88.

Lindblom, C.E. (1968) *The policy making process,* Englewood Cliffs, NJ: Prentice Hall.

Lindblom, C.E. (1980) *The policy making process* (2nd edn), Englewood Cliffs, NJ: Prentice Hall.

Lindblom, C.E. and Cohen, D.K. (1979) *Useable knowledge: Social science and problem solving,* New Haven, CT: Yale University Press.

Lomas, J. (2000) 'Using "linkage" and "exchange" to move research into policy at a Canadian foundation', *Health Affairs,* vol 19, no 3, pp 236-40.

Lundberg, G. (1947) *Can science save us?,* New York: David McKay.

Lynd, R. (1940) *Knowledge for what? The place of social science in American culture,* Princeton, NJ: Princeton University Press.

Lyons, G.M. (1969) *The uneasy partnership: Social science and the federal government in the twentieth century,* New York: Russell Sage Foundation.

MacCoun, R. and Reuter, P. (2001) 'Evaluating alternative cannabis regimes', *The British Journal of Psychiatry,* vol 178, pp 123-8.

MacDonald, R. and Das, A. (2006) 'UK classification of drugs of abuse: an un-evidence-based mess', *The Lancet,* vol 368, no 9535, pp 559-61.

MacIntyre, A. (1973) 'The essential contestability of social concepts', *Ethics,* vol 84, pp 1-9.

Majone, G. (1989) *Evidence, argument and persuasion in the policy process,* New Haven, CT: Yale University Press.

Majone, G. (1996) *Regulating Europe*, London: Routledge.

Mann, K. (2009) 'Remembering and rethinking the social divisions of welfare: 50 years on', *Journal of Social Policy*, vol 38, no 1, pp 1-18.

Mannheim, K. (1952) 'Competition as a cultural phenomenon', in K. Mannheim (ed) *Essays on the sociology of knowledge*, London: Routledge and Kegan Paul, pp 191-229.

March, J.G. and Olsen, J.P. (1976) *Ambiguity and choice in organisations*, Oslo: Scandinavian University Press.

Marmot, M.G. (2004) 'Evidence-based policy or policy-based evidence', *British Medical Journal*, vol 328, no 7445, pp 906-7.

Marsh, D. and Rhodes, R.A.W. (eds) (1992) *Policy networks in British government*, Oxford: Clarendon Press.

Marsh, D. and Smith, M. (2000) 'Understanding policy networks: towards a dialectical approach', *Political Studies*, vol 48, no 1, pp 4-21.

Marsh, D. and Smith, M. (2001) 'There is more than one way to do political science: on different ways to study policy networks', *Political Studies*, vol 49, pp 528-41.

May, T., Warburton, H., Turnbull, P.J. and Hough, M. (2002) *The times they are a-changing*, York: Joseph Rowntree Foundation.

Mazey, S. and Richardson, J. (1999) 'Interests', in L. Cram, D. Dinan and N. Nugent (eds) *Developments in the European Union*, Basingstoke: Macmillan, pp 105-29.

McLaughlin, E., Muncie, J. and Hughes, G. (2001) 'The permanent revolution: new labour, new public management and modernization of criminal justice', *Criminology and Criminal Justice*, vol 1, no 3, pp 301-18.

Melrose, M. (2006) 'Young people and drugs', in R. Hughes, R. Lart and P. Higate (eds) *Drugs: Policy and politics*, Maidenhead: Open University Press, pp 31-44.

Merton, R.K. (1957) *Social theory and social structure* (revised edn), Glencoe, IL: Free Press.

Miller, R.B. (1995) 'The information society: A brave new world', *Social Science Computer Review*, vol 13, no 2, Summer.

Miller, W. and Dickson, M. (1996) *Local governance and citizenship*, Strathclyde: University of Strathclyde, ESRC.

Mills, J.H. (2003) *Cannabis Britannica: Empire, trade and prohibition*, Oxford: Oxford University Press.

Monaghan, M. (2008) 'Appreciating cannabis: the paradox of evidence in evidence-based policy making', *Evidence & Policy*, vol 4, no 2, pp 209-31.

Monaghan, M. (2010) 'The complexity of evidence: reflections on research utilisation in a heavily politicised policy area', *Social Policy and Society*, vol 9, no 1, pp 1-12.

Moore, T.H.M., Zammit, S., Lingford-Hughes, A., Barnes, T.R.E., Jones, P.B., Burke, M. and Lewis, G. (2007) 'Cannabis use and risk of psychotic or affective mental health outcomes: a systematic review', *The Lancet*, vol 370, no 9584, pp 319-28.

MORI (2002) *Policing the possession of cannabis: Residents' views on the Lambeth Experiment*, London: The Police Foundation.

Morton, A., Airoldi, M. and Phillips, L. (2009) 'Nuclear risk management on stage: a decision analysis perspective on the UK committee on radioactive waste management', *Risk Analysis*, vol 29, no 5, pp 764-79.

MPA (Metropolitan Police Authority) (2002) *The Lambeth cannabis warning pilot scheme*, London: MPA.

Mulgan, G. (2005) 'Government knowledge and the business of policy making: the potential and limits of evidence-based policy', *Evidence & Policy*, vol 1, no 2, pp 215-26.

Murji, K. (2010) 'Applied social science? Academic contributions to the Stephen Lawrence Inquiry and their consequences', *Journal of Social Policy*, vol 39, no 3, pp 343-57.

Nakamura, R. (1987) 'The textbook policy process and implementation research', *Policy Studies Review*, vol 7, no 1, pp 142-54.

NAO (National Audit Office) (2001) *Modern policy making: Ensuring policies deliver value for money*, London: The Stationery Office.

National Academy of Sciences (1968) *The behavioural sciences and the Federal Government*, Washington, DC: National Academy of Sciences.

National Science Foundation (1968) *Knowledge into action: Improving the nation's use of social sciences*, Washington, DC: National Science Foundation.

Newcombe, R. (2007) 'Trends in the prevalence of illicit drug use', in M. Simpson, T. Shildrick and R. MacDonald (eds) *Drugs in Britain: Supply, consumption and control*, Basingstoke: Macmillan, pp 13-38.

Newman, J. (2002) *Modernising government: New Labour, policy and society*, London: Sage Publications.

Newsweek (2009) 'Everything you need to know about Obama's news conference (but were afraid to ask)', Washington (www.newsweek.com/blogs/the-gaggle/2009/07/23/everything-you-need-to-know-about-obama-s-news-conference-but-were-afraid-to-ask.html).

Nutley, S.M. and Webb, J. (2000) 'Evidence and the policy process', in H.T.O. Davies, S.M. Nutley and P.C. Smith (eds) *What works? Evidence-based policy and practice in public services*, Bristol: The Policy Press, pp 13-41.

Nutley, S.M., Walter, I. and Bland, N. (2002) 'The institutional arrangements for connecting evidence and policy: the case of drug misuse', *Public Policy and Administration*, vol 17, no 3, pp 76-94.

Nutley, S.M., Walter, I. and Davies, H.T.O. (2003) 'From knowing to doing: a framework for understanding the evidence-into-practice agenda', *Evaluation*, vol 9, no 2, pp 125-48.

Nutley, S.M., Walter, I. and Davies, H.T.O. (2007) *Using evidence: How research can inform public services*, Bristol: The Policy Press.

Nutley, S.M., Morton, S., Jung, T. and Boaz, A. (2010) 'Evidence and policy in six European countries: diverse approaches and common challenges', *Evidence & Policy*, vol 6, no 2, pp 131-44.

Nutt, D. (2009) '"Equasy" – an overlooked addiction with implications for the current debate on drug harms', *Journal of Psychopharmacology*, vol 23, no 1, pp 3-5.

Nutt, D. (2010) 'Science and non-science in UK drug policy', *Addiction*, vol 105, no 7, p 1154.

Nutt, D., King, L.A., Saulsbury, W. and Blakemore, C. (2007) 'Development of a rational scale to assess the harm of drugs of potential misuse', *The Lancet*, vol 369, no 9566, pp 1046-53.

Oakley, A. (2003) 'Research evidence, knowledge management and educational practice: early lessons from a systematic approach', *Review of Education*, vol 1, pp 21-33.

Oakley, A. (2005) 'Who's afraid of the randomized control trial? Some dilemmas of the scientific method and "good" research practice', in A. Oakley (ed) *The Ann Oakley reader*, Bristol: The Policy Press, pp 233-44.

Obama, B. (2009) Remarks by the President at the National Academy of Sciences annual meeting, 27 April, Washington, DC: National Academy of Sciences.

Oldham, G. and McLean, R. (1997) 'Approaches to knowledge-brokering', Paper presented in advance of the Search Conference, 15-16 May, organised by the Institute for Sustainable Development and others (www.iisd.org/publications/pub.aspx?id=829).

Oppenheim, F. (1981) *Political concepts: A reconstruction*, Oxford: Blackwell.

Ostrom, E. (1990) *Governing the commons*, Cambridge: Cambridge University Press.

Page, R.M. (2010) 'The changing face of social administration', *Social Policy and Society*, vol 44, no 3, pp 326-42.

Pan, D. (1990) 'Ivory tower and red tape: reply to Adler', *Telos*, vol 86, no 12.

Parker, H., Aldridge, J. and Measham, F. (1998) *Illegal leisure: The normalization adolescent of recreational drug use*, London: Routledge.

Parker, H., Bakx, K. and Newcombe, R. (1988) *Living with heroin: The impact of a drugs 'epidemic' on an English community*, Milton Keynes: Open University Press.

Parker, H., Williams, L. and Aldridge, J. (2002) 'The normalization of "sensible" recreational drug use: further evidence from the North West England longitudinal study', *Sociology*, vol 36, no 4, pp 941-64.

Parsons, T. (1937) *The structure of social action*, New York: McGraw-Hill.

Parsons, W. (1995) *Public policy*, Cheltenham: Edward Elgar.

Parsons, W. (2002) 'From muddling through to muddling up: evidence-based policy making and the modernising of British government', *Public Policy and Administration*, vol 17, no 3, pp 43-60.

Pawson, R. (1989) *A measure for measures: A manifesto for empirical sociology*, London: Routledge.

Pawson, R. (2002) 'Evidence-based policy: in search of a method', *Evaluation*, vol 8, no 2, pp 157-81.

Pawson, R. (2006a) *Evidence-based policy: A realist perspective*, London: Sage Publications.

Pawson, R. (2006b) 'Digging for nuggets: how "bad" research can yield "good" evidence', *International Journal of Social Research Methods*, vol 9, no 2, pp 127-42.

Pawson, R. and Tilley, N. (1997) *Realistic evaluation*, London: Sage Publications.

Pearson, G. (1987) *The new heroin users*, London: Blackwell.

Pels, D. (2003) *Unhastening science: Autonomy and reflexivity in the social theory of knowledge*, Liverpool: Liverpool University Press.

Peters, B.G. (1994) 'Agenda-setting in the European Community', *Journal of European Public Policy*, vol 1, no 1, pp 9-26.

Petticrew, M. and Roberts, H. (2006) *Systematic reviews in the social sciences: A practical guide*, Oxford: Blackwell.

Pierre, J. (2000) 'Introduction: understanding governance', in J. Pierre (ed) *Debating governance: Authority, steering and democracy*, Oxford: Oxford University Press, pp 1-10.

Pierre, J. and Stoker, G. (2000) 'Towards multi-level governance', in P. Dunleavy, A. Gamble, I. Holliday and G. Peele (eds) *Developments in British politics 6*, Basingstoke: Macmillan, pp 29-45.

Pitts, J. (2000) 'The new youth justice and the politics of electoral anxiety', in B. Goldson (ed) *The new youth justice*, Lyme Regis: Russell House, pp 1-13.

Plewis, I. (2000) 'Educational inequalities and education action zones', in C. Pantazis and D. Gordon (eds) *Tackling inequalities: Where are we now and what can be done?*, Bristol: The Policy Press, pp 87-100.

Police Foundation, The (2000) *Drugs and the law: Report of the Inquiry into the Misuse of Drugs Act 1971*, London: The Police Foundation.

Prideaux, S. (2004) 'New Labour old functionalism: the influences of older sociological functionalist ideas from the USA upon "New" Labour thinking on welfare reform', Unpublished PhD thesis, Leeds: School of Sociology and Social Policy, University of Leeds.

PSS Consultancy Group (2002) *Evaluation of Lambeth's pilot warnings of possession of cannabis*, London: PSS Consultancy Group.

Radaelli, C.M. (1999) 'The public policy of the European Union: whither the politics of expertise?', *Journal of European Public Policy*, vol 6, no 5, pp 757-74.

Ramsay, M., Baker, P., Goulden, C., Sharp, C. and Sondhi, A. (2001) *Drug misuse declared in 2000: Results from the British Crime Survey*, Home Office Research Study 224, London: Home Office Research and Development Statistics Directorate.

Rein, M. (1976) *Social science and public policy*, Harmondsworth: Penguin.

Reiner, R. (2007) 'Media-made criminality: the representation of crime in the mass media', in M. Maguire, R. Morgan and R. Reiner (eds) *The Oxford handbook of criminology* (4th edn), Oxford: Oxford University Press, pp 302-37.

Reuter, P. and Stevens, A. (2007) *An analysis of UK drug policy: A monograph prepared for the UK Drug Policy Commission*, London: United Kingdom Drug Policy Commission.

Rhodes, R.A.W. and Marsh, D. (1992) 'Policy networks in British politics: a critique of existing approaches', in R.A.W. Rhodes (ed) *Policy networks in British government*, Oxford: Clarendon Press, pp 1-26.

Richardson, J.J. (1996a) 'Policy making in the EU: interests, ideas and garbage cans of primeval soup', in J. Richardson (ed) *European Union: Power and policy making*, London: Routledge, pp 3-23.

Richardson, J.J. (1996b) 'Actor-based models of national and EU policy making', in H. Kassim and A. Menon (eds) *The European Union and national industrial policy*, London: Routledge, pp 26-51.

Richardson, J.J. and Jordan, G. (1979) *Governing under pressure: The policy process in a post-parliamentary democracy*, Oxford: Martin Robertson.

Ritter, A. and Bammer, G. (2010) 'Models of policy-making and their relevance for drug research', *Drug and Alcohol Review* (www3.interscience.wiley.com/journal/121638199/issue).

Rodger, J.J. (2008) *The criminalisation of social policy: Anti-social behaviour and welfare in a de-civilised society*, Cullompton: Willan.

Rolles, S., Kushlick, D. and Jay, M. (2006) *After the war on drugs: Options for control*, Bristol: Transform Drug Policy Foundation.

Rosenthal, R. and DiMatteo, M.R. (2001) 'Meta-analysis: recent developments in quantitative methods for literature reviews', *Annual Review of Psychology*, vol 52, pp 59-82.

Rossi, P.H. (1987) 'No good applied social research goes unpunished', *Society*, vol 25, no 1, pp 73-9.

Rossi, P.H. and Freeman, H.E. (1985) *Evaluation: A systematic approach*, Beverly Hills, CA: Sage Publications.

Rothschild, L. (1971) *A framework for government research and development*, Cmnd 4814, London: HMSO.

RSA (Royal Society of Arts) (2007) *Drugs – Facing the facts: The report for the RSA Commission on Illegal Drugs, Communities and Public Policy*, London: The Royal Society for the Encouragement of the Arts, Manufacture and Commerce.

Rüdig, W. (1993) 'Sources of technical controversy: proximity to or alienation from technology?', in A. Barker and B.G. Peters (eds) *The politics of expert advice: Creating, using and manipulating scientific knowledge for public policy*, Edinburgh: Edinburgh University Press, pp 17-32.

Ryan, M., Savage, S.P. and Wall, D.S. (eds) (2001) *Policy networks in criminal justice*, London: Palgrave.

Sabatier, P.A. (1987) 'Knowledge, policy oriented learning and policy change', *Knowledge*, vol 8, pp 649-92.

Sabatier, P.A. (1988) 'An advocacy coalition framework of policy change and the role of policy oriented learning therein', *Policy Sciences*, vol 21, pp 129-68.

Sabatier, P.A. (1993) 'Policy change over a decade or more', in P.A. Sabatier and H.C. Jenkins-Smith (eds) *Policy change and learning: An advocacy coalition approach*, San Francisco, CA: Westview Press, pp 13-39.

Sabatier, P.A. and Jenkins-Smith, H.C. (1993a) 'The Advocacy Coalition Framework: assessment, revisions, and implications for scholars and practitioners', in P.A. Sabatier and H.C. Jenkins-Smith (eds) *Policy change and learning: An advocacy coalition approach*, San Francisco, CA: Westview Press, pp 211-36.

Sabatier, P.A. and Jenkins-Smith, H.C. (eds) (1993b) *Policy change and learning: An advocacy coalition approach*, San Francisco, CA: Westview Press.

Sabatier, P.A. and Jenkins-Smith, H.C. (1999) 'The Advocacy Coalition Framework: an assessment', in P.A. Sabatier (ed) *Theories of the policy process*, Boulder, CO: Westview Press, pp 117-66.

Sabatier, P.A. and Pelkey, N. (1987) 'Incorporating multiple actors and guidance instruments into models of regulatory policymaking: an advocacy coalition framework', *Administration and Society*, vol 19, pp 236-63.

Sabatier, P.A. and Zafonte, M. (1995) 'The views of Bay/Delta water policy activists on endangered species issues', *Hastings West-Northwest Journal of Environmental Law and Policy*, vol 2, pp 131-46.

Sanderson, I. (2002) 'Evaluation, policy learning and evidence-based policy making', *Public Administration*, vol 80, no 1, pp 1-22.

Sartori, G. (1984) *Social science concepts*, Beverly Hills, CA: Sage Publications.

Saunders, L. (2005) 'Research and policy: reflections on their relationship', *Evidence & Policy*, vol 1, no 3, pp 383-90.

Savage, S.P. and Charman, S. (2001) 'The bobby lobby: police associations and the policy process', in M. Ryan, S.P. Savage and D.S. Wall (eds) *Policy networks in criminal justice*, Basingstoke: Palgrave, pp 24-54.

Scharpf, F. (1986) 'Policy failure and institutional reform: why should form follow function?', *International Social Science Journal*, vol 38, no 2, pp 179-89.

Scharpf, F. (1999) *Governing in Europe: Effective and democratic?*, Oxford: Oxford University Press.

Schlager, E. (1995) 'Policy making and collective action: defining coalitions within the advocacy coalition framework', *Policy Sciences*, vol 28, pp 242-70.

School of Health and Related Research, University of Sheffield (no date) 'Systematic reviews: what are they and why are they useful' (www.shef.ac.uk/scharr/ir/units/systrev/index.htm).

Science and Technology Select Committee (2006a) *Scientific advice, risk and evidence-based policy making*, London: House of Commons.

Science and Technology Select Committee (2006b) *Drug classification: Making a hash of it?*, London: The Stationery Office.

Scott, R.A. and Shore, A.R. (1979) *Why sociology does not apply: A study of the use of sociology in public policy*, New York: Elsevier.

Seddon, T. (2007) 'The hardest drug? Trends in heroin use in Britain', in M. Simpson, T. Shildrick and R. MacDonald (eds) *Drugs in Britain: Supply, consumption and control*, Basingstoke: Macmillan, pp 60-75.

Seddon, T. (2010) *A history of drugs: Drugs and freedom in the liberal age*, Abingdon: Routledge.

Seddon, T., Ralphs, R. and Williams, L. (2008) 'Risk, security and the "criminalization" of British drug policy', *British Journal of Criminology*, vol 48, no 4, pp 818-34.

Shepherd, J. (2006) '"I felt very isolated", says stunned critic', *Times Higher Education Supplement*, 1 December.

Shiner, M. (2003) 'Out of harm's way? Illicit drug use, medicalisation and the law', *The British Journal of Criminology*, vol 43, no 4, pp 772-96.

Sin, C.H. (2008) 'The role of intermediaries in getting evidence into policy and practice: some useful lessons from examining consultancy-client relationships', *Evidence & Policy*, vol 4, no 1, pp 85-103.

Smith, M.J. (1993) *Pressure, power and policy: State autonomy and policy networks in Britain and the United States*, Hemel Hempstead: Harvester Wheatsheaf.

Smith, S. (ed) (2007) *Applying theory to practice*, Aldershot: Ashgate.

Solesbury, W. (2001) *Evidence-based policy: Whence it came from and where it's going*, Working Paper 1, London: ESRC UK Centre for Evidence-based Policy and Practice.

South, N. (1997) 'Drugs: use, crime and control', in M. Maguire, R. Morgan and R. Reiner (eds) *The Oxford handbook of criminology*, Oxford: Oxford University Press, pp 925-60.

South, N. (1999) 'Debating drugs and everyday life: normalization, prohibition and otherness', in N. South (ed) *Drugs: Cultures, controls and everyday life*, London: Sage Publications, pp 1-15.

Spencer, H. (1891) *Essays: Scientific, political and speculative*, London: Appleton.

Stevens, A. (2007a) 'Survival of the ideas that fit: an evolutionary analogy for the use of evidence in policy', *Social Policy and Society*, vol 6, no 1, pp 25-35.

Stevens, A. (2007b) 'When two dark figures collide: evidence and discourse on drug related crime', *Critical Social Policy*, vol 27, no 1, pp 77-99.

Stevens, A. (2010: forthcoming) 'Telling policy stories: an ethnographic study of the use of evidence in making policy on drugs and crime', *Journal of Social Policy*.

Stimson, G. and Lart, R. (1994) 'The relationship between state and local practice in the development of a national policy on drugs between 1920-1990', in J. Strang and M. Gossop (eds) *Heroin addiction and drug policy: The British system*, Oxford: Oxford University Press, pp 331-41.

Stimson, G., Hickman, M., Quirk, A. and Frischer, M. (1997) *Estimating the prevalence of drug misuse in Europe*, Strasbourg: Council of Europe.

Stoker, G. (1998) 'Governance as theory: five propositions', *International Social Science Journal*, vol 50, no 155, pp 17-28.

Stokes, P. (2007) *Philosophy: The great thinkers*, Royston: Eagle Editions.

Strang, J. and Gossop, M. (1994) 'The British system: visionary anticipation or masterly inactivity', in J. Strang and M. Gossop (eds) *Heroin addiction and drug policy: The British system*, Oxford: Oxford University Press, pp 342-51.

Sutton, S. and Maynard, A. (1993) 'Are drug policies based on "fake" statistics?', *Addiction*, vol 88, no 4, pp 455-8.

Taylor, D. (2005) 'Governing through evidence: participation and power in policy evaluation', *Journal of Social Policy*, vol 34, no 4, pp 601-18.

Tizard, B. (1990) 'Research and policy: is there a link?', *The Psychologist*, vol 10, pp 435-40.

Tonry, M. (2004) *Punishment and politics: Evidence and emulation in the making of English crime control policy*, London: Willan.

Toynbee, P. and Walker, D. (2001) *Did things get better? An audit of Labour's successes and failures*, Harmondsworth: Penguin.

Turner, S.P. and Turner, J.H. (1990) *The impossible science: An institutional analysis of American sociology*, London: Sage Publications.

van het Loo, M., van Beusekom, I. and Kahan, J.P. (2002) 'Decriminalization of drug use in Portugal: the development of a policy', *Annals of the American Academy of Political Science*, vol 582, no 1, pp 49-63.

Verdun, A. (1999) 'The role of the Delors committee in the creation of EMU: an epistemic community?', *Journal of European Public Policy,* vol 6, no 2, pp 308-28.

Vickers, G. (1965) *The art of judgement: A study of policy making*, London: Chapman and Hall.

Warburton, H., May, T. and Hough, M. (2005) 'Looking the other way: the impact of reclassifying cannabis on police warnings, arrests and informal action in England and Wales', *British Journal of Criminology*, vol 45, no 2, pp 113-28.

Ward, V., House, A. and Harmer, S. (2009) 'Knowledge brokering: the missing link in the evidence to action chain?', *Evidence & Policy*, vol 5, no 3, pp 267-80.

Webster, C. (2007) 'Drug treatment', in M. Simpson, T. Shildrick and R. MacDonald (eds) *Drugs in Britain: Supply, consumption and control*, Basingstoke: Macmillan, pp 141-61.

Weible, C.M., Sabatier, P.A. and McQueen, K. (2009) 'Themes and variations: taking stock of the advocacy coalition framework', *Policy Studies Journal*, vol 37, no 1, pp 121-40.

Weiss, C.H. (1977) *Using social research in public policy making*, Lexington, DC: Heath.

Weiss, C.H. (1986) 'The many meanings of research utilisation', in M. Bulmer (ed) *Social science and social policy*, London: Allen Unwin, pp 31-40.

Weiss, C.H. (1993) 'Where politics and evaluation research meet', *Evaluation Practice,* vol 14, no 1, pp 93-106.

Weiss, C.H. (1995) 'The haphazard connection: social science and public policy', *International Journal of Education Research*, vol 23, no 2, pp 137-50.

Weiss, C.H. (1998) 'Have we learned anything about the use of evaluation?', *American Journal of Evaluation*, vol 19, no 1, pp 21-33.

Weiss, C.H. (1999) 'The interface between evaluation and public policy', *Evaluation*, vol 5, no 4, pp 468-86.

Weiss, C.H. and Bucuvalas, M. (1980) *Social science research and decision-making*, New York: Columbia University Press.

Weiss, C.H., Murphy Graham, E., Petrosino, A. and Ghandi, A.G. (2008) 'The fairy godmother and her warts: making the dream of evidence-based policy come true', *American Journal of Evaluation*, vol 29, no 1, pp 29-47.

Whorf, B.L. (1956) *Language, thought and reality: Selected writings*, Cambridge, MA: MIT Press.

Wilensky, H.L. (1997) 'Social science and the public agenda: reflections on the relation of knowledge to policy in the United States and abroad', *Journal of Health Politics, Policy and Law*, vol 22, no 5, pp 1241-65.

Young, J. (1971) *The drugtakers: The social meaning of drug use,* London: MacGibbon and Kee.

Young, K., Ashby, D., Boaz, A. and Grayson, L. (2002) 'Social science and the evidence-based policy movement', *Social Policy and Society*, vol 1, no 3, pp 215-24.

Zafonte, M. and Sabatier, P.A. (1998) 'Shared beliefs and imposed interdependencies as determinants of ally networks in overlapping subsystems', *Journal of Theoretical Politics*, vol 10, no 4, pp 473-505.

Zito, A. (2001) 'Epistemic communities, collective entrepreneurship and European integration', *Journal of European Public Policy*, vol 8, no 4, pp 585-603.

Index